T0283234

Feh

Feh

SHALOM AUSLANDER

RIVERHEAD BOOKS

NEW YORK

2024

RIVERHEAD BOOKS
An imprint of Penguin Random House LLC
penguinrandomhouse.com

Scriptures taken from the Holy Bible, New International Version®, NIV®.
Copyright © 1973, 1978, 1984, 2011 by Biblica, Inc.™ Used by permission of Zondervan.
All rights reserved worldwide. www.zondervan.com. The "NIV" and "New International
Version" are trademarks registered in the United States Patent and Trademark
Office by Biblica, Inc.™

Library of Congress Cataloging-in-Publication Data

Names: Auslander, Shalom, author.
Title: Feh : a memoir / Shalom Auslander.
Description: New York : Riverhead Books, 2024.
Identifiers: LCCN 2023041253 (print) | LCCN 2023041254 (ebook) |
ISBN 9780735213265 (hardcover) | ISBN 9780735213289 (ebook)
Subjects: LCSH: Auslander, Shalom, | Authors, American—21st century—Biography. |
Jews—United States—Biography.
Classification: LCC PS3601.U85 Z46 2024 (print) |
LCC PS3601.U85 (ebook) | DDC 813/.6 [B]—dc23/eng/20231115
LC record available at https://lccn.loc.gov/2023041253
LC ebook record available at https://lccn.loc.gov/2023041254

Printed in the United States of America
1st Printing

Book design by Alexis Farabaugh

For Craig Markus, the best Feh I ever knew

Feh (fɛ)

YIDDISH ORIGIN

An expression of disapproval or disgust.

Those who do not have power over the story that dominates their lives, power to retell it, rethink it, deconstruct it, joke about it, and change it as times change, truly are powerless.

SALMAN RUSHDIE

1.

The morning of my blinding began like any other.

I was in the first grade, six years of age, perhaps seven, at the ultra-Orthodox Yeshiva of Spring Valley in a town in rural New York named Monsey, waiting for class to begin. Some boys stood at the back of the classroom, laughing and joking and flipping baseball cards. Others sat on the floor and played *kugelach*, the Jewish version of jacks. Suddenly the door flew open, and a bearded man in a long black coat hurried in. He sat down and flipped open the very old black book that lay on his desk. The pages were yellowed. The cover was frayed. It was held together with duct tape along its spine. Then he blinded me. The way the man blinded me was this:

He blinded me with a story.

The story he blinded me with is called *Feh*.

Feh was the first story I was ever told. I was told *Feh* before *Cinderella* and before *Frog and Toad*, before *Winnie the Pooh* and before *Peter Rabbit*, before *The Berenstain Bears* and before *The Three Little Pigs*. Rabbis tell this story. Their rabbis told it to them. Priests tell this story, pastors tell this story, imams tell this story. The story is told by thousands of people to thousands of other people, thousands of times a day, in thousands of different forms. The book from which the original story derives is the oldest, most influential book of stories ever written, so influential that even people who weren't told the story know the story. Soon they end up telling it too.

It was, the storytellers said, the story of me.

It was, the storytellers said, the story of all human beings.

This is how it goes:

FEH

Once upon a time, there was a man named God who was perfect and never wrong. One day, He created Earth. He liked Earth very much. He liked the land and He liked the sea. He liked the trees and He liked the grass. He liked the moon and He liked the stars. He liked the birds and He liked the beasts. Every day, after creating something, God would stand back, wipe His hands on His smock, and say, - It is good.

So proud was God of His work that He called the angels Gabriel and Elijah over to see it.

- What's that? they asked.

- That's the aurora borealis, said God.

- Amazing, they said. - What's that?

- That's the Grand Canyon.

- Spectacular, they said. - What's that?

- That's a field of dew-dusted lavender bellflowers, awakening in the early-morning sun.

- Breathtaking, they said.

That was Thursday.

On Friday, God created Man.

Man wasn't great. He wasn't even good. Supplies were low. All God had left was some dirt. He made Man out of dirt.

- What do you call *that*? the angels asked, unable to hide their disdain for the hideous lumpen mass laid out on God's workbench.

- Man, said God.

- So you're his father? asked Gabriel.

- Kinda, said God.

- Who's his mother? asked Elijah.

- It's complicated, said God.

- What's that? asked Gabriel.

- A penis, said God.

The angels shrugged.

- Meh, said Elijah.

- *Feh*, said Gabriel.

- It needs work, said Elijah.

- It needs pants, Gabriel replied.

God wasn't crazy about Man either. In the entire story of the beginning of the earth and the universe and all that is in it, Man was the only creation after which God did not say, *It is good*.

He didn't say anything.

He said *bupkis*.

Bupkis is Yiddish for *nothing*.

How do we know how God felt about his son? Here's a clue: He named him *Adam*, from the Hebrew word *Adamah*, which means *dirt*.

He named his son Dirt.

Dirt wasn't happy in God's world. Dirt had nothing to do. Dirt was lonely. Before long, Dirt was getting on God's nerves.

The angels tried to cheer God up.

- He's a first draft, they told God. - All first drafts are shit.

But they didn't really believe that, and neither did God. After all, dogs came out perfect – wet noses, fluffy tails, unconditional love. Draft One, nailed it. Sunset didn't need a rewrite. The Great Barrier Reef was a masterpiece. So God started Man over.

- Oh well, He said. - Writing is rewriting.

God took Dirt, laid him back down on his workbench, and ditched everything but a single rib.

One rib, that was all that was worth saving. The rest was trash.

The second draft, which God named Woman, was an improvement. He turned Physical Strength down a bit, but ramped up Emotional Complexity and doubled Self-Awareness.

Better.

Not great.

Not even good.

But better.

He named her *Chava*, from *Chai*, the Hebrew word for *alive*. He named her Alive.

Alive isn't exactly high praise, but it's better than Dirt.

Now they were a couple. The Dirts. A minimal standard. The store brand. The first thing the Dirts did was to break the rules. Well, one rule. Once. But God was very angry.

- Get out, said God.

The Dirts left, but the story only got worse. The Dirts had children. Two boys. The older Dirt murdered the younger Dirt. The very first man born of man, and what does he do? He kills. He stabs. He butchers.

These are my ancestors.

This is my *mishpacha*.

Hebrew for *family*.

Up in Heaven, God is depressed. God needs a drink. God creates a pub.

- The usual? the bartender asks.

God nods.

- How's the human thing going? the bartender asks.

God sighs.

- My spirit will not contend with mankind forever, He says. - I am going to put an end to all people. I am surely going to destroy both them and the earth.

- 'Bout time, says the bartender.

- Cursed is the ground because of them, says God.

- True that, says the bartender.

Gabriel was right about human beings, God thinks as He throws back His drink.

They're *feh*, from top to bottom.

Totally, irredeemably *feh*.

The End

It's a miserable story.

It's a downer.

It's a bummer.

My life would have been immeasurably brighter if they'd taught me *The Three Little Pigs* instead.

Alas, Soul-Crushing Storytime wasn't over. It was only beginning. The story of *Feh* is just the first story in a long book of similar stories, the collection of which is a book called *You Suck*. The first part of *You Suck* is known as *The Old Testament*.

Spoiler alert: Moses, the main character, dies before reaching his goal.

Why?

Because he was *feh*.

The second part of *You Suck* is known as *The New Testament*.

Spoiler alert: It ends with God making a huge wine press, filling it with millions of people, and crushing them to death.

Why?

Guess.

Most people who read the Old Testament don't read the New. Most people who read the New Testament don't read the Old. They don't have to. They're the same story:

Feh.

The name of the man who blinded me was Rabbi Hammer. People in Monsey went to him for advice. *Tell us how to see*, they beseeched him. But Rabbi Hammer was blind too. When he finished telling us *Feh*, he closed the book of *You Suck*, leaned forward, and kissed it. Then he called us up, one by one, and gave us each a small copy of the book.

- To keep in your hearts and minds, he said, all the days of your lives.

Then he handed us our book and shook our hands.

- *Mazel tov*, he said.

Hebrew for *good luck*.

He wasn't kidding. I am fifty years old now and still I am blind. It is a strange blindness. It is not a darkness, not a blackness, not an absence of light. Rather, I go through life as if beneath a shroud; I can see the sky, the earth, the trees, the animals, all the flora and fauna without deviation, without distortion or diversion. But mankind appears to me grotesque, vile, foul, ignominious, none more so than myself. With others I can occasionally be fair. With others there is a chance of expiation. With myself, though, I am a hanging judge. To myself I show no mercy. There is no criticism I don't believe, no compliment I accept. I avoid mirrors. Mirrors are bad. Catching a glimpse of my reflection in a store window is enough to ruin my whole day. This is what I think when I do:

Feh.

- I wish you could see yourself, says my wife Orli, the way I see you.

As if wishing could make a blind man see.

I was very young when they told me that I am *feh*, and that you are *feh*, and that all of us are *feh*, so young that I don't remember exactly how young I was. But I remember this: It was the days of laughter and joking. It was the days of flipping baseball cards. It was the days of *kugelach*. It was the days of light.

Then people began telling me this story.

And behold, the world and all that is in it turned to darkness.

2.

Recently, according to my psychiatrist Ike, I tried to kill myself.

I disagreed.

It was late in the evening. Ike was at home in New York City; I was two hours away in Northern Dutchess Hospital, tubes running in and out of my arms, machines around me beeping wailing flashing blinking.

- I didn't try to kill myself, I said.

- You drank poison, said Ike.

- I didn't know it was poison.

- It said *Poison* on the bottle.

- No, it didn't.

- What did it say?

- It said *Danger.*

- And?

- And *Toxic.*

- And?

- And *Not for Human Consumption.*

- You drank something that said *Danger, Toxic, Not for Human Consumption*, Ike said. - That sounds like suicide to me.

I had been in agony for days, my insides knotted and aflame. Some malefi-cent creature, red-eyed and furious, had burrowed its way into my stomach and was desperately trying to claw its way back out. I lay in bed, sweating, wincing, unable to move.

- Something's wrong, I finally moaned to Orli.

I'd waited awhile to tell her because I knew that this pain, whatever it was, was my fault. I knew that I had caused it. And I knew Orli knew that too. Self-destruction's my whole thing. When at last I began vomiting bile, she drove me to the ER, her jaw set in anger.

- How's Orli? Ike asked.

Meaning, *Have you destroyed your marriage?*

- Fuck you, I said.

Meaning, *Probably.*

I hung up.

The doctor entered, Orli behind him, her countenance grim.

- Your pancreas, Doctor Superior said, is eating itself.

- Why is it doing that? I asked.

- You tell me, he said.

I hate doctors because doctors judge me. Everyone judges me, and I judge everyone, but I'm *paying* doctors. That's why people become doctors, after all – to pass judgment. It's the best part of the job. The salary is good, and the respect is nice, but nothing compares to the joy of judging strangers. It's like being a priest, only you get to have sex. And a Porsche.

I tried not to picture my sons Paix and Lux, just twelve and seven years old at the time, waiting for me at home. They are utterly beautiful, those boys, inside and out. I have no idea how they came from me. They seem to love me, though I cannot fathom why. I can only assume they're idiots. I can't think of any other reason. Gullible, young – soon they will learn. Orli and I both emerged from severely dysfunctional families, and it has been our life's mission to give our own children the loving, stable home neither of us ever had. I would rather die than hurt them or imperil our little family. Which is exactly what it seemed, from the look on Doctor Superior's face, I had just done.

Earlier that afternoon, as we left for the hospital, the boys watched from the front porch as I staggered, doubled over in pain, to the car.

- I'll be fine, guys, I lied.

Paix reached for his younger brother's hand.

- Okay, Dad, he said.

Lux buried his face in Paix's chest.

- There's pizza in the fridge, Orli said.

Pain slashed through me; I lowered my face a moment so they wouldn't see their father in agony. Paix waved and forced himself to smile. Lux cried.

- I love you, Dad, Paix called.

- I love you, Dad, Lux called.

Idiots.

Doctor Superior took out his chart and clicked open his pen.

- Did you drink anything? he asked.

- No.

- Did you eat anything?

- No.

- Did you take anything? Pills, supplements, drugs?

- No, I said.

Back home, twenty miles away, in a bag in a box in a case in a drawer in my bathroom, lay a small, amber-colored dropper bottle. *GW501516*, it said on the label.

Danger.

Toxic.

Not for Human Consumption.

I wanted Doctor Superior to leave. I wanted Orli to leave. Loneliness is oxygen to the fire of self-reproach, and I wanted to burn. I wanted my pancreas to eat itself. I wanted it to eat my liver, my lungs, my heart, my soul.

- Are you a drinker? Doctor Superior asked.

- Of water?

- Of alcohol.

- A bit.

- How much?

- A few martinis.

- A day? he asked.

- A week, I said.

Orli scoffed.

- A few? she said icily.

- A few, I said icily.

The doctor wrote on my chart. I gave Orli the finger. She glared at me with rage-red eyes and brushed a bitter tear from her cheek.

Orli didn't know about the GW501516 I had been taking. She didn't have to, because she knew me. She knew I had a thing for poison. She knew that sometimes I drank it, that sometimes I smoked it, that a while back I had injected it.

The only thing to do, Doctor Superior determined, was to shut my system down.

- Shut it down? I asked.

No food, no water, no nothing, he explained. For at least a week. They would take scans, MRIs, look for cancer. Tubes would deliver the necessary nutrition and hydration to keep me alive. The hope, he said, was that my pancreas would stop self-destructing.

- But self-destruction's my whole thing, I said.

Orli turned on her heel and walked out.

Orli and I are alike in many ways, but in our fundamental approach to Life, Being, Self, and Mankind, we are opposites.

- Fuck me, I say.

As a rule.

The problem, I know, as a rule, is me. Whatever is, is wrong, and whatever is wrong is wrong because of me.

Whereas she says, - Fuck them.

The problem, she knows, is them.

At least we agree on the fuck part.

We're a lot of fun at parties.

Being of Middle Eastern descent, Orli is forever on DEFCON 1. She treats our small four-person family like a biblical homeland that needs constant defending. At the slightest threat, real or imagined, her Early Warning Defense System lights up, jets scramble overhead. Come into our life and you can expect to have your passport checked, your bag searched, questions asked. If we didn't rent, she'd install a metal detector at the front door.

- I know you're from FedEx, she says, but you're going to have to take off your shoes and step through the scanner.

The FedEx guy is confused.

- If you'd prefer a body search, she says as she pulls on her latex glove, we can do that too.

- But you *ordered* this package, he pleads. - It has your name on it . . .

- Are we going to have trouble here? she snaps, reaching for her Taser. - Because if you want trouble, I CAN GIVE YOU TROUBLE.

She has a defiance to which I aspire, and as the hospital door closed behind her, the room felt suddenly empty; I knew that once she left me for good, my life would feel empty too. We've been together for twenty-five years now, and I still wake every morning expecting to find her gone.

You were right about you, the note she will leave on my nightstand will read. *Feh.*

- We actually have a wonderful marriage, I said to Doctor Superior.

- Mm-hmm, said Doctor Superior.

And then he left too.

Once upon a time in Harlem, New York, I met a beautiful girl with emerald-green eyes and a sun-filled laugh that banished all my darkness. Her laugh was free and unabashed and total, it was lustful and devilish and joyous, and the very first time I heard it I experienced a desire even more overwhelming than my overwhelming sexual urges: the desire to see her laugh, to listen to her laugh, to help her laugh, every day for the rest of eternity. Her laugh gave me hope for myself, for the world. Her name was Orli, Hebrew for *my light*. And she was. We fell ridiculously, insanely, achingly in love. She made me want to write love poems, which I loathe; she made me nod knowingly at syrupy sweet Hallmark cards, which before I'd have happily piled on the floor of the pharmacy and set on fire. Together we went to hockey games at Madison Square Garden, and we walked the leaf-strewn paths of Central Park, and we browsed the endless shelves of the Strand Book Store, and soon we rented a tiny basement apartment in Queens and moved in together. She had boxes of art supplies, crates of paints, she had lightboxes and canvases and a drawing table; I had a bong and a notebook half-filled with abandoned ideas for novels. One afternoon a few months later, I took the subway to Forty-sixth Street in Manhattan, between Fifth and Sixth Avenues, a street known as the Diamond District for the diamond shops that line it, most of them owned by ultra-Orthodox Hasidic Jews. I knew the street well, not because of diamonds, but because of books. I was a reader, with thoughts of becoming a writer myself, and many times I visited the only non-diamond store on the street, a dimly lit bookshop with exquisitely creaky wood floors named the Gotham Book Mart.

The diamond shops were full of customers.

The bookstore was empty.

Wise Men Fish Here, read the weathered wooden sign that hung above the bookstore.

Well, I thought. *That explains the emptiness.*

- Can I help you? the man at the counter had asked the first time I went in.

- Yeah, I said. - What's funny?

Ever since I was a child, laughter has been my salvation, my underwastewater breathing apparatus, my Davidian slingshot against the Goliath of being, created by God, I am certain, on the evening of Day Six, when He realized that the man He created that afternoon wouldn't survive a week without it. I imagine a Genesis before Genesis, a prequel, Genesis 0:1, in which Adam didn't steal from God's tree but hanged himself by the neck from it.

- Uh-oh, saideth the Lord.

- That's the third one in a row, said Gabriel. - Better give the poor bastards laughter.

It's not much, I know. Laughter, to borrow Camus's phrasing, is a man charging a group of machine guns with only a sword. But it's the only weapon I've got.

The bookseller led me down a narrow, book-lined aisle, wonderfully musty, perfectly dusty. I was a student in an Orthodox yeshiva high school at the time, my yarmulke stuffed in my pocket, my tzitzit stuffed in my pants. The only writers I knew were Moses and Solomon. He pulled out a book called *The Trial*, by someone named Franz Kafka.

- What's it about? I asked.

- It's about a guy who gets arrested, he said, but they won't tell him what he did.

- What did he do?

- We don't know.

- Does he know?

- No.

- Do they know?

- No.

- What happens?

- They find him guilty.

- And then?

- And then they kill him.

- That's not funny, I said. - That's my life.

- That's why it's funny, he said.

This particular day, though, I hurried right past Gotham Book Mart to the diamond shop on the corner of Sixth Avenue. I had decided to ask Orli to marry me. I was broke, earning just two hundred dollars a week at a small advertising agency on East Eleventh Street, but I wanted to buy her the biggest diamond in the world. She wasn't materialistic, I just couldn't imagine any other reason she would agree to marry me.

- Can I help you? the heavy Hasidic man behind the counter asked through his bushy black beard.

I looked over the diamonds beneath the glass countertop, and my heart sank. Even the smallest ones, some no larger than the head of a pin, cost thousands of dollars.

- Yes, I said, pointing to the large stone at the center of the display. - I'd like to steal that diamond. Would you mind looking away so I can grab it and run for the door?

He looked me over.

- *Farshteyn d'yiddish?* he asked.

Yiddish for *Do you understand Yiddish?*

- *A bissel,* I said.

A little.

- *Kum,* he said. - Let me show you something.

He led me to the far end of the counter, where, from a low glass shelf, he produced a tray of diamonds, each one delicately wrapped in its own soft velvet bag, tied with a golden string. He opened one, and the precious stone tumbled into his hand.

- You like? he asked.

I did.

- You want? he asked.

- I can't, I said. - Unless you're okay with the whole stealing thing.

- *Gib a kik,* he said — Yiddish for *take a look* — as he passed me his jeweler's loupe. I pressed it to my eye as he held the diamond up to the light.

- You see? he asked.

I did. There in the center of the stone was a thin cloud, invisible to the naked eye, wispy and white, like a soul trapped in ice that would never melt.

- What is that? I asked.

- A flaw.

- Can it be fixed?

He shook his head.

- It's internal, he said, pointing to his chest as he did. - Can't be fixed. But God willing, no one will ever see it. And I can give it to you for cheap.

We obviously had very different ideas of God. And very different ideas of cheap. He knocked a hundred dollars off the price and agreed to throw the setting in for free. I reached into my pocket and handed him all the money I had in the world.

That evening, I sat on our futon beside Orli and held the ring out to her.

- Will you marry me? I asked.

Tears filled her eyes, eyes that to this day make my soul dance, eyes that give me hope in this dark, despoiled world.

- It's beautiful, she said.

- It's flawed, I said, pointing to the soul trapped inside. - Like me.

- Yes, she said softly.

- Yes you will, or yes I'm flawed?

She laughed.

- Yes. She nodded. - Yes, yes, yes, I will.

- Are you sure? I asked her, my own eyes beginning to fill with tears. - You can do better.

She threw her arms around me and hugged me tightly.

I wondered if she thought I was fat.

That was twenty-five years ago, the promising act 1, in storytelling terminology, of a stirring romance I never expected and probably don't deserve. Of late, though, our love story has been veering precipitously toward tragedy; darkness has been overwhelming light, resignation has been smothering hope. And so I've begun to think of our marriage like that diamond, beautiful and precious and marred by one fatal, irreparable flaw:

Me.

I lay in the hospital bed, listening to the beeps and whirrs of the machine trying to save me from myself. The morphine was beginning to wear off, and I pressed the button for the nurse, desperate for the release from myself that the drug would provide.

- The laughter thing's not working, said Gabriel. - Another one hanged himself this morning.

- Damn, said God. - What else we got?

- Opioids.

- Aww, God whined. - I was keeping those for myself . . . What about humor?

- What's humor?

- It's this thing I made. It seems to cause laughter.

Gabriel was skeptical.

- It *causes* laughter? he asked. - How does it *cause* laughter?

- I'm not sure. It doesn't always work. Sometimes it just causes anger.

Gabriel shrugged.

- It's worth a shot, he said.

A few moments later, the nurse entered. I tugged at the too-thin hospital bed linen, trying to cover myself, to hide myself from her view. I wondered if she thought I was fat.

- Are you in pain? asked the nurse.

- Who isn't? I said.

- You're crying, said the nurse.

- Who isn't? I said.

3.

- God, Rabbi Hammer told us, needed to breathe life into the man made of dirt, but where could He do so?

He couldn't breathe life into the man's mouth, he said, because He knew that with that mouth the man would lie.

He couldn't breathe life into the man's eyes, he said, because He knew that with those eyes the man would look upon women with lust.

He couldn't breathe life into the man's hands, he said, because He knew that with those hands the man would kill.

He couldn't breathe life into the man's feet, he said, because He knew that with those feet the man would run to commit sin.

So God breathed life into the man's nostrils.

- Why his nostrils? asked Rabbi Hammer.

- Because He knew that with his nose, said Rabbi Hammer, the man could smell the stench of his own foulness.

The End.

4.

- Noah, Rabbi Scold said to our third-grade class, was a man without sin.

I doubted it.

Men had not exactly been the noble heroes of the stories he'd been teaching us. Adam had stolen from God and blamed it on his wife; Cain had murdered Abel; Lamech had murdered Cain; and to top it all off, a bunch of monstrous male giants were running around Earth raping Canaanite women.

And we were only up to chapter 6.

A man?

Without sin?

That didn't sound right.

I, too, lived in a world of monstrous male giants. My father was a fearsome, violent man, barrel-chested, hairy-armed, thick-wristed, and filled with terrible rage and resentment. He cursed, he roared, he slammed the bedroom doors so hard that the walls of our home shook. I worried/hoped that one day his rage would bring the whole house down and kill us all. On Friday night, the night of Shabbos (Hebrew for the Sabbath), my father would get drunk, slur the words to the traditional Shabbos songs, bang his heavy fists on the table, and slap my brother in the face.

- Fuck you, my brother would shout.

- Cocksucker, my father would reply.

Afterward, I would lie in my bed, wide-eyed and terror-struck, blanket pulled up under my chin, waiting for my bedroom door to burst open and one of them to appear, knife in hand, having at last realized it was all my fault, whatever it was.

My rabbis at school were fearsome male giants too. They pinched our arms, pulled our ears, slapped our hands, and smacked our faces. Rabbi Scold was the most fearsome rabbi of all, a stocky, furious man with a white beard and a red face. One time he shook a student so hard that he broke the student's arm. He slapped another so hard that the boy's nose bled.

- Now the earth was corrupt in God's sight, Rabbi Scold continued with the story of Noah, and was full of violence, and every inclination of the human heart was evil.

Now *that* sounded right.

That afternoon, after yeshiva, as the school bus lurched to a stop in front of my house, I looked out the window to find my father mowing the front lawn.

Shirtless.

Goddammit, I thought.

My father was a heavy man, and his belly hung over the waistband of his pants as he tossed the lawn mower around the yard like he tossed my brother around the dining table. A cigarette dangled from his lips, and with every furious jerk of the mower, gray ash fell onto the gray hair that covered his chest. His body jiggled and shook, and it filled me with dread to know that someday I would look like him.

And Adam looked down at himself, and he felt shame.

At least Adam had the good sense to put on a shirt.

I averted my eyes from the grotesque specter of my inexorable future and headed straight for our mailbox. One of my few joys in those days was reading the comics of the Rockland *Journal News*; the laughter the strips provided was weak, the jokes lame, but how desperate I was for even a brief respite from the tumult around and within me. A joke could change a mood. A joke could stop a fight. A joke could make my father laugh when he was getting ready to shout or slap or hit. And so every afternoon after yeshiva, I raced to the mail-box to grab the paper before my siblings could.

- *Gonif*, my father would say.

Yiddish for *thief*.

That day, though, as I tugged open the rusty door of the old black mailbox, a curious pink catalog tumbled into my waiting hands. On the cover was a woman of such otherworldly beauty that I gasped to see her, a blonde-haired, ivory-skinned goddess draped across an elegant red velvet couch, wearing nothing but her *gatkes*.

Yiddish for *underpants*.

Her legs, endless and lean, were dipped in white silk pantyhose, and her long blonde hair tumbled over the armrest, a waterfall of gold and sunlight. Above her, in the calligraphic handwriting of an angel, were these inscrutable words:

Victoria's Secret.

The lawn mower coughed and died.

- Piece of shit, my father grumbled.

He looked over and saw me holding the newspaper.

- Don't go disappearing with my newspaper, he said. - Lousy *gonif*.

Actually, I was a fantastic *gonif*, and later that night, as my brother slept soundly in his bed across from mine, I slid the Victoria's Secret catalog out from beneath my mattress and flipped through page after page of beautiful women in beautifully appointed rooms wearing nothing but beautiful *gatkes*. I was only eight years old at the time, and the seeds of sexual desire had not yet begun to bear their wicked fruit, so that what I was overcome with as I turned one glossy page after another was not lust but jealousy. Bitter, all-consuming jealousy.

Women were graceful and refined; we men were clumsy and coarse. Wom-en's underpants were crafted of the finest silk and satin; mine were made of dingy white cotton with an ugly elastic waistband that Nechemya Leibo-witz, the class bully, would grab, yank up, and snap painfully against my skin.

Women's underpants were made of lace and straps and beads and pearls and said *Delicate* on the label, *Hand Wash Only*. Mine had a cartoon of an apple and grapes on the tag and said *Fruit of the Loom*. Even their shoes had feathers on them.

Feathers!

On shoes!

Victoria used words I had never heard before, words like music, words like flowers — *chemise* and *charmeuse* and *teddies* and *bodice* and *boudoir* — available in colors I never knew existed: *mauve* and *lavender* and *aubergine* and *lilac*.

Victoria's Secret for *purple*.

On one page, an angelic woman was seated on a Parisian chair, her long legs tucked off to the side, her back arched, swanlike, her eyes closed with the sheer ecstasy of being female.

In her boudoir, Victoria wrote beneath her, *a woman prepares for an evening of intrigue. A final fascination: the lacy ruffle at your hip. In rose and honey beige.*

I had no idea what Victoria was talking about. I didn't need to. How utterly delighted these women seemed with themselves! They held their heads up, their shoulders back, their breasts proud and high. I couldn't imagine such self-contentedness. What must it be like, I wondered, to wake each morning and find such beauty in the mirror? To not merely be beautiful, but to be Beauty itself? How fortunate they were to have been born women, I thought; what a lucky flip of the coin. Heads, you go through life as purest poetry, your every movement a symphony, your very being the envy of all creation.

Tails, you're a man.

Through page after page I turned, each seraphic beauty more breathtaking than the one before; white-skinned women in black *gatkes*, black-skinned women in white *gatkes*, blonde-haired women in red *gatkes*. And then, on the last page, as if to remind me of my own vile loathsomeness, a man. A foul, hairy, thick-fingered man, despoiling with his mere presence this Eden of female beauty.

Wearing nothing, God help me, but his *gatkes*.

The hideous beast's back was turned to the camera, *Baruch Hashem* (Hebrew for *Blessed is God*), so I was spared a preview of the grotesque transformation that lay ahead for my doomed male genitalia. But the rear view wasn't exactly good news either. The backs of the beast's thighs were covered in a hideous undergrowth of wiry hair that only grew denser the closer it crept to the swampy morass of his fetid haunches. I pitied the smooth-skinned, raven-haired beauty beside him, who would no doubt have run screaming from the room had he not been restraining her about her waist with his thick arm, it too covered in a dark coat of fur. She smiled, the poor thing, but surely it was with relief to be wearing silk long-sleeve Christian Dior classic pajamas in azure with delicate eggshell trim, which kept her from having to touch the hideous ape who would soon be dragging her screaming up the side of the Empire State Building.

And here's a secret, wrote Victoria. *It's machine washable!*

Bullshit.

Victoria wasn't fooling me. Her secret wasn't laundry. Her secret was this:

Women were beautiful.

And I was hideous.

I heard my father upstairs, fee-fi-fo-fumming his way to the kitchen like a rampaging Canaanite giant, and quickly buried the catalog beneath my pillow. I switched off my bedside lamp, pulled the bedcovers up under my chin, and shut my eyes tight, as tight as I could, so tight they burned, imagining that for one brief, blissful moment there was nothing beneath my covers, nothing below my neck — no torso, no arms, no legs, no body, and nobody, at all.

...

The following morning, I pulled on my non-silk yeshiva pants with no curve-enhancing waistline, stepped into my non-stiletto yeshiva shoes that had no delicate ankle straps, and looked in the mirror.

Stupid God, I thought. The creation of Eve was a clear admission that he had blown it with Adam. He should have named her Whoops. He should have named her Mulligan. Women were the update, the new and improved; car manufacturers did it all the time, so why was God still creating the first version? Ford didn't still make Model Ts. They had a better model now. So why was God still making Model T people? And why did I have to be one?

- What are you so *broyges* about? my mother asked as I trudged into the kitchen.

Yiddish for *glum*.

Easy for you to say, I thought. *You're a woman.*

I slumped down at the kitchen table, poured myself some Rice Krispies, and watched her shuffle about the kitchen, one hand on her aching lower back, the other massaging her aching temple.

- *Oy*, she said. - *Vey iz mir.*

Yiddish for *woe is me.*

My mother was possessed of a glamorous, classic beauty. With her dark, almond-shaped eyes, high cheekbones, and elegant arched brows, she could have been a film star. Alas, that was from the neck up. From the neck down, it was a different story, a story of aches and pains, poor design and cheap materials.

Here's another story Rabbi Hammer told me. It's called *Why Women Deserve Pain*. This is how it goes:

WHY WOMEN DESERVE PAIN

Once upon a time, God created a woman named Eve. She was a better design than Adam, but she still had many flaws. She was too curious. She was too strong-willed. She wanted to vote. When she tossed her hair, Adam's penis grew stiff and his mind went blank.

One day, she ate an apple.

It was God's apple.

God was very angry. He pinched her arm and slapped her hand and decreed that Eve would suffer terrible agony when she gave birth.

- What's birth? Eve asked.

- It's when you have a baby, said God.

- What's a baby? asked Eve.

- Keep tossing that hair, bitch, said God. - You'll find out.

God was so angry that He decided punishing Eve wasn't enough, and so God declared that all women, for all time, all over the earth, for ever and ever, would suffer agonizing pain when they gave birth too.

The End

My mother must have eaten more than just an apple, though, because her suffering didn't end at childbirth. Her back hurt and her shoulders ached. Her sinuses were congested and her feet were sore. Her neck was tight, her stomach was upset, her nails were ingrown, her eyesight was failing, her head was splitting, her throat was sore, her hands were stiff, her knees were creaky, her skin was dry, her lips were chapped, her feet were numb, her nerves were pinched, her teeth were cracked, and her gums were inflamed.

And she wasn't the only one.

All the women in *shul* – Yiddish for *synagogue* – seemed condemned to eternal agony. Mrs. Goldstein was bent at the waist and went with a walker, which she clutched with her clawlike arthritic hands. Mrs. Balsam had swollen ankles and *gut-unt-himmel*ed with every step. Mrs. Mayefsky needed a cane to climb the stairs. Men and women sat in separate sections, as per the ancient law, but why they put the Women's Section up two flights of stairs I'll never know; by the time they all *oy vey*ed their way up there, the services were over and it was time for them to start *vey iz meer*ing their way back down. And so, watching my mother in agony that morning, I found my mood mysteriously . . . improving.

I found myself strangely relieved.

Victoria, I realized, was a liar.

She was a fraud. A phony. This right here, holding her lower back with one hand and spraying Afrin nasal decongestant up her nose with the other, *this* was a *real* woman. The women in Victoria's Secret catalogs weren't real; it was lighting, makeup, tricks, no different than the Sea-Monkeys I had ordered from the Johnson Smith novelty catalog the summer before. After waiting an eternity for them to arrive, I poured the packet of dried Sea-Monkey eggs into a bowl of water, waiting, hands clasped, for the creatures from the advertisement to emerge: the handsome Father Sea-Monkey, the smiling Child Sea-Monkeys, the pretty Mother Sea-Monkey with a delicate pink bow in her hair. But all the eggs brought forth were tiny, squirming *shrutzim*.

Yiddish for *bugs*.

Sea-Monkeys, it turned out, were just shrimp.

- *Treyf*, my mother said as she flushed them down the toilet.

Yiddish for *nonkosher*.

The realization cheered me; the women in the Victoria's Secret catalog were as fake as Sea-Monkeys. Real women didn't hold their heads up. Their shoulders rolled forward, and they carried their breasts neither proudly nor high, but like sins, like burdens they were desperate to set down but had been cursed by God to carry for eternity. Were breasts punishments too? I wondered. Did God consider bras cheating? *Woe unto she who strappeth her breasts to her shoulders.*

I laughed at my own gullibility. When did real women ever dress like the women in Victoria's Secret? When had I ever seen a real woman wearing feathered shoes? I wasn't thrilled with being male, not by a long shot, but the women around me weren't making a great case for being female either. And so later that morning, as we gathered in the yeshiva synagogue to pray, I called out the traditional male prayer – *Blessed are you, Lord our God, Ruler of the Universe, who has not made me a woman* – and meant every word of it. I decided I would throw out Victoria's catalog of lies when I got home, and I would have, too, if I hadn't gone to Dov's house after school.

I loved going to Dov's house. Dov was my best friend, and his house was a joyful place filled with laughter and jokes. His father was a large but gentle man, and his mother wasn't in constant agony. Sometimes she was even happy.

- Grass stains mean you had fun! she laughed that afternoon as we tumbled in from playing outside. - No grass stains, kiddo, you're in big trouble!

She sat us in the kitchen and placed a plate of cookies before us.

Cookies!

Before dinner!

But cookies were only the first miracle of that day, for a moment later there appeared in the doorway a vision of beauty as otherworldly as any I'd beheld in the pages of Victoria's Secret. I thought for a moment I must have been dreaming; she was tall and graceful, all curves and long limbs and proud breasts, and she floated into the kitchen as if upon wings, her auburn hair tumbling over her bare, olive-skinned shoulders, the air trailing behind her as she floated by kissed with the most delicate scent of rarest flowers.

- Hey, Raizy, Dov said without so much as a glance in her direction.

Yiddish for *rose.*

Raizy? I thought.

That was Raizy?

I had seen Dov's older sister before, of course, but it had been a while. In that time, she had somehow transformed into an otherworldly being of heart-stirring magnificence. She smiled at me as she entered, her teeth white as brand-new tzitzit, her lips the same deep red as my favorite yarmulke. With the tips of her long, elegant fingers, she playfully snatched a cookie from Dov's plate.

- That's mine! Dov wailed. - Mom!

Raizy threw her head back and laughed, a gleeful, wicked laugh, a laugh that lit my soul, before spreading her wings and sweeping back out of the room as miraculously as she had swept in.

I couldn't breathe.

I couldn't move.

Kina hora, I thought.

Yiddish for *holy fuck*.

I lost all sense of time and that other thing. Dov said something, and then his mother said something else. She did a thing, and then he did a thing, and then some other thing happened, and then he went somewhere. It was only the loud, angry blare of my father's car horn that roused me from my reverie.

- I think that's for you, Dov's mother said.

I thanked her for the cookies, hurried out, and climbed into the front seat of my father's car. He squinted through his dreary cigarette smoke at the grass stains on my pants.

- You think we're made of money? he asked.

- No.

- Grass stains don't come out.

I could have argued Dov's mother's point – that perhaps grass stains, though financially lamentable, could also be seen as positive indicators of a well-spent youthful afternoon – but I didn't want my father to punch my best friend's mother in the face. My father was like God – loud, violent, reactionary – and Yahweh, I knew, was never prouder of His children than when they were being as violent as He was. I wondered if perhaps I could appease my father by being violent too.

- Dov pushed me, I lied.

- Did you push him back?

- Yes.

- Hard?

- Really hard. He fell down.

- Good.

I eyed his thick, hairy, male hands strangling the steering wheel as he drove – the cracked and yellowed fingernails, the blisters he'd been picking at, the dead skin sloughing off – and then I turned to the window and thought of Raizy. I thought of her long, elegant neck and her white painted fingernails and I thought of the way she held that cookie between her thumb and forefinger, and of the way the rest of her fingers gently fanned out when she did, like the petals of the delicate flower for which she was named, and I tried to imagine how it must have felt to be possessed of such beauty that even the most mundane of motions was somehow made song.

My father pulled into our driveway, parked the car, and belched, a deep rumbling quake that roiled up from the subterranean recesses of his vast abdominal netherworld. He trapped the toxic gas in his cheeks, and I thought for a moment he was trying to save me, to protect his child from the deadly reactor core meltdown that was occurring within him – *Run, child! Save yourself!* – but he merely twisted his lips in my direction and blew the noxious fumes out.

I smelled borscht.

I tried not to breathe, to think only of Raizy, but all I could think of was gas chambers.

He killed the engine.

- You better hope those grass stains come out, he said. - Money doesn't grow on trees.

He belched again, climbed out of the car, slammed the heavy door, and trudged inside to rape some Canaanite women.

And that, more or less, was when I decided to steal my mother's pantyhose.

· · ·

- Fuck you, my father said to my brother.

- No, fuck you, my brother said to my father.

It was Shabbos and for once, I had been looking forward to their fighting, as it would provide me cover to sneak down the hallway to my parents' bedroom. Raizy was living proof that women like those in Victoria's Secret did exist, even in Monsey, and I wanted to experience, if only for a moment, what it would be like to be her.

He who wears the clothes of a woman, said God, *is an abomination.*

Easy for God to say, I thought. *He doesn't even have a body.* Who was He to tell me what to do with mine? Besides, if God was cruel enough to make me a First-Draft Man, I didn't see why I shouldn't take matters into my own hands and edit myself into a Second-Draft Woman.

My father grabbed my brother by his collar and shook him.

My brother swung his fist at my father.

My mother sang Shabbos songs.

My sister cried.

I slipped out and headed to my parents' bedroom, where I went straight for my mother's underwear drawer. I grabbed the first pair of pantyhose I could find, stuffed them into the pocket of my dark-blue Shabbos pants, and was back at the table before my brother was even bleeding.

Lousy *gonif*, my ass.

...

Once upon a time, Rabbi Scold had told us, Jacob wrestled with an angel. They wrestled all night, hour after hour, from evening to morning, neither one willing to relent or surrender, but it was nothing compared to how I wrestled that evening with my mother's pantyhose. For what seemed like hours, I tried to figure out how to get the damned things on, as it was impossible to tell the front from the back, or even if there was a front or back. I grew irritated, angry. Would a label have killed them? Every time I tried to slide my foot down one leg of it, the other leg seemed to disappear, leaving me no choice but to back my first foot out, find the other leg, and start all over again. It was as if they didn't want me to get them on, as if they knew I was committing a sin. I tried to get both feet into both legs simultaneously, but the nail of my big toe snagged painfully on the fabric, threatening to tear my mother's pantyhose or rip off my toenail. My frustration grew; every minute I spent in the bathroom was another minute my father could come downstairs, kick the bathroom door open, and catch me. At last, from a combination of exasperation and fear, I gave up. I would not contend with pantyhose forever.

I trudged back to my bedroom, climbed into bed, and took out the Victoria's Secret catalog, hoping that within it lay some revelations, some instructions, some clues. I flipped glumly through the pages, careful not to rouse my brother, who was sleeping just a few feet away, wondering where it was that women gathered to pass along the ancient secrets of pantyhose, when I happened upon the image of a woman sitting on the edge of a yellow tufted chair, pulling some parma violet tights onto her long, graceful leg. She had pulled them only halfway up, but I noticed that she had first gathered them in her hand, bunching the leg together all the way to the toes, and only then sliding them up her leg.

Of course! I thought.

Like Torahs.

Pantyhose are like Torahs.

In synagogue, before the Torah is returned to the Holy Ark, it is raised overhead, the scrolls rolled back up, and its cover replaced. In order to get the cover back over the scrolls, you first have to gather the cover in your hands, slip the openings over the scroll handles, only then pulling the cover down around the scroll itself.

A moment later I was back in the bathroom, door locked, blinds closed, successfully unrolling the pantyhose up my legs. I shivered at the wave of delightful sensations it sent through me. Cool yet warm, tight yet soft, restrictive yet utterly freeing. I looked down in amazement at my once-hideous form. My legs were now smooth, my calves were now shapely, my thighs were now long and lean. From the waist up, I was still a hideous male, but from the waist down I was a beautiful woman.

I was elated, and I was furious. Why the hell were these magical garments reserved for *women?* Men were the ugly ones. If anyone needed pantyhose, it was us.

I was desperate to see my new form in full, but the only mirror in the bathroom was the door of the medicine cabinet above the sink. I tiptoed back to my bedroom in my pantyhosed feet, heart pounding, alert for the slightest creak of a floorboard overhead, the tiniest squeal of a mattress spring from my parents' bedroom that would signal my doom. If my father caught me, he'd kill me; if my mother caught me, she'd cry so much I'd kill myself. I crept in, quietly opened my closet door, and had to silence a gasp as I stared in wonder at my reflection in the full-length mirror that hung behind it.

- And the Lord, Rabbi Scold had taught us, saw that it was good.

Good? I thought as I admired my shapely legs.

I was fucking *fantastic.*

...

- Today, Rabbi Scold announced, his eyebrows furrowing even deeper than usual, we are going to read a story about a terrible city called Sodom.

- God destroyed Sodom, Rabbi Scold continued, because the men who lived there were *feigeles.*

Yiddish for *fags.*

Everyone laughed.

Of all the insults in the Yiddish language, none was so mortifying as *feigele.* Sure, we called one another *schmuck* and *putz* and occasionally, if no rabbis were around, *asshole.* But *feigele* was worse than them all. It had nothing to do with sex, which we knew nothing about at the time. To be a *schmuck* or a *putz* was to be a fool – but to be a *feigele* was to be weak, mincing, effeminate. To be a *feigele* was worse than being a woman, who had no choice but to be a woman. A *feigele* was a man who *wanted* to be a woman. And that was unforgivable.

Rabbi Scold smiled along with my snickering classmates. Nechemya, sitting beside me, did his best *feigele* impression – hands out to his sides, wrists dangling limply as he swiveled his hips in his seat – and the laughter began again.

Over the past week, pantyhose had led to skirts. Skirts had led to blouses. Blouses had led to perfume.

Was I a *feigele*? I wondered as they laughed, feeling myself redden with bitter shame. How could I know for sure? Did *feigeles* know they were *feigeles*? Did they *want* to be *feigeles*? And could I un*feigele*ize myself if I was?

Rabbi Scold had taught us that to combat the temptations of the Evil Inclination, we should repeat to ourselves the names of the seven Canaanite nations: Canaanites, Amorites, Girgashites, Hittites, Hivites, Jebusites, and Perizzites. This, he said, would remind us of the wages of sin.

I was up to Girgashites when the mockery of my classmates turned my shame to anger. So I put on pantyhose, so what? So I put on a skirt? Why were pants for men and skirts for women anyway? It seemed so arbitrary. What was everyone's obsession with fabric?

- I know you're my son! the *feigele*'s father shouts. - But in my house, boys wear fabric formed into two tubes and connected at the top, not one single cylinder of fabric that goes around the waist! A single cylinder of fabric that goes around the waist is for girls!

To hell with them, I thought. I was just doing what God Himself did when He created Eve, trying to undo the hideous blunder that was Man. This was God's screwup, not mine. Here I was, cleaning up His mess, fixing His mistake – and *I* was the sicko?

School came to an end, but my mood did not. I felt uglier than ever, as sick inside as I was revolting outside, and needed something to cheer me up.

Something like high heels.

Finding the house empty when I returned from yeshiva, I hurried to my mother's bedroom closet. On the floor at the back where she kept her Shabbos shoes, I found the white chunky heels she wore on Yom Kippur, the Day of Atonement. They were no stilettos, and they had no feathers, but they would do.

Downstairs in my bedroom, I pulled on my mother's pantyhose, slipped on her shoes, and all that was hideous disappeared – Rabbi Scold, Nechemya, my father, myself, all were gloriously gone – and behold, I was beautiful again, more beautiful than ever before. The heels made me taller, longer; they made my hips tilt forward, my lower back arch, my shoulders drop.

I hurried again to my closet mirror. Unfortunately, though, while from the waist down I had my mother's physique – a tiny woman who shopped for clothes in the Petites department in Bamberger's – from the waist up I had my father's build – a squat, barrel-chested man who shopped for clothes in the Auto Department at Sears. Consequently, my body looks as if God, running out of parts during my creation, jammed the top half of a strongman onto the bottom half of a ballerina, glued a penis on it, and called it a day.

I lifted the mirror off its hook, set it on the floor, and tilted it forward, angling it so that my upper body was not in frame.

I was all lower half.

And I was beautiful.

I turned my back to the mirror, put my hands on my waist, and cocked my hips to one side as I'd seen the women in Victoria's Secret do, then peered over my shoulder at the half reflection of my half-beautiful self. I may have been an abomination, but Christ Almighty, what an ass I had on me.

...

The next day, Sodom was destroyed.

Rabbi Scold shook his fist, pounded on his desk. The *feigeles* of Sodom had tried to rape some angels, and God was furious.

- Burning sulfur rained down upon the city! Rabbi Scold bellowed. - All were killed!

Everyone cheered.

- Can I come over after school? I asked Dov.

I wanted to see Raizy. I wanted to watch her, study her. I wanted to memorize how she held her head, how she walked, how she moved through time and space, so that I could try to do the same in the twelve-inch-wide mirrored world behind my bedroom closet door, that secret narrow portal to a world in which I was beautiful too.

Mostly, though, I just wanted to raid her closet.

My mother's tan and beige palette was beginning to bore me. As Victoria herself had wisely noted, there's more to life than earth tones.

Me and Dov played tag. We played baseball. We played football. I was careful not to fall and get any grass stains.

- What do you want to play now? Dov asked.

- I don't know, I said. - How about something . . . indoors?

We went inside to find his older brother Lazer in the living room watching the TV show *M*A*S*H*. Klinger, the cross-dressing corporal, was wearing a dress.

- I'm nuts, said Klinger.

Lazer and Dov laughed.

As they did, I crept upstairs, trying not to make a sound, where I happened upon Raizy in her bedroom, blow-drying her hair. I hid at the edge of the doorframe and watched her, bent over at the waist, her long hair dancing and whirling in the warming air, and my soul danced with it.

I watched her and I watched her. Now and then I heard Dov and Lazer laugh. I thought I heard someone coming up the stairs and turned to check. When I turned back, my blood froze. Raizy had straightened up and was staring at me in her mirror. I waited for her to shout, to berate me. *Pervert! Peeping Tom! Police!* But she didn't. Instead, with her perfect index finger she tucked her perfect hair behind her perfect ear and turned her head upon her long, elegant neck to face me, a gentle smile on her face. It was as if she knew — knew what poetry she was, knew how lucky she had been to have been born female, knew and understood why I would long to be so too.

- I think that's for you, she said, her voice a song.

Her hair dryer?

Was she offering me her hair dryer?

I could use a hair dryer.

- It . . . is? I asked, reaching out my hand.

- Your father, she said, nodding toward the window. - Isn't that him?

Only then did I hear the furious car honking coming from the driveway. I turned and raced downstairs. On the TV, Klinger was talking to Radar.

- I have to burn my froufrou, he said.

Everyone laughed.

I climbed into the car. My father glared at me.

- What took so long? he growled. - Something wrong with your ears?

I stared glumly out the window.

Something was wrong with my everything.

We drove home in silence. He dropped me off in front of the house, told me to fold the laundry and clean my room, and sped off to Sears.

Nobody was home. I went to my mother's bathroom, where I found her round hairbrush and blow-dryer. I brought them to the downstairs bathroom and wet my stupid short male hair in the sink. I leaned over as Raizy had and pressed my meager locks forward over my forehead. I turned the hair dryer on and began whipping it back and forth, feeling the warm air flowing through my hair.

It felt beautiful.

I felt beautiful.

The warmth upon my face, my hair twirling and swirling; was this what she felt like? Was this what all women felt like, every moment of every day, this delicious freedom, this inexpressible joy?

I switched the blow-dryer off, straightened up, and jumped.

There in the doorway stood my father, the pack of cigarettes he'd forgotten in his hand, a look of utter disgust upon his face.

- *Feigele*, he said.

...

I avoided my mother and father for the rest of the evening and went to bed early. I desperately wanted to put on my mother's shoes.

I took them out. I put them away. I took them out. I put them on.

Feigele, I thought.

I took them off.

I put them away.

Canaanites, I thought to myself. *Amorites, Girgashites* . . .

I left for yeshiva early the following morning, hoping not to see my parents, but I passed my mother on my way to the front door and her eyes fixed on mine with a look of such disappointment that I had to turn away.

Maybe I was a *feigele*. Maybe I was a sinner. Maybe I was no better than the angel-raping Sodomites whom God in His disgust had turned to ash. Maybe I should be turned to ash too.

When I got to yeshiva, a terrible commotion was under way. It was early, morning prayers had not yet begun, and the boys were scurrying in and out of the bathroom, laughing and shouting. Inside, I found them pressed together in the last stall, where Nechemya was flipping through the pages of a glossy, colorful magazine. I pressed my way through them to get a better view, hoping it was Victoria's Secret.

The magazine was called *Honcho*.

There was a cowboy on the cover.

He was wearing sunglasses.

His shirt was unbuttoned to his hair-covered stomach.

Feh, I thought.

It was no Victoria's Secret.

Nechemya opened the magazine, revealing a full-page photograph of two half-naked construction workers, staring into each other's eyes and holding each other's penis.

- *Feigeles!* Nechemya shouted. - *Feigeles!*

Everyone laughed, and this time, I joined them too.

I was elated. I was jubilant. I was overcome with relief.

That's a feigele? I thought.

That can't be me, I thought. *I hate men! Men disgust me!*

A huge weight had been lifted from my shoulders, and I laughed as loud as I could.

- Gross! said Nechemya.

- Gross! I joined in.

Nechemya turned the page, but this time, instead of laughing in mockery at what he found there, he shouted in genuine horror – a shout of shock and revulsion and disgust. I looked over his shoulder, expecting to see more *feigeles*, but what I saw instead, at the top of the page, was a photo of a woman. She was quite beautiful, with long blonde hair, full red lips, and matching red heels. She held one hand over her open mouth, her eyes wide, as if caught being naughty. With the other, she held up the front of her skirt, revealing, between her legs, an erect penis.

Nechemya pretended to vomit.

- Bluuuurrgghhh! he shouted, and shoved the magazine into my hands.

The photo was an advertisement for an 8mm film.

The film was called *Chicks with Dicks*.

Nechemya ran from the stall, still pretending to puke. The other boys did the same, shouting and fake retching as they went. I dropped the magazine, afraid for my life, terrified they would discover the pantyhose I was wearing beneath my yeshiva pants.

I decided to play along to avoid suspicion, and raced with them from the stall, screaming and fake puking all the way. We raced toward the bathroom exit as if fleeing from Sodom, never looking back, but before we could reach it, the door swung open and Rabbi Scold walked in, fists clenched and eyes afire, a furious male giant, as monstrous and wrathful as God Himself.

...

Nechemya was crying. I tried not to look at him. All the boys Rabbi Scold caught in the bathroom had been sent to the office of Rabbi Ream, the fearsome yeshiva principal. He ordered us to stand against the back wall and watch as he interrogated Nechemya, spittle flying from his lips as he demanded to know where Nechemya had gotten the magazine. Nechemya's face was red with shame, and he kept his eyes lowered. Between heavy sobs, he said he'd found the magazine in the tall grass beside the road on his way to yeshiva.

Rabbi Ream slapped his face.

- What other *dreck* do you bring to yeshiva? he bellowed.

Yiddish for *trash*.

- Are you a garbageman? Rabbi Ream roared.

The control top of my mother's pantyhose pinched at my waist. I was terrified they were going to discover me, punish me, humiliate me, phone my parents. If my father thought I was a *feigele* just for blow-drying my hair, then pantyhose and *Honcho* were going to remove all doubt. He would do to me what God did to Sodom.

Nechemya was suspended for a week. The rest of us were sent back to class, our punishments to be decided later. Later, I watched from the classroom window as Nechemya's father dragged him by the ear to his car.

When I got home, I hurried to my bedroom to purge it all – the pantyhose, the heels, the blouses, the catalog – only to find my mother already there, standing beside my bed, the same look of sorrow on her face as when I'd left that morning.

In her hand was the Victoria's Secret catalog.

She had been cleaning my room, she said, changing the bedding, when she found it hidden under my pillow.

- What would your uncle say? she asked.

My uncle was a rabbi.

I couldn't answer. All I could think about was my secret stash of lingerie and high heels hidden just below the bed, inches from where she now stood, and what might have happened if I'd gotten home just moments later.

- If you want to look at naked women, she said, do it somewhere else.

She turned and went back upstairs, taking Victoria with her. I sat on my bed, burning with shame. My father thought I was a *feigele*. My mother thought I was a pervert. But the truth was far more dire than either of them suspected.

I didn't want to have sex with men.

I didn't want to have sex with women.

I wanted to *be* a woman.

I wanted to be beautiful.

I wasn't a *feigele*.

I was worse.

I was a chick with a dick.

Feh.

I gathered my mother's clothes from beneath my bed, brought them to the laundry room, and mixed them in with the rest of the family laundry. I would return the heels to her closet when she wasn't home.

When God was destroying Sodom, Rabbi Scold taught us, He commanded Lot and his wife not to look back at the city as they fled. He didn't want them to see what He was doing.

Was God ashamed of Himself too? I wondered.

Of His anger?

Of His rage?

Of His being a violent, hideous First-Draft Man?

We ate dinner in silence. Afterward, I went to bed, climbed under the covers, and turned to face the lamp on my nightstand. I switched it on and stared into the bright, blazing white bulb until my eyes began to water. I didn't allow myself to look away. I didn't allow myself to blink. When at last I could bear it no more, I fumbled for the switch and turned the light off.

I was blind. Wonderfully, blissfully blind. I couldn't see – not the walls, not the windows, not the moon, not myself. I lay back in bed, with no sense of physical being at all but for the tears of shame running down my cheeks.

Now the earth was formless and void, and darkness covered the deep.

How nice it must have been before birth.

How nice it must have been before Being.

How nice it must have been to have no form at all.

5.

On the holiday of Purim, Rabbi Chagrin told us the story of Haman, the evil vizier of the Persian king Ahasuerus, who wanted to kill the Jews. The story begins with Queen Vashti refusing to dance naked for her husband and his guests.

- Why did she refuse to dance? Rabbi Chagrin said. - Because God had cursed her.

How did He curse her?

He cursed her by causing her to grow a tail.

- A tail? we asked.

- By tail, Rabbi Chagrin explained, the rabbis meant penis.

God cursed Vashti with a penis.

The End.

6.

The upside to midlife, of course, is that the damned thing is half over. The race is half run. Twenty years old, thirty years old – sorry, kid, you've still got a lot of miles ahead of you. Death when it comes is no guarantee of release – God could always send you back for a consecutive life sentence, the sick fuck – but as for this particular go-around, you hit midlife and it's all downhill.

- Hello? the old lady in the room down the hall called, her voice weak and terrified in the dark. It was well past midnight.

- Hello? she called. - Hello? Help me, hello?

She'd been at it for hours.

Where the fuck, I wondered, *are the fucking nurses?*

They probably couldn't hear her over Sean Hannity.

- Our nation, proclaimed Sean, is under attack.

The patient in the room across the hall had been watching Fox News, full volume, ever since he'd been admitted earlier that afternoon. The man was morbidly obese, and I had watched from my bed as it had taken half a dozen health-care workers to transfer him from his double-wide gurney, through the doorway, to his bed. Anyone entering his room was required to wear full hazmat suits, which I thought a bit much just because he was watching Fox News.

The nurse told me it was because he was infested with vermin.

I was pretty sure that was the same thing.

One morning, some years ago, like millions of other innocent men and women around the world, I found myself suddenly bombarded by miserable stories. They were stories of despair, cruelty, and evil. There was no escape from them. They came at me every minute, every second, without cease. The stories were called *news*, though there was nothing new about them. They'd been around for years, but now they appeared on my phone, on my laptop, on my desktop, as texts, as videos, every minute of every hour of every day and night, a vomit of stories spewed upon the world by the foul coupling of the twenty-four-hour news cycle and the internet. Some of these stories were delivered to my phone. Some were delivered to my email. Some were told to me by friends, some were told to me by coworkers, all of whom had been bombarded themselves. *Did you hear about this?* they asked. *Did you read about that?* The specifics of the stories were always different – some were about war, some were about climate change, some were about scandals or racism or antisemitism – but the name of the stories was the same:

Feh.

Feh is the only story the news ever tells, and soon I could take it no more. I needed the barrage of contempt, criticism, and condemnation to end.

- Did you hear what happened in Israel? my friend Craig asked one morning. I was in no mood.

- Something horrible? I replied.

- A bomb, he said with a shake of his head. - In a pizza shop.

- Why are you telling me that?

- I don't know.

- You don't know?

- I thought I'd let you know.

- It's nine thirty in the morning, and you thought you'd just let me know people had been blown to bits five thousand miles away?

- I thought you might want to know.

- I already know, it's the fucking Middle East! Bombs go off in pizza shops!

That's what pizza shops in the Middle East are for – blowing up! So tell me, how the *fuck* does my knowing about this particular fucking bombing change *anything* in the world except to make me feel even more hopeless than I did before?

He shrugged and took a bite of his chocolate doughnut.

- Good thing I didn't tell you about the oil spill, he said. - It was a doozy.

Later that day, determined to dam up the flood of miserable stories, I added a note to the bottom of my emails:

Any emails containing links, pics, or news stories of any kind will be deleted immediately. I don't care if you think they're funny or LOL or WTF. I don't care, and I don't want to know. Share them with your other friends. Do not fuck with my fucking bubble.

In response, Craig sent me a link to the story about the oil spill.

My editor sent me a link to the pizza shop bombing story.

I have good friends.

Eventually, though, the stories stopped coming. My digital levee held. But here in the hospital, I could not escape.

- *Feh*, said Sean Hannity. - We'll be right back.

Like Hannity himself, Hazmat hadn't stopped complaining since he'd arrived. He complained about the doctors he proclaimed were Liberals, he complained about the black maintenance man he proclaimed lazy, he complained about the Latina nurse he proclaimed *can't speak no good English*. His God Hannity hated, so behold Hazmat hated too.

- I want a fucking nurse, Hazmat shouted from his bed, who speaks fucking English!

Note: The nurse did speak English.

Note: The fat fuck was Latino himself.

I'm in Hell, I thought. I wasn't in a hospital; it only looked like a hospital. I had died and been sentenced to Hell, where bitter men with lice-infested genitalia complain ceaselessly about the heat, where the only TV channel is news, and where the painkillers never arrive.

- Hello? the old woman called again. - Hello?

The old woman's name was Ida. I'd overheard some nurses discussing her earlier. She was a hundred and three years old, and her mind was shot. She thought it was 1922. She thought she was twelve years old.

- I'm going to be late for school! Ida called out in a weak and wavering voice. - Hello?

Listening to a woman at the end of her life made me consider the middle of my own, and about how I had come to find myself in this hospital bed, hooked up to machines, my system forcibly shut down so that it didn't destroy itself.

I was in my forties and unemployed, having been fired some time ago from my advertising job of fifteen years. God works in mysterious ways, and that time He worked through a dim-witted, dough-faced Scandinavian creative director in a sweater-vest who called me into his office, took off his gold Rolex, laid it down on the desk, and told me they couldn't afford me anymore. I nodded, stood, and told him that someday, a dumb fuck in a sweater-vest would sit *him* down, take off *his* Rolex, and fire *him*.

Note: That has not happened.

He's doing great.

He runs IKEA or something.

I was good at advertising because I hate myself. Advertising is a *feh*-based industry; the more *feh* you can make someone feel, the more inclined they will be to purchase the product that promises to un*feh* them. Some years earlier, I had been hired by Saatchi & Saatchi to come up with fake words. Not commercials or billboards. Fake words. The fake words would be used to advertise a midlevel brand of supermarket hair-care products, by turning the fake words into fake hair problems that their products could offer fake solutions to. The word I came up with was *follicalization*. The shampoo, the ad would claim, increases the follicalization of your hair. Guess what happens if you have poor hair follicalization:

Feh.

But three years now since being fired, I still hadn't been able to find a job.

Craig suggested I try writing for Hollywood. Craig is a Feh, too, and so feels the need, as we Fehs often do, to fix everyone's problems. It's not because we're nice; it's because we're pretty sure there's no other reason for you to love us; we're like the shop owner paying the mob to let him stay open.

We're the shop owners.

You're the mob.

- They pay a lot, Craig said. - You'd be good at it.

But the idea of writing for Hollywood made me feel even more *feh* than I already did.

- I just think I should give doing hard-core pornography a chance first, I said.

My situation was grim. I had two mortgages, two leases, two children, and no income. I was forty-something in a world that considered twenty-two over the hill. I tried my best.

- Data social bandwidth content? the interviewers asked me.

- Optimization analytics geo-tagging, I replied. - Insta.

They concurred, but they sensed that my heart wasn't in it.

Sometimes, in my darkest moments – when my heart gets broken or my dreams collapse or I can't find a job to provide for my family – I suspect I am God's favorite comedy.

- I could use a good laugh, God says as He drops onto His couch and aims His remote at the TV. - Let's watch a little *Auslander*.

Gabriel enters, holding a bowl of popcorn, and sits down beside Him.

- Is this the unemployment episode? Gabriel asks. - I *love* this one.

I couldn't eat. I couldn't sleep. All I could do was obsess about money. Monsey, the town of my youth, was a wealthy community, and I went to a yeshiva with wealthy children. Their parents drove Cadillacs and Mercedes. On Sundays they played on their tennis courts and swam in their pools. My family was not wealthy. My father drove an old station wagon; on Sundays my mother clipped coupons, went to Marshalls, sighed, and put clothes on layaway. My relationship to money is thus a tortured one: nothing makes me feel more secure than having it, but upon having it, I can only worry about losing it. Capitalism and religion are more alike than their disciples care to admit: The striving in both is perpetual, the goal selfish, winners scarce, and losing unforgivable. Yahwists and Mammonists exist side by side on the razor's edge of ruin, and I am sat right between them. And so, desperate for work, I attempted to make myself look younger.

I bought skinny jeans that made me look fat. I bought tooth whitener that burned my gums. I paid a bald man in SoHo for what his hair salon called the Camo, a dye job that promised to get rid of my gray hair without making me look like a middle-aged fool. I went home, looked in the mirror, took out the hair trimmer, and shaved my head. I didn't want my sons to see me, to see that I thought age mattered, to see that I thought appearances made a difference. To see that I was a middle-aged fool.

- Did you get a haircut? Paix asked that evening.

- Yeah, I said. - What do you think?

- You look like a soldier, he said approvingly.

He picked up his phone, held it out, and took a photo of us. He smiled. He saw a beautiful young boy and his dad. This is what he said when he looked at it:

- Cool.

I saw a beautiful young boy next to the fat failure who couldn't provide for him. This is what I thought when he showed it to me:

Feh.

And so, in a fateful decision that led to my eventual hospitalization, I decided to lose weight.

Again.

My first diet was over thirty years ago. I was nine years old, and my mother had taken me to Sears to buy pants. I went into the dressing room and pulled on a pair of Toughskins jeans, sized Slim.

Nope.

I tried on a pair of Regulars.

Nope.

- You're a Husky, said my mother.

- I'm a what?

- A Husky.

- What does that mean?

- It means you're chubby, she said.

I stopped eating. I would have made myself vomit, but I felt guilty for wasting the food my mother had spent money on. A few days later, I went to the nearby Caldor department store, shoplifted a handgrip strengthener and a chest expander, and began to exercise. A chest expander is two plastic handles connected by long metal springs. It doesn't expand your chest; it tears the flesh off it.

That's what you get, I reproached myself as I expanded my chest, flaying myself while fighting back bitter tears of agony, *for being a fat husky fuck.*

A lifetime of diets has followed in its bloody wake – diets and workouts and weight-gainer shakes and weight-loss pills. Antisemites like to claim that Jews are shape-shifters, but riddle me this, Grand Wizard: If I could pick my shape, do you really think I'd have picked *this* one? I'd have picked the Brad Pitt. I'd have picked the Serena Williams. I'd have picked anything but the Shalom Auslander.

Size Husky.

Pride, of late, is in. I confess I don't get it. All around me, I see people dressed in tight, revealing clothing, and I wonder if they can possibly be as okay with themselves as they seem to be. I cannot imagine being proud, of anything, and so I take note of the non-slim men tugging uncomfortably at their slim-fit shirts, of the young women pulling down their belly shirts to cover the bellies that the shirts are designed to expose. I'm projecting, I know, but they seem terribly uncomfortable, glancing about to see if anyone's watching as they adjust themselves. I can't believe they actually want to dress this way; perhaps they have merely chosen the lesser of two evils – feeling physically uncomfortable wearing trendy clothing over feeling socially uncomfortable for not wearing trendy clothing. I hope I'm wrong. I hope they're truly okay with themselves. I am not and never have been. But then I worry about the follicalization of my hair, and I made the fucking word up.

Which brings me back to the poison in the amber-colored dropper bottle hidden at the back of my bathroom drawer.

GW501516 is a selective androgen receptor modulator, or SARM, that had shown promise in triggering fat loss until it was banned by the World Anti-Doping Agency when it had also been shown to trigger cancer cells. But to a certain self-loathing, self-destructive state of mind such as my own, *banned* just means it works. *Banned* is good. It doesn't get better than *banned*. I ordered GW501516 from a shady website, and it arrived soon after, along with a page of legalese indemnifying said website from any negative effects its product might have upon people self-loathing enough to use it. Now, after two months of using it, my pancreas was eating itself.

- Hello? Ida called out. - Is anybody there? Hello?

- FOR FUCK'S SAKE, I shouted, WILL SOMEONE PLEASE HELP THAT WOMAN?

The nurse stormed into my room.

- If you need something, she said with barely contained fury, press the red button.

I pressed the red button.

- Yes? she said.

- That old woman is terrified.

- She thinks she's twelve years old, said the nurse. - She thinks she's late for school.

- It's midnight.

- She thinks it's daytime.

- Tell her it's nighttime.

- I did, said the nurse. - She forgets. I tell her she's not twelve years old, but she forgets that too.

- Then tell her she *is* twelve years old, but it's Sunday. School's closed, kid, chill the fuck out.

- I'll try that.

- Thank you.

- Is there anything else?

I wanted to ask her if she hated herself. I wanted to ask her if she hated the way her ill-fitting nurse uniform accentuated the rolls of her belly fat, if she hated her thinning hair, if she hated the bags under her eyes. Or if, somehow, inexplicably, she didn't – if she liked her hair, if she liked the baby blue of her uniform, if she didn't particularly care about the veins on her legs, if she went home, fell into bed, smiled, and thought, *I like myself*, because if she did, if she genuinely liked herself, then she was fucking bananas and shouldn't be walking the streets, let alone administering medication.

- I'm in pain, I said.

- I'll get you some painkillers, she said.

She turned to leave.

- I'm sorry, I said.

- It's okay, she said. - It's nice that you care about her.

- I'm a wonderful person, I said. - Would you mind telling that fat fuck to turn down that Fox News shit?

- I tried that too, she said. - I'll try again.

She went to Hazmat's room; a moment later, he was shouting again. He shouted that the nurse was violating his constitutional rights, that the doctor was a libtard quack, that the hospital was substandard because of immigrants, that the care was insufficient because of Democrats, that the food was too cold, and that his room was too hot.

I didn't blame him. He was only repeating the story Sean Hannity had been telling him, a story in which Conservatives were the beleaguered Gods, beset by stiff-necked Liberals and mainstream media and transgender pervert pedophiles who knew them not.

I phoned Ike.

It was one a.m.

Fuck you, I was going to say to him.

- Call whenever you need me, he'd said early in our relationship, and there had never been a time in those many years when he didn't take or return my call, including the day his own father passed away.

There was no answer.

I phoned back.

No answer.

I phoned back.

He answered.

- Fuck you, I wept.

I told him this was all his fault. I told him that for years he had laughed at my jokes about self-loathing, my jokes about shame, my jokes about guilt, like everyone did, like everyone always had, but that he was my shrink, god-damn it, and he should have known it was never mere jest, he should have known the pain I was in, should have known that I've lived my life from Day Fucking One locked in an endless battle with my own despised being – judging, condemning, deriding, belittling, unforgiving, without cease.

- Is that why you tried to kill yourself? he asked.

- I didn't try to kill myself! I shouted. - Jesus Christ, I was trying to fucking *like* myself! A few drops of poison a day, under the tongue, to lose weight, to like myself when I looked in the mirror – vainly, superficially, yes, but *like*, finally, somehow, after this eternity of disgust. Fuck my fucking pancreas; cut the damned thing out. It'll save me a few pounds.

There was a long silence.

- Hello? Ida called.

Ike apologized, though we both knew he wasn't at fault. But he insisted, adamantly, that neither I nor anyone else has ever hated themselves from Day One.

- We don't hate ourselves naturally, he said. - Nobody is born hating them-selves. Someone, consciously or not, intentionally or not, taught you to do that.

I hung up and texted Orli.

- I'm sorry, I said.

- About what?

- About me.

There was a long pause.

Hazmat turned up Fox News.

- You should get some sleep, she finally replied.

- I can't.

- Then write, she said.

I imagined her at home, surrounded by cardboard boxes and Bubble Wrap, whistling a happy tune while packing my shit up in the hopes I was going to drop dead.

That night, as Orli packed and Ida called for help and Fox News called for blood, I wrote a story about a bug who woke up one morning to find himself transformed into a hideous Franz Kafka. He was in Franz Kafka's body, in Franz Kafka's house, in Franz Kafka's bedroom. Bug lay on his back and with great effort lifted his oversize human head to peer down at his hideous naked being: at his pigeon chest, his flabby belly, his spindly legs, a meager two now, when the night before he'd had a magnificent six.

What's happened to me? he wondered.

He dropped to the floor, naked, and crawled to the closet mirror to get a better look at himself. He was horror-struck at first, but soon, as the shock of his transformation lessened and the warm orange light of the rising morning sun began to fill the room, Bug began to like what he beheld. His Kafka eyes were dark and soulful; his thin, almost feminine hands were long and graceful; his legs were scant but strong. He was on his hands and knees, looking backward over his shoulder to examine his external human genitals in the mirror when the bedroom door flew open and Kafka's father burst in, jaw clenched, eyes red with anger.

- *Feigele*, growled Kafka's father.

Bug didn't know what the word *feigele* meant, but he knew from the harsh sound of it that it must be critical, hateful. That it was meant to hurt him. Later, as Bug went about his first human day, he discovered that his father wasn't the only human who stood in judgment, who pointed his crooked finger and chose words to cause harm; it seemed something all humans did, all the time, to all other humans. His boss called him lazy; other car drivers told him he was stupid; billboards told him he was ugly; and in the evening, the grim news anchor told him the situation was hopeless and mostly his fault. Bug cursed his terrible humanness and decided to take his own life.

Why stay? he asked himself.

That night, after the Kafkas had gone to sleep, Bug crept to the kitchen, where he found, in the cabinet beneath the kitchen sink, a can of Instant-Kill bug spray.

Danger, said the can.

Toxic.

Not for Human Consumption.

Bug sat at the kitchen table, uncapped the poison, and pointed the nozzle directly at his face.

One press, he thought, *and all this pain and anguish and self-loathing will be over.*

He placed his thumb on the spray button, ready to commit an act of terrible self-harm that when he was vermin he would never have imagined. He closed his eyes, took a deep breath – and stopped. A warm and wonderful scent had filled his nostrils, something sweet and peaceful, something like joy. He opened his eyes and spotted, on the nearby stovetop, a tray of fresh-baked brownies. He had never smelled anything so delightful, and so he stood, and he went to the stove, whereupon he lifted a brownie out of the pan, soft and sweet and flaky, and placed a delicate morsel in his mouth.

My God! he thought. *What a blessed life I was ready to end! What a heaven of sensation I was ready to quit, what a paradise I was ready to leave!*

Just then, though, the lights came on, blinding him a moment, and Bug turned in horror to see Kafka's father standing in the doorway behind him, seething, red-faced, full of fury and contempt, an aluminum baseball bat in his hands. His eyes narrowed to see the brownie in Bug's hand.

- *Gonif,* growled Kafka's father.

And he beat Bug to death.

The End.

I sent Orli the story and waited. If she laughed, if she read my story, there was hope for us after all.

Time passed slowly.

She was probably packing my books.

Hasn't even read most of them, she thinks, dropping *Finnegans Wake* into a box. *Feh.*

At last, my phone buzzed.

- Ha, she texted. - Funny.

Our marriage was okay. For now. For the moment. For how long, I couldn't say.

- Hello? Ida called out again. - Help me, please!

The nurse hurried past my door, on her way to soothe her. But I knew it wouldn't matter what the nurse told Ida. It wouldn't matter what Ida saw outside her window. Day was night in her world, night was day. No amount of proof would change her mind.

At last, morning came, and Ida, believing it night, fell asleep.

7

THE MAN WHO DID NOTHING
WRONG AND WAS WRONG

Once upon a time, in a country far away, there lived a man named Job. Job was happy. Job did nothing wrong. Someone must have been telling lies about him, though, because one day his world turned to darkness. His children were murdered. His money dried up. His wife despised him. He bought skinny jeans. He tried to lose weight. His pancreas began to eat itself.

Job became distraught. He wished he had never been born. Job fell to his knees in misery and pain, and he called out to his God, wanting to know why He had brought such suffering upon him. This is what God said when he did:

- *Feh.*

- Oh, right, said Job. - Good point.

The End

To be *feh* is to be born upon a gallows. From the moment you are, you are guilty. There is no trial, no investigation, because the judgment is never in doubt. There is no reading of the crimes because the crime is you, your severest punishment a foregone conclusion. The case is closed before it is ever opened.

Still, as I lay in my hospital bed, waiting for my next dose of painkillers, I couldn't resist the too, too human temptation of causality – of wondering what particular sin I had committed this time, what specific law I had broken, what apple I had eaten to earn God's pancreatic wrath. I glanced over at my laptop resting on the table beside the hospital bed, the laptop I am never without, and it didn't take me long to figure it out:

My sin was writing.

Some years earlier, I had written a book about my relationship with God. I might have called Him an asshole. He was not amused. Somehow, despite His feelings, the book was published. This infuriated God even more, so He made sure, in the months following, that there was no film interest from Hollywood. One morning, soon after the book's release, on a steep canyon road in Los Angeles, a producer in his Porsche veered inexplicably off the side of the road. The car flipped over the guardrail, tumbled down the embankment, and burst into flames, incinerating as it did the screenplay for the film of my book on the front passenger seat beside him.

- What a shame, says Gabriel, peering down at the wreckage.

- He was a movie producer, says God. - Who gives a shit?

- I was talking about the Porsche, says Gabriel.

They laugh.

But God wasn't done. God plays the long game. God holds a grudge. Jews are *still* commanded to destroy Amalek, a nation that hasn't even existed for thousands of years and may never have. And so, in the years following the book's publication, our dear friend Lisa died from breast cancer; Paix was rushed to the ICU with swine flu and a collapsed lung; Lux was attacked by a swarm of bees; and, just so I didn't mistake it all for a simple run of bad luck, God killed our beloved dog Harley.

On Yom Kippur.

The Day of fucking Atonement.

I hate to pull an Adam here and blame a woman for my mistakes, but the whole damned writing thing was Orli's idea. From the very first, she encouraged me to write. I thought it a ludicrous idea.

- Why is it ludicrous? she had asked.

Because I had dropped out of college after four weeks, I'd said. Because I had never been to the Iowa Writers' Workshop. Because I'd read *The Art of Fiction* and *The Art of the Novel* and *Aspects of the Novel,* and I still hadn't written a goddamned thing. Because Joyce Carol Oates would never blurb me, and because Michiko Kakutani would never like me.

- Who's Michiko Kakutani?

- A book critic.

- Why won't she like you?

- Because I don't limn.

- You don't what?

- Limn. She likes writers who limn; I don't limn.

- So what if she doesn't like it? Orli said. - Fuck her.

- She's very influential.

- People will read you.

- Who?

- Me.

- Because you have to, I said. - Because I'm your husband.

- Because you're crazy, she said. - And I like crazy. All the crazy people are dead. Writers, artists, musicians – everyone's so sane these days, it's fucking boring.

She put her arms around me and hugged.

I wondered if she thought I was fat.

The next day, I went to the ad agency at which I worked, locked myself in my office, and wrote a story. The story concerned an advertising executive who dies and wakes sometime later to find that he has been reincarnated as a toilet in a men's room at the Port Authority Bus Terminal in New York City. He loudly bemoans his fate and curses the vengeful God who would punish him so cruelly.

- Surely there can be no fate worse than mine! he wails.

His lamentations are soon rebuffed by the toilet paper, who, in her previous life, had been an accountant in Westchester.

- You? she cries. - You have it easy!

A fierce debate ensues as to whose punishment is worse, whose existence more wretched. At least, argues the toilet paper accountant, the toilet advertising executive has the blessing of being rinsed clean after each humiliation, whereas she is ripped apart, piece by agonizing piece, smeared with fecal matter, and flushed away forever.

- How blessed are you! the toilet advertising executive retorts. - Soon the perforated roll of your existence will come to an end and with it your punishment, whereas I am made of porcelain and shall be here forever!

The plunger, standing in a puddle of filth in the corner of the restroom, can remain silent no longer.

- You both have it easy, the former podiatrist weeps. In his plunger form, he exists quite literally to suck shit, a punishment perhaps befitting a Hitler or a Stalin but certainly not a foot specialist from San Diego. His only respite is the few blessed moments he enjoys face-down on the urine-soaked restroom floor until it is time once again to be dunked into the murky depths of his porcelain hell.

The toilet paper accountant has no pity for the podiatrist plunger.

- What I wouldn't give, she says, for a cool rinse in the clear waters you decry!

- What I wouldn't give, the podiatrist plunger replies, to know I am only fifty sheets away from death!

Back and forth go these existential complaints, ultimately involving the urinal (an actuary from Staten Island), the automatic hand dryer (a screenwriter from Pasadena), and the paper seat protectors (a group of nuns whose minivan had been T-boned by a tractor trailer on the way to Disneyland), each one arguing that his or her fate was worse than the others'. None can imagine a despair more despairing than their own, nor offer any pity for their fellow sufferers. They argue and debate, getting nowhere, until all at once the bathroom door flies open and a man named Shalom Auslander rushes in. Auslander, bowels aflame, hurries headlong into the first filthy stall, sweating profusely as he is wont to do because he's fat. He lays some nuns down on the seat, defiles the advertising executive, wipes himself with the accountant, uses the podiatrist to clear a clog, downs three Imodium with a chug of his Pepto-Bismol, tries masturbating, fails, tries again, fails, gives up, and checks his emails.

The condemned souls witness this hideous spectacle in appalled silence. They have seen horrors before in their lavatorial hell, unspeakable horrors, it's true, but none as revolting as Auslander. At last Auslander finishes, washes his hands (inadequately), wipes them on his (soiled) pants, and leaves. As the door closes behind him, the toilet and the toilet paper and the urinal and the hand dryer and all the other pitiful souls trapped in that public bathroom at last agree that though their reincarnated forms are indeed loathsome, at least they hadn't come back as *that* guy.

That, they knew, would be truly unbearable.

That night I showed Orli the story, and she laughed. I told you about her laugh a few chapters back, but whatever you imagined as the laugh of all laughs, you were way off. You weren't even close. Orli laughs with her soul, she laughs with her being, she laughs with her hair and her toes. Her laugh is not just a light in the darkness, it is a light against darkness, a defiant light, a *Fuck you* to all that would dare to darken her world. She is under no illusions that life is not a bowl of cherries, far from it, but when she happens upon the rare cherries, she devours them. When we go for walks, she stops to smell the roses. Literally. It's annoying.

- Smell them, she says.

- I'm not smelling them.

- Why not?

- Because it's ridiculous.

- Just smell the fucking roses.

I smell them.

I sneeze.

My eyes water.

Later I will take Claritin.

The Claritin will give me nosebleeds.

Soon that became our tradition – the writing, not the rhinitis. I would write a story, and Orli would read it, in bed, or in the tub, or in the car on our way to dinner, and she would laugh, and I would laugh to see her laugh, and it felt like it was me and her against the world, and the world didn't stand a chance.

Now, though, from my bed in the darkened hospital, writing seemed a sin.

And the days of laughter very far away.

8.

The story of Job is one of the most famous stories in the world. Millions of people know it and tell it and retell it, and have done so for thousands of years.

- Therefore, Job says at the end of the story, I despise myself.

That's the happy ending.

The book of Job is the beloved tale of a man learning to despise himself.

This is what God says when he does:

- Good.

The End.

9.

- How did Pharaoh stop the plagues? asked Rabbi Scold.

- By despising himself, said Rabbi Scold.

- I and my people are wicked, Pharaoh finally admits.

English for *feh*.

All were *feh*, not just the leaders, not just the soldiers, not just the slave drivers – the painters and the writers were *feh*, the cellists and the poets were *feh*, the hungry and the homeless, the singers and the songwriters, the caregivers, the abolitionists, the kindergarten teachers, the doctors, the nurses, the abused, and the sick and the weak and the poor.

- *Feh* and *feh* and *feh*, said Pharaoh.

- Duh, said God.

And the plagues ceased.

The End.

10

Flynn, our chihuahua, is a fucking asshole. I could probably spend time wording that more eloquently and perhaps set myself up for a literary award of some kind that will make me feel momentarily better about myself, but I think it important to convey, without gloss or gild, his fucking assholeness.

Gloss or gild, how was that?

Pulitzer?

Guggenheim?

No?

Anyway.

Flynn snarls. He barks. He growls. At everyone and everything. He has cause. As a puppy, Flynn was terribly abused. The shitpile of a human being who owned him then ran a day-care center out of her home; in order to keep the children occupied in the backyard while she went inside to masturbate to *Schindler's List*, she would tie Flynn to the clothing line and let the little psychopaths torture him.

And they did. They chased him, poked him, grabbed him. He was eight weeks old at the time.

This is the story Flynn was raised with:

People Suck.

When at last he bit one of the bad children, the bad owner shouted, *Bad dog!*

and decided to put him down. A kindly foster family took him in, but it was too late. Flynn already knew the story. He mistrusted the foster family, as he did all human beings now, and he barked and growled at them too. Soon they put him up for adoption. We answered the advertisement, and they brought Flynn over to meet us. He growled at me, he growled at Orli, he growled at the boys, and he growled at our other dog, Natasha.

- Can we keep him? the boys asked.

I believe I already mentioned their poor judgment.

Some years before, when Orli and I learned that she was pregnant with our first son, I went to Ike in a panic. I had no idea what a father did. I didn't want to break this perfect, innocent being; I didn't want to ruin him, hurt him.

- Tell me, I begged him. - What does a father do?

- It's simple, said Ike. - It's not easy, but it's simple.

- What is it?

- Unconditional love.

- I'm not familiar with that, I said.

- Exactly, said Ike.

It sounded foolishly sentimental, but Ike had been a father to me himself. I had been suicidal when I first went to see him; in those dark first months he kept me from death, and in the months that followed, he gave me life. So Orli and I took his advice. We're trying the whole unconditional thing. This is the story we've endeavored to raise our sons with:

You are loved, without question, without reservation, no matter what you do, no matter what you become, from the moment you are born until the end of time.

The End.

Now the boys wanted to teach Flynn that he was loved too. I tried to pick him up, but he scurried beneath Orli's car and growled if any of us came near.

- Please, Dad, the boys begged. - We'll love him! He'll get better!

I told them it wouldn't be easy. I told them it would take patience and effort to get him to trust us, and it was possible he never would. The boys said they understood but wanted to try. I looked to Orli.

- Well, she said with a shrug, he's had a shitty childhood and hates people. He's an Auslander.

The boys cheered. It was hours before Flynn emerged from underneath the car, and another hour before he took his first wary step into our home. Over time, though, Flynn has changed; after years of love and affection, of treats and belly rubs, he now snuggles with us on the couch. He climbs into our laps, lies back, and sighs with relief. This is his new story:

Most People Suck.

But some don't.

Some people care.

Some people love.

Some people pick you up when the thunder rattles the windows, and some tuck you under the covers where it's warm when it's cold, and some scratch you behind the ear in that spot you just can't reach yourself.

Fair warning, though: If you happen to meet Flynn, even now, years later, and you happen to touch that spot on his back, that spot by his tail where the children grabbed him and pulled him and shook him, he will bite your fucking hand off.

Stories are powerful things.

11.

After a week in the hospital, my pancreas stopped eating itself. I was discharged, but the medical team warned me there was no guarantee it wouldn't start doing so again. I still hadn't confessed the drug I had taken, so they were still looking for an answer. I would need further MRIs, liver tests, kidney tests, and regular blood work, but for the moment I had stabilized enough to go home. Doctor Superior had stopped by my hospital room to judge me one last time before I left.

- Now remember, he said, you only have one pancreas.

- Really? I said. - I didn't know that. What's the one we have two of again?

- Kidneys.

- Oh, I said. - I was thinking of testicles, but maybe that's just me.

- Live clean, said Doctor Superior. - Don't drink, don't smoke, don't take drugs. Second cases of pancreatitis don't always respond to treatment.

I hadn't told Orli about the weight-loss drug I had taken either. I'm aware of the irony of my spinelessness: I had taken something dangerous because I was ashamed of myself, and now, because I was ashamed of what I had taken because I was ashamed of myself, I couldn't admit it to the woman who loved me that I had taken something because I was ashamed of myself.

Which I was ashamed about.

We got home and Orli helped me to the couch, a bottle of prescription pain-killers clutched in my hand.

Caution, it read.

A black skull and crossbones.

The good stuff.

I watched Orli at the kitchen table, going through the week's mail: sighing at the Amex statement, shaking her head at the notices from the bank, flinging the latest threat from the IRS onto the growing pile of bills.

- What? I asked.

- Nothing, she said.

- Not nothing. Something.

- It can wait.

- Jesus, I snapped, just fucking tell me.

She closed her eyes, took a deep breath, and shook her head.

- We can't afford this anymore, she said.

- This what?

- It can wait.

- No.

- Yes.

- This *what?*

- This house! she said. - This fucking house!

We'll be back with more hilarious Auslander *after these commercial messages.*

Of all the drugs I've taken in my life to ease my *feh*, none has been more potent than money. Psychiatrists should prescribe it.

- I'm awful, Doc, says the patient. - I'm a failure. I'm hideous.

- Have you tried money? asks the psychiatrist. - I think you should try money.

Like any medication, though, money has some nasty side effects. Capitalism tells its own stories, stories as destructive as any of those in the Bible. It tells them every day, in advertisements and films, in ghettos and gated communities, in Compton and in Bel Air, on television and in newspapers and on social media. There are two fundamental stories in capitalism, stories as old as the system itself, stories upon which the entire system is built and without which it would collapse.

The first is called *The Man Who Was Lazy.*

This is how it goes:

THE MAN WHO WAS LAZY

Once upon a time there was a man who was poor.

He was poor because he was lazy.

Feh.

The End

The second story works in concert with the first.

It's called *The Man Who Deserved It.*

This is how it goes:

THE MAN WHO DESERVED IT

Once upon a time there was a man who was rich.

He was rich because he worked hard.

The End

As with other religions, capitalism never fails its adherents; it is only failed by them. That is the real cardinal rule. God/The Market is never questioned; Heaven/Money is worth any sacrifice; and if you find yourself in Hell/

Poverty, you must have Sinned/Not Worked Enough to be sent there. The most remarkable thing about money, though, is that it doesn't just make *you* forget you're *feh*, it makes *other* people forget you're *feh*. Trump without money is just an insufferable prick. Would even the most die-hard Republican vote for a poor Donald Trump? Would anyone sit across from a destitute Elon Musk for more than ten seconds without punching him in the face? That's a challenge even *with* his billions. The religions of the world may argue about the nature of God and the afterlife, but they all agree on this: The wealthy tax cheat sits up front with the holy man, while the poor man stands in the back. In synagogue, the rich man puts some coins in the *pushke* – Yiddish for *charity box* – and all praise his generosity, but the prayer shawl he drapes over his shoulders is threaded with gold, sterling silver ornaments are sewn into his neckband, and he secures it all about his chest with golden clasps in the shape of the Ten Commandments. Because Jews love money, sure sure, but once upon a time a Jew named Jesus condemned the hypocrisy of the wealthy clergy of his time; today the church that calls him God is worth thirty billion dollars and has spawned the perverse Prosperity Theology, which claims that God wants nothing more from His followers than for them to be filthy rich. You want to blame Jews for the death of Christ's body, go ahead, but it is Christians who crucified his soul.

- Don't fight over my worldly possessions, said Mohammed to his brothers as he felt death approaching.

Guess what they fought over.

I first experienced money's miraculous healing power in my early twenties. Theater was my first love – Beckett, Ionesco, Albee. Soon, like most playwrights, I was broke. *Try again, fail again, fail better,* wrote Beckett, but he had a Pulitzer Prize on his shelf when he wrote that, so fuck him. I put away my word processor and interviewed for a job at an ad agency.

- What's the pay? I asked.

- Eighty thousand dollars, they said.

And behold, in an instant, my *feh* disappeared. Money was better than pot, better than gin, better than Prozac. I bought a TV. I bought a car. I bought a cabin in the woods. I parked my car at my cabin and stood in my living room beside my TV, and I looked out my window overlooking the valley, and I felt . . . good.

Not great.

But not *feh*.

Money un*feh*ed me like nothing before ever had. And now it was gone. I may have had a pancreas, but what good was it without a job?

Orli shoved the pile of bills away.

- I didn't want to bother you with this now, she said.

- I'll get a job, I grumbled.

- It's not about the job . . .

- I'll *get* a *job*!

She crossed to the living room window, which overlooked our pool, which overlooked a valley. We lived in the majestic woods of the Hudson Valley, a place the Native Americans who once lived here regarded as magical and holy. And it was. Woodstock had been our Eden, our Walden, our place of quiet and peace and solitude. We took long meandering walks in the forest behind our house; we made love among the pines and oaks. Sometimes, after watching the sun set softly behind the mountains, we lay on our backs on the deck, smoked a joint, and marveled at the starry heavens above. Soon our boys were born, and we were very happy.

Dear Mr. Thoreau,

Your mortgage payment is overdue.

- Do we really need this? Orli now asked. - This house, this pool, this . . . bullshit?

- What bullshit?

- This! she said. - This stainless-steel fridge, these high ceilings. What are they costing us? What are they costing *you*? Anxiety? Worry? Who is it for? I don't want this; I don't need this!

- I'll get a job, I said.

- You have a job, she said. - You write books. It's enough if we just . . .

- I'll get a job . . .

- It's not about the job!

- I'LL GET A FUCKING JOB.

Orli snatched her car keys from the table and headed for the door.

- I have to pick the boys up from school, she said. - They're excited to see you.

I listened as her car wound its way down the long dirt road. When I was certain she had gone, I stood, tentatively, and staggered outside to the front porch. I hadn't walked more than a few steps all week and had to stop now and then to catch my breath and find my equilibrium. Holding on to the railing with both hands, I limped down the porch steps, then wobbled across the gravel driveway to the small storage shed across the way, where, on a low shelf behind some old paint cans, I kept an emergency pack of cigarettes.

Don't drink, don't smoke, don't take drugs.

Being my pancreas isn't an easy gig.

Here's another story they told me when I was young. It's called *Money Buys Love*. This is how it goes:

MONEY BUYS LOVE

Once upon a time, there was a young man named Isaac who wanted to get married but was very bad with women. He was shy. He was reserved. Perhaps this was because when he was a child his father Abraham tied him to an altar and tried to slit his throat. Anyway, Abraham was very rich, and he had many servants, and so he appointed his servant Eliezer to find his traumatized son a wife. Eliezer set out for the town of Nahor, where he met a beautiful young maiden named Rebecca.

- Wanna marry my boss's son? Eliezer asked.

- Is he handsome? asked Rebecca.

- No.

- Is he smart?

- Not particularly.

- Strong?

- Weak.

- Is he confident?

- Nope.

- Is he funny?

- Funny ha-ha? asked Eliezer.

- Yes.

- No.

- Then why should I marry him? asked Rebecca.

At this, Eliezer reached into his bag and brought forth a handful of jewels. He gave Rebecca a golden nose ring. He gave her golden bracelets. He gave her silver, and he gave her clothing. Rebecca took Eliezer to her home, where he gave additional bling to her mother and her brother.

- There's more where that came from, said Eliezer.

- I shall marry Ezra! Rebecca declared.

- Isaac.

- Whatever.

And they lived happily ever after.

The End

I lit a cigarette, drew the smoke deep into my lungs, and looked back at the house I could no longer afford: a three-bedroom, two-bath monument to my own failure. But the house wasn't all we were losing. Soon after Paix was born, I came home to find Orli going out of her fucking mind. She is an artist, but since she had become pregnant, her art had been both literally and metaphorically packed up and stored away. That afternoon, in a paroxysm of paint, passion, and postpartum depression, she had dug out one of her old rolls of canvas, sliced it into eight-foot-long, three-foot-wide strips, and hung them all over the living room and dining room, ceiling to floor: over the walls, the windows, the doors, the cabinets, the closets. Each one she had then attacked with paint, covering every inch of them in subtle gradations of color from top to bottom – this one blues, this one reds, this one oranges – the artist version of *The Shining*'s "All work and no play makes Jack a dull boy" typed over and over across hundreds of pages.

- Uh, hey, hon, I said when I got home.

- Hey.

- You . . . okay?

- Yeah, she said as she sliced up another section of canvas. - Why?

She looked both exhilarated and borderline insane.

- Well, it's just that . . .

- I need more paint!

- Right.

- Like, a *lot* more paint!

- Sure. Okay. Let's get more paint.

- And canvas. I thought I had more canvas. Where is all my canvas? Did you throw it out? Why would you throw out my canvas???

It was obvious she didn't just need materials, she needed a place away, to herself, where she could paint and draw and not drown our baby in the bathtub. We found an old, dilapidated barn for rent a few miles down the road, at the far end of an old homesteader's property, tucked beside the woods and a gentle creek, for two hundred dollars a month. What it lacked in heat, running water, and natural light, it made up for in mice and spiders and mud.

- It's perfect, Orli had said.

Now, because of my failure, the barn, too, would have to be surrendered. The guilt consumed me.

Feh, I thought.

Orli could insist she didn't want money, but I knew it would solve our problems. I decided that I had no choice. I would take Craig's advice.

I would write for Satan.

Hollywood.

This is what's known, in storytelling terminology, as the break into act 2.

I heard Orli's car coming back up the dirt road, took a final drag of my cigarette, and stubbed it out, burying the butt under the gravel so the boys wouldn't find it. I hobbled back to the front porch and sat on the steps as if I'd been waiting for them to arrive.

The boys bounded out of the car.

- Dad! they called, and they ran to me, hugging me and kissing me and telling me how happy they were that I was safe and home.

Idiots.

12.

- Bring me another beer, Gabe, calls God, feet up on the table as He watches another episode of me. - Auslander's going Hollywood.

Gabriel enters.

- Hollywood? asks Gabriel.

- He's writing scripts, says God. - What a jackass.

Gabriel shrugs. He doesn't love this new direction.

- Is this going to be one episode, Gabriel asks, or like a whole mini-arc?

- Why?

- Dunno, he says. - It's not . . . believable. I mean, Auslander's an idiot, but he must have *some* capacity for self-preservation.

- That's what's so funny, says God. - He thinks he *is* saving himself. Wait till you see the earthquake episode.

- Earthquake?

- Season finale.

- Feels like I've heard that plot point before, says Gabe. - Genesis, Pompeii, Lisbon . . .

- Yeah, chuckles God. - But this one's in *Beverly Hills.*

Gabriel smiles.

- That *does* sound funny, he says.

13.

Once upon a time I discovered a wonderful land, a land of magic and delight, a land where there was no God and no sin, where nobody judged and nobody condemned and nobody hid trays of half-eaten brownies underneath their beds because their father would get angry if he found out they ate them.

I wanted to live there.

I was ten years old, and it was Shabbos, so my family was fighting. As my mother served the chicken soup, my brother mocked my father, my father threatened my brother, my sister had an asthma attack, and my mother wept. Under cover of their violent antipathies, I crept away from the dinner table to steal my father's new silver pen.

I may have been a *gonif*, and possibly a *feigele*, but I was also a reader. I loved books, all books, and I spent my evenings and weekends at the Suffern Free Library, returning the books I had borrowed the previous week before searching for new books to get me through the week ahead. I had never seen another library, but I knew, without question, that this one was the most beautiful library in the world. The original building was a simple stone farm-house with white wooden shutters, dating back to the 1800s, but the com-munity had outgrown it and had recently added on. The old farmhouse now held the children's library; the new addition beside it, all modern angles and iron and glass, was the adult library, with skylights and murals and soft chairs and miles upon miles of bookshelves. So often did I go, and so many hours did I spend cross-legged on the floor with a pile of books before me, that the head librarian issued me an adult library card even though I was still a child, the grandest honor of my young life. It soon became my un-home away from home, quiet and peaceful, with warm rays of sunshine cascading down through the skylights, filling the tranquil two-story atrium with gold, illuminating the endless rows of books full of stories and voices of people I had never met, people from around the world and across time and not from Monsey.

I wanted to live there.

Sometimes sitting in that sunlit room I even allowed myself to dream that one day I would become a writer myself, of tomes and epics, of philosophy and wisdom, and those dreams of literary greatness gave rise in me to a terrible *taiva* for elegant pens like my father's.

Yiddish for *lust*.

I had first seen him writing with it the week before, all gleaming silver from the tip to the end of the barrel, with a narrow section etched near the tip to provide grip to the hand of the creator lucky enough to possess it. He had stepped away for a moment, and while he was gone, I dared to take it into my hand, feeling its weight and import. It said *Cross* on the pocket clip, which made me think of my father, who was always cross, and of Jesus Christ, whom God made die on a cross because he said he was the Messiah and was going to save everyone. We were forbidden from saying Jesus's name, but I didn't blame Christ – I was a liar too, and the world was so full of violence and hate that it certainly seemed to need saving. Perhaps with such a pen, I thought, I could write books that would save the world. And so that Friday night, as my family fought and cursed and kicked and slapped, I tiptoed down the hallway to my parents' bedroom, and slowly, slowly, slowly slid open the small drawer of my father's bedside table, careful so as not to jangle the metal pull. If my father caught me in his bedroom, let alone searching through his drawers, he would beat me black and blue. But the pen was exquisite, a work of art that created works of art, and it deserved better than my brutish father's thick-fingered hand.

- Drop dead, I heard my brother shout at my father.

- Rotten kid, I heard my father shout at my brother.

And there it was: the pen, gleaming, even in the dark of the drawer. I knew God was watching, and I knew that it was forbidden to write on Shabbos, forbidden even to touch a pen lest you be tempted to write, but I assured God I wouldn't write with it until Shabbos ended, and I lifted it up, feeling its wonderful heaviness in my hand. As I did, though, I noticed in the drawer, buried beneath my father's spare yarmulkes and cigarettes, a small magazine, no larger than an *Archie Comics Digest*. Hoping for a Veronica-themed issue, I took it out; on the cover was a woman wearing nothing more than red thigh-high leather boots, her red-fingernailed hands bound behind her back with red leather handcuffs.

The magazine was called *Penthouse Variations*.

It was no *Archie Comics*.

Shabbos, Rabbi Gavel had told us, was a day of rest, but that night I didn't sleep a wink. I read the magazine from cover to cover, and then I read it again. I had seen pornographic magazines before – my brother hid them beneath his dresser, my father hid them beneath his mattress – but this one was different. Other magazines were filled with photos, images – but this one was filled with *words*. It was filled with *stories*, and the stories were from real people, incredible stories of lust and desire and utter abandon – of whips and clips, of trysts and fists and cuffs on wrists, of twosomes and threesomes and foursomes, oh my.

Dear Penthouse Variations, the stories began, each one as astounding and inconceivable as any of the stories Rabbi Gavel read us from the Torah. *You'll never believe what happened to me at work.*

On a cruise.

On a plane.

With my wife.

With our neighbor.

With my wife, our neighbor, their doctor, his nurse, and her brother.

I trembled as I read them. Compared to these stories, what was Exodus? What was the splitting of the sea? What was Queen Esther Versus Haman (though the whole Vashti-with-a-penis subplot was suddenly more compelling than it had been)? Here were stories from people, real people, all over the world, from New York and Los Angeles, from Paris and London, from businessmen and religious men, from doctors and lawyers.

And plumbers.

There were a lot of stories from plumbers.

The only people not in the magazine were Jews. There were no Chaims or Ephraims, no Frumas or Fievels, no Schimmels or Kimmels. The more I read, the more I began to feel about the world described in *Penthouse Variations* as I had about the one I had seen some years earlier in Victoria's Secret: Here was another Eden I had no place in, another paradise I was excluded from — the first because I was male, the second because I was a Jew.

Dear Penthouse Variations,

Yesterday I sat on my plumber's face.
It's good to be a shiksa.

— *Mary C. Wichita*

Yiddish for *non-Jewish woman*.

Rabbi Gavel told us that in Paradise, Adam and Eve had everything they wanted; they would only have to think of it, and it would appear. But the Land of Penthousia was miraculous for something it *didn't* have: shame.

In my family, all was shame. My father was ashamed of his *feigele* son. My mother was ashamed of my furious father, who waited for her outside synagogue on Saturday afternoon, arms crossed and red-faced because she was taking too long talking to her friends who had cancer (they all had cancer; Penthousians didn't have that, either).

Dear Penthouse Variations,

Doctor Silverberg slowly unbuttoned my blouse.
He took my heaving breast in his warm hand.
- It's cancer, he said.

— Leah N. Monsey

My brother was ashamed of my sister, who was overweight and had messy hair and was deaf in one ear, and my sister was so ashamed of herself for being overweight and having messy hair and being deaf in one ear that late at night she would raid the kitchen, eat all the Shabbos brownies, and hide the empty cooking trays underneath her bed. I was ashamed of everything – of my violent father, of my mournful mother, of my cruel brother, of my sickly sister, of my desires, of my lusts, of my stealing Shabbos brownies because I knew my father would blame my sister, of the dark hairs beginning to appear on my genitals, and of the acne beginning to appear on my face.

In the land of Penthousia, though, nothing was disgusting.

In Penthousia, nobody judged.

In Penthousia, nobody said *Feh*.

...

Monday morning, Mrs. Mendlowitz assigned us the writing of a poem. Everyone groaned.

- A poem? Mordechai asked. - About what?

- Whatever you like, said Mrs. Mendlowitz. - Shabbos. Torah. It's up to you.

Mrs. Mendlowitz was a heavyset woman with turquoise eyeshadow, yellow-brown teeth, and a dusty rat's nest of a wig who liked me because I was a good student. I was a good student so that Mrs. Mendlowitz would like me. If Mrs. Mendlowitz liked me, I would get a good grade, and if I got a good grade, my parents would be happy, and if my parents were happy, maybe, possibly, nobody would fight.

I glanced across the way to Sarah Pomerantz, who was crestfallen by the assignment. Sarah was a quiet girl I was desperately in love with, with gleaming jet-black hair and jet-black eyeliner, and when she smiled, deep, dark dimples appeared on her cheeks like bottomless pools of joy.

- I can't write a poem, she sighed. - I'm *terrible* at rhymes.

I had recently switched to this yeshiva; this one, unlike the previous, was for both boys and girls. Still, only English and math classes were mixed, so this was a rare opportunity to talk to her.

- P-poems don't have to rhyme, I said.

- They don't? she asked.

- Of course not, I said, happy to make her happy.

Mordechai overheard us.

- Mrs. Mendlowitz, he called, do poems have to rhyme?

- Of course they have to rhyme, said Mrs. Mendlowitz. - That's what makes it a poem.

Sarah was even more distraught than before. Her friends Deena and Drorit tried to cheer her up, but to no avail. The bell rang, and she headed, frowning and dimple-less, for the classroom door.

- I'll write it for you, I blurted out after her.

Sarah stopped and turned to me.

- You . . . will? she asked.

It was a rash decision, I knew, but I wanted her to be happy. I wanted her to smile. I wanted to go on a Shabbos walk with her, and I wanted to hold her hand; and when the walk was over, I wanted to kiss her dimple. No boy in my class had ever kissed a girl, but the Penthousians had inspired me. People were sitting on each other's faces in Kansas, why couldn't I kiss a dimple in New York?

- You write poems? Sarah asked.

I didn't.

- I do, I said.

I wasn't concerned. If Mrs. Mendlowitz's standards for poetry were as low as her standards for wigs, I could write a limerick and get an A.

And maybe, just maybe, a Shabbos walk with Sarah.

- You're the best, Sarah said with a smile.

We both blushed.

Drorit and Deena giggled.

Dear Penthouse Variations,

You'll never believe what happened at yeshiva today.

— *S. Auslander*

I went home afire with lust and raided my father's bedroom for further issues of *Penthouse Variations*. Where there's smoke there's hellfire, and at the back of his underwear drawer at the bottom of his dresser, I found the April issue. On the cover, a woman, naked but for her trench coat, was flashing the camera as a horny policeman looked on.

In Penthousia, *women* flash *men*.

I really wanted to live there.

Later that afternoon, I emerged from my locked bedroom and found my mother in the kitchen, sitting forlornly at the table. She had been crying. Seeing my mother smile made my whole world shine, but her sadness was unbearable.

- What's wrong? I asked.

- It's Baba, she said.

Baba, my grandmother, had begun showing signs of dementia. Sometimes she watered her plastic plants. Sometimes she forgot the names of her grandchildren. Recently she had gotten lost coming home from the market and couldn't remember the address of the home she had lived in for decades. The doctors wanted to do some tests.

- What kind of tests? I asked.

- Alzheimer's, my mother said, beginning to cry again.

She headed for the door.

- I – I want to be a doctor, I blurted out after her.

She stopped and turned to me.

- You . . . do?

It was a rash decision, I know, but I wanted her to be happy. I wanted her to smile.

- You want to be a doctor? she asked.

I didn't.

- I do, I said.

In the Orthodox Jewish community, no profession ranks higher than doctor. Lawyer is a close second but has an air of sleaze about it. Rabbi is third, if his synagogue is big enough. CPA is fourth. There is no fifth. Any other occupation is met in the Court of Synagogue Mothers with mild shame and a defeated shrug.

- What's Yaakov doing?

- He's in marketing.

Mild shame.

- How's Shalom?

- He's a writer.

Defeated shrug.

I had never seen my mother prouder than when my cousin Josh graduated medical school. Now she looked at me with similar pride.

- Why do you want to be a doctor? she asked, wiping the tears from her cheeks.

- So I can cure Baba, I said. - So I can cure everyone.

She smiled.

- And I bet, she said as she hugged me close, you *will* cure everyone.

I wondered if she thought I was fat.

The following day, my mother drove me to the library, where I took out

Gray's Anatomy, The Merck Manual of Diagnosis and Therapy, and a massive tome called *The Making of a Surgeon, Atlas of Human Anatomy Volume 1 (Head, Neck, Upper Limb)* and *Atlas of Human Anatomy Volume 2 (Trunk, Viscera, Lower Limb)*. I also picked up an impressive, gilt-edged anthology of contemporary poems, a two-inch-thick history of classic poetry, and a guide to writing poems in an hour or less. I heaved the pile of books onto the library counter, and the librarian smiled. My mother beamed.

This was going to be easy. She was already proud, and I wasn't even a doctor yet.

And so, for the first time in my life, I liked myself.

Maybe I wasn't awful.

Maybe I wasn't bad.

Maybe, sometimes, I was even good.

...

Baba's symptoms were growing worse every day, and my mother's grief grew worse with them. Friday night, as she blessed the Shabbos candles, she wept. I sat on the nearby couch with my medical books on my lap, wanting her to see me reading them while trying my best not to puke.

I had run into a problem:

The medical books were making me sick.

Lump-in-my-throat, stomach-turning sick.

If my rabbis really wanted to keep me from thinking about sex, they should have just handed me a copy of *Gray's Anatomy*, an enormous, anxiety-inducing parts catalog of the shlocky, poorly designed human machine: fragile parts, weak parts, parts that should never have passed inspection, parts that, once they broke down, could never be replaced. The more I read, the more repulsed I became. Sweat glands, bile ducts, urea, oil, phlegm, mucus; reading *Gray's Anatomy* was like peeking under the hood of my father's station wagon while he tried in vain to fix it.

- Lousy piece of crap, he would growl. - What idiot designed this piece of shit?

At least with the station wagon, you could go to the parts store. Where do you go if you need a duodenum, or a jejunum, or a pancreas? What happens if your pancreas is shot, then what?

- *We're sorry, that item is not in stock.*

- *Can you order it?*

- *The manufacturer only made one.*

- *One? He made one?*

- Fucked, my father would grumble as he slammed shut the hood of the car. - The whole thing's fucked.

The Merck Manual was even worse, a grim compendium of the myriad ways the shoddy parts in *Gray's Anatomy* failed, split, ruptured, cracked, backed up, and broke down, closed when they should have opened, opened when they should have closed.

The more I read, the more paranoid I became. What inside me, right this moment, was breaking down, failing, leaking, shorting out, rusting through? Late at night, I lay in the dark and listened to the thin beating of my flimsy heart. A fist-size spasmatic muscle was all that stood between me and the grave. What idiot designed this piece of shit?

- Mom, I asked one afternoon, do we have a blood pressure monitor?

- What do you need a blood pressure monitor for?

- To take my blood pressure.

- Your blood pressure's fine, she said.

- It might be high.

- You're ten.

- So?

- So it isn't high.

High blood pressure can cause aneurysms. An aneurysm is when a blood vessel explodes. When it happens in your brain, it's called a brain aneurysm. A brain aneurysm can lead to death.

- They call it the silent killer, I said.

- What?

- High blood pressure.

- Why are you so concerned about having high blood pressure?

- I'm not concerned about having high blood pressure, I said. - I'm concerned about having a coronary.

A coronary occurs when an artery bursts, resulting in a coma. A coma is a persistent state of unconsciousness. A lack of activity in both cortices is called brain death.

The medical books were causing me anxiety, which caused me sleeplessness, which is an early sign of dementia, which caused me more anxiety. I felt my cardiac arresting, my pulmonaries embolizing, my brain deathing.

I went into the kitchen and sat solemnly across from my mother. She was clipping coupons. I took a deep breath and gave her the news:

- I have emphysema, I said.

- You don't have emphysema.

- I've been coughing for days.

- That's not emphysema, she said. - That's a cold.

- But Dad smokes.

- So?

- So, smoking causes emphysema.

- Then Dad would have emphysema.

- Dad has emphysema? I asked, perhaps a bit too brightly.

- Nobody has emphysema, she said. - I think you should stop reading those medical books.

But she wasn't the one who had to cure Alzheimer's.

A few days later, I was playing on the swings in the backyard when I slipped off the plastic seat, flipped over, and landed flat on my back. Pain tore through me, my every cell afire, and for a moment I couldn't breathe.

I had shattered my spine.

I had severed my spinal cord.

Damage to the spinal cord can result in paralysis. Paralysis is a loss of motor function. A loss of motor function can lead to an inability to breathe, which can lead to death.

I tried not to panic. I tried not to pass out. I gathered every ounce of my strength, forced whatever air I could into my collapsing lungs, and screamed.

- HELP! I'M PARALYZED!

Nothing.

- HELP!

At last, I saw the back door open and my mother step outside, a bit casually for my liking. She was holding a dish towel and a dinner plate.

- What on earth are you shouting about?

- I'm paralyzed, I gasped.

My breath was getting shallow. The world seemed to dim and darken around me.

- I broke my spine, I managed to say. - I've . . . lost control of . . . all my . . . basic motor functions . . .

She tossed the dish towel over her shoulder.

- Come here, she said. - I'll take a look.

I rolled slowly onto my side, not wanting to cause secondary damage, got to my feet, and limped carefully across the lawn, my hand on the small of my back.

- I heard a crack, I said once I reached her. - L1. Could be L2.

- You *walked* here, she said.

- Where?

- Here, she said. - To me.

- So?

- So, you're not paralyzed, she said.

The fool had obviously never heard of delayed-onset paralysis.

- I think you should stop reading those medical books, she said. - I have enough to worry about as it is.

A veil of sadness fell over her. She was referring to Baba.

- Did the tests come back? I asked.

- Not yet, she said.

Her eyes filled with tears.

- You know what this is called? I asked, pointing to the muscle on the side of my neck.

- What is it called? she asked.

- The sternocleidomastoid, I said.

She smiled.

Bingo.

- My little doctor, she said.

Stop reading medical books, my ass.

. . .

Monday morning, I hurried into English class and situated myself at a desk where Sarah couldn't miss me, my shiny silver pen in my hand, the impressive poetry anthology strategically propped up on my desktop. Gilt-side out.

- What's that? she asked.

- Oh, this? I said, as casually as I could. - *Contemporary English Poetry.*

She smiled.

- My poet, she said.

My plan to win Sarah's heart was working. The heart is responsible for pumping blood throughout the body. When blood fails to get to the brain, it's called a stroke. Strokes can lead to paralysis.

- Sarah? I called after her.

- Yes? she replied.

Between Baba's diagnosis, *Gray's Anatomy*, and *The Merck Manual*, it was beginning to dawn on me that life was terribly fragile, death waiting around every corner. I could go at any time – and so could Sarah.

- Do you . . . Do you want to go on a Shabbos walk? I asked.

Technically, there was nothing remarkable about a Shabbos walk; it was just a walk, on Shabbos, that a girl and boy took together, usually to nearby

Viola Park. But symbolically, it meant everything. I could feel everyone watching us – boys, girls, even Mrs. Mendlowitz.

- Sure, Sarah said with a smile.

Dimples.

Bingo.

...

The week passed slowly, like fecal matter passing through an obstructed colon. If a colon is damaged, it may require a colostomy.

Don't ask what a colostomy is.

Friday night, my mother sobbed as she covered her face with her hands and blessed the Shabbos candles. Her shoulders shook as she wept. The doctors had phoned. Baba had been officially diagnosed with Alzheimer's disease.

Some doctors think Alzheimer's is caused by plaque in the brain. Some think it is caused by neurofibrillary tangles. The one thing they agree on is that there is no cure. After a somber Shabbos dinner, my mother went to her bedroom, closed the door, and cried. Across the hall, in her own bedroom, my sister shamefully wolfed down the brownies she had taken from the freezer and hidden beneath her bed. In the kitchen, my father angrily slammed the cabinet doors, demanding to know where the brownies were, proclaiming his certainty that the *gonif* who stole them was the same *gonif* who had stolen his silver pen.

- When I get my hands on you, he vowed to no one. - When I get my hands on you.

I went down to my bedroom, closed the door, and took out the *Penthouse Variations*. I wasn't feeling lustful; I just wanted to be in Penthousia for a little while, just for a moment, in that magical place without disease or pain, that place without strokes or Alzheimer's, that distant paradise free of shame and weeping and sorrow and neurofibrillary tangles.

It didn't help.

Dear Penthouse Variations,

Today I forgot the names of my children.

— Baba

The following afternoon, I kissed Sarah Pomerantz.

She was waiting for me for our Shabbos walk at the end of her driveway, wearing her fancy Shabbos dress and her shiny Shabbos shoes. She was all sunlight and patent leather and dimples and joy. We walked for hours. We walked from her house to Viola Park, where we sat on the swings and climbed the jungle gym and slid down the slide and tried to catch fireflies in the tall grass of the fields. Once, as we did, my hand grazed hers, and I couldn't believe a hand could be so warm and so soft, couldn't imagine that inside that hand was the same hideous mess of bone and cartilage and ligament that *Gray's Anatomy* said was inside mine. Soon Sarah needed to go home. Her father was a rabbi, and he wasn't happy about our Shabbos walk to begin with. We walked hand in hand to Carlton Road, where I would turn left to head home, and she would turn right. We stood there for some time.

- Well, she said.
- Well, I said.
- That was fun, she said.
- That was, I said. - Fun, I mean.
- Bye, she said.
- Bye.

I turned and headed back home, a mile trek in stiff Shabbos shoes that cut into my ankles, to that dark place I called home, where my father would be searching for stolen brownies and my mother would be weeping and my brother would be making fun of my sister and my sister would be running down the hallway from him and locking herself in her room.

- Sarah? I called.

She stopped.

- Yes? she asked.

- I had a good time.

- Me too.

She blushed and looked down at her shiny shoes, and as she did, I leaned forward and kissed her dimple. She smiled, and with her perfect index finger she tucked her perfect hair behind her perfect ear.

- Okay, I said.

- Okay, she said.

- Bye, I said.

- Bye, she said.

Sunday, I closed myself in my bedroom, took out my father's silver pen, and wrote Sarah's poem, which I titled *Aftermath*. It was about a wooded forest the morning after a violent overnight storm. Branches had snapped, trees had fallen, devastation was everywhere. But now the storm was over, and golden rays of sunlight were breaking through the forest canopy. Newts were paddling in the puddles, the birds were beginning to sing, and with the promise of a bright afternoon, all the world had forgotten about the darkness of the night before.

My mother spent the day on the phone with Baba's doctors. My father found the empty tray of brownies beneath my sister's bed, along with a plate of half-eaten chicken, and loudly announced he was going to put a lock on the refrigerator door. My sister cried from shame and ran out of the house. My brother mocked my father, saying that the brownies were kept in the freezer, not the fridge.

My father said: I'll put you in the freezer.

My brother said: I'm so scared.

Monday came, and I waited excitedly for lunch. When at last it came, I slid the poem from my backpack, careful not to bend the corners or crease the page, hurried to the cafeteria, and walked over to the girls' table to present it to Sarah. Deena stopped me before I could reach her.

- You can't, she said.

- Can't what?

- Can't see her.

I was confused.

- I have her poem, I said.

Deena shook her head. - You can't talk to her.

- Why not?

She tutted with annoyance.

- She doesn't want to talk to you, she said.

I looked past her to the girls' lunch table. Everyone was watching us. Sarah turned away. The other girls eyed me with disgust.

- What's going on? I asked.

- You're too fast, said Deena.

- Fast?

- Kissing? said Deena. - On your first Shabbos walk? What's wrong with you?

I felt foolish, guilty, leaden with shame.

- But . . . but I love her, I said.

- You see? Deena declared as she tossed her hands up and walked away. - Fast!

Deena sat back at the girls' table, where the girls began to whisper and laugh. Sarah laughed too. My shame turned to anger, my anger to rage. I crumpled the poem into a tight ball, threw it onto the girls' table, and stormed off.

- Ooh, is that the poem? Drorit asked as she lunged for it. - Can I have it? I'm terrible at poems!

Everyone laughed.

Somewhere in Penthousia, someone was being desired. Someone was kissing, and someone was being kissed. Nobody blushed. Nobody felt ashamed. Nobody said *feh*.

But I wasn't in Penthousia. I was in Monsey, where even the plumbers never had sex, where desire was shameful and where love was foolish, where babas got Alzheimer's, and where everyone sat in harshest judgment of everyone else. Even God only judged us one day a year; here on Earth, though, among mankind, every day was judgment day, every night a night of bitter self-reproach.

Four long hours later, the school bell rang. I hurried out of the classroom and down the hallway, hoping to get out of school before seeing any of the girls. I wanted to go home and burn the *Penthouse Variations* and throw the silver pen as far as I could into the dark woods behind our house. Save the world? I wanted to burn it down.

Drorit was waiting for me at the school's front door. In her hand was my poem. She had unfolded it and smoothed all the creases.

- Take it, she said.

- I don't want it. You use it.

- I can't, she said.

- Why not? I sneered. - It rhymes, doesn't it?

She looked down at the poem. Her hair fell across her face.

- It's about hope, right? she asked, her voice soft, her eyes lowered.

- It's about trees.

The hallway was beginning to fill with students, shouting and yelling and laughing, probably at me. Drorit gently placed the poem in my hand, and I could feel her hand on mine, and it was as soft and warm as Sarah's.

- You should be a writer, she said.

Then she turned and hurried back to her classroom to get her bag. I watched her go. Her pretty blue skirt went *swish-swish-swish* as she walked.

The muscles that comprise the buttocks are known as the glutei maximi. They are the among the largest muscles in the body. Prominent gluteal muscles are associated with virility and fertility.

I wanted to kiss her.

I wanted to feel her glutei maximi.

I wanted to tell her I loved her.

Feh.

14.

- You seem down, said Ike.

- I'm in a psychiatrist's office, I said. - I'm supposed to be down. If I wasn't down, I could understand your mentioning it, I could understand your feeling somehow compelled to draw attention to the fact that I *wasn't* down, what with it being a psychiatrist's office and all and my being up, but it seems pretty fucking obvious to say to a patient sitting *in* a psychiatrist's office, You seem down. *Really? Do I? Fuck, maybe I should go see a psychiatrist?*

Ike wrote something on my chart.

Asshole, I assumed.

- I meant more than usual, he said. - How's the job search going?

It was Thursday. Earlier that week, Orli and I had put our house up for sale.

- The searching is going great, I said. - It's the finding that's difficult.

The house had made me feel less *feh. Wow,* people said when they came to visit, and I allowed myself to believe they were saying it about me. Orli had already vacated her barn, her art supplies and canvases and artwork back in boxes in the basement. She assured me she was okay with it all. She was anxious about money too, but she was happy to leave the house and happier still for me to be free of its burden.

- Did your heroes live like this? she had asked. - Did Beckett, did Kafka, did Gogol? Did anyone you admire have a fucking pool?

- Yes.

- Who?

I thought about it.

- Voltaire.

- He literally won the lottery, she said.

- Groucho.

- Marx?

- Yes.

- Groucho Marx had a pool?

- Probably.

- He doesn't strike me as a big swimmer.

- I think he probably just floated around.

- I'm done with this, she said.

She meant the house. She meant money. I was pretty sure she meant me too.

God, according to the Bible, loves money. He has a particular interest in gold, but copper and silver make Him happy too. In story after story, God punishes with death but rewards with money – with gold and with silver, with camels and with sheep, with oxen and with donkeys. Before we are even told the story of how Adam met Eve (Genesis 2:21), we are told where on this new earth to find gold and jewels (Genesis 2:11). When Moses leads his people out of Egypt, this is the All-Knowing God's advice:

- Grab the gold.

Exodus 11:2.

The Holy Temple? Blinged out. Golden lamps, golden walls, golden posts, golden altars. If it had a golden toilet, it could be Trump's house.

This is what we learn about Job, three verses into his story: He was loaded. The narrator is tax-return specific: Job had seven thousand sheep, three thousand camels, five hundred oxen, five hundred donkeys, and an army of servants. Money was Job's happy act 1. Then, one day, Satan decides to fuck with him.

How?

He takes his money.

Only after he takes his money does he take Job's children and health. So Job apologizes. He was wrong to question God, wrong to speak out.

God is pleased. So God rewards Job.

How?

With money.

God gives Job money:

42:12: *The Lord blessed the latter part of Job's life more than the former part. He gave him fourteen thousand sheep, six thousand camels, a thousand yoke of oxen, and a thousand donkeys.*

42:13: *And also He gave him seven sons and three daughters.*

First money.

Then, y'know, what's it called.

Children.

15.

Philip Seymour Hoffman was sleeping.

It was lunch hour, and we were in the bustling lounge of the Norwood, an elegant members-only club in the Chelsea district of Manhattan, where I was pitching him a film script. I was halfway into my pitch, just warming up. And Philip Seymour Hoffman was out cold.

- So, the protagonist, I continued, is trapped, you see. In, in, in the very home that he thought would, uh, you know. Free him.

Uptight, angular club members walked by, sharpy dressed and neatly coiffed, wondering why Philip Seymour Hoffman (who was neither uptight, angular, sharply dressed, nor neatly coiffed) was asleep on the elegant rolled-arm Chesterfield couch in the main lounge in the middle of the day. And why I was speaking to him as if he weren't.

These were both good questions.

We were there to discuss a novel of mine that he was interested in turning into a film, which I was desperate to make happen. I'd put off novels to write TV and film scripts, but the screenplay form was more restrictive than I'd anticipated, the industry more conservative, and so, while writing prose left me feeling free and light, writing for Hollywood left me dark and heavy. Tensions were high at home. Every repair to the roof, every appliance that broke down, every required maintenance on the car set off a firestorm of anxiety.

- *Required* maintenance? I shouted. - I own this car, how can they require me to do anything?

- It's just an oil change, said Orli.

- I don't understand, I continued. - *They* built a car that needs oil, and *I* have to pay for it? That is fucking bullshit.

My book editor was skeptical of my Hollywood plan. He assured me I could write my way out of my financial problems through publishing, and likened writers in Hollywood to condoms: They're irritating, he said, nobody wants to use them, and once they do, they toss them in the gutter.

- That's beautiful, I said.

- Thank you.

- You should write poetry.

- Nobody buys poetry, he said.

I assured him Hollywood would be different with me. I had published books, after all; they would respect that. Orli was even more skeptical. She'd had nothing but contempt for advertising and was certain Hollywood would be even more dispiriting. Her plan for us was Fuck It – fuck the house, fuck the pool, fuck the car, fuck everything. I made enough money from books, she said – not a fortune, but enough to live on – and she wanted me to write the books I needed to write.

- Didn't Hollywood drive Faulkner to drink? she asked.

- Mississippi drove Faulkner to drink, I said. - Hollywood just paid the tab.

She needn't have worried. After a year of trying, the only thing I had managed to sell was the option to a story I had written about a trip we had taken years earlier to the Caribbean. It had been an emotionally painful time for me, as I was just beginning to reckon with my dysfunctional family, my religious upbringing, and my crippling neuroses. So, we decided to get away for a bit, to escape mothers and fathers and history and sadness and sorrow. We spent money we didn't have on a peaceful, white-shuttered room with French doors in a remote villa on the sandy beach of a hidden cove. It was everything we had hoped for – quiet, private, and, most of all, deserted. There was only one other guest at the hotel, a kindly, gentle old man who introduced himself to me the evening of our first day there.

- I'm Alan, he said. - What's your name?

- Shalom, I said.

He smiled.

- Are you Jewish? he asked.

Uh-oh, I thought.

- Yes, I said.

His smile disappeared.

- I'm a survivor, he said.

Cancer, I hoped.

- Holocaust, he said.

Fuck, I thought.

- I'm sorry, I said.

- I could tell you stories, he said.

And, for the next ten days, he did. He sat uninvited beside me on the pristine sandy beach, a relentless Scheherazade of misery, regaling me with nightmarish stories about death camps and gas chambers and mass graves.

- Auschwitz was bad, he said as the azure waters lapped gently at the shore. - But Treblinka, now *that* was a death factory.

The film version of the story, as I envisioned it, would be a dark comedy about history and memory — *What About Bob?* meets *Schindler's List*, in the mix-and-match, lowest-common-denominator parlance of the film industry. I called it *Auschwitz on the Caribbean*. Robert De Niro's company phoned, wanting to turn it into a film.

I was excited to talk to them.

They had one question.

- Does it need the whole Holocaust thing? they asked.

I thought that it did.

A second company phoned.

I was excited to talk to them.

They had one question.

- Does it need the whole Holocaust thing? they asked.

I thought that it did and offered to write it myself, but they decided to hire a screenwriter best known for her social media feed about the squirrels living in her backyard. The first thing she did was ditch the Holocaust thing.

The project soon died.

Make it six million and one.

And then, one day, I received an email saying that Philip Seymour Hoffman wanted to adapt a novel of mine for the screen. I was elated. It felt as if the Nobel Prize committee had phoned to tell me I'd won. Orli was less excited.

- He wants to meet! I said. - To talk about a script!

- Did you write today? she asked.

- Write? I asked.

- Write.

- No, I said. - I mean, yes. Some notes. For the script.

- Mm-hmm, said Orli.

This is what Samuel Beckett's wife, Suzanne, said when a man from the Nobel Prize committee phoned and told her Sam had won:

- *Quelle catastrophe.*

French for *What a catastrophe.*

I spent weeks compiling notes for the script, sketching out scenes, while at the same time trying to find a time Phil could meet. The latter was the more difficult task. Every time we scheduled a get-together, his producer called at the last minute to cancel it.

- He's busy, I said to Orli. - He's a busy guy.

- Mm-hmm, she said.

At long last, though, here I was. After months of worry and stress and second mortgages and unpaid Amex bills, here I was, in the lobby of the Norwood Club, pitching my novel to Philip Seymour Hoffman.

And Philip Seymour Hoffman was asleep.

I cleared my throat, hoping to rouse him.

Nothing.

- And so, I continued, I think it has an interesting unity, of, of time and place. And, uh. You know. Time.

His producer Emily, sitting beside him, tried her best to pretend he wasn't out cold.

- It really does, she said loudly, hoping to wake him. - That's what we love about it.

Philip Seymour Hoffman began to snore.

- It's, uh, subversive, Emily continued. - But heartfelt.

That was literally the blurb on the cover.

Of my book.

That she was holding in her hand.

Snore.

- Yes, I said. - That's an interesting way to put it.

Snore.

She nudged him with her knee.

- Why Phil, she said, you haven't even touched your burger.

She nudged him again, harder this time, and he came to, rubbing his eyes and tugging the brim of his red baseball cap down over his face as he glanced sheepishly around the room to see if anyone had noticed his sleeping. Ordinarily, I would have made a joke about the situation – *Riveting, huh? When do we start filming?* – but he seemed so terribly ashamed for having fallen asleep, so utterly mortified with himself, like a child caught napping in class, that I could only pretend it hadn't happened.

- Which I think adds to the dark humor, I said.

He glanced at me from under the brim of his cap, reached over, and patted my knee, as if to thank me for not humiliating him further.

- It's a great book, he said.

He offered me half his burger, but I explained that I had a two-hour bus ride back to Woodstock and severe gastrointestinal issues.

- I wish I did, Phil said with a chuckle. - Maybe I'd eat less.

- My anxiety keeps me fit, I replied. - If it weren't for my hypochondria, I'd be a complete drug addict.

And then Phil laughed, a laugh like rolling thunder, a laugh that roused the living dead members of the Norwood Club, Dionysian, booming, healing, a laugh like freedom itself. It wasn't quite as good a laugh as Orli's, but it was close.

The Norwoodians turned and scowled. Fame brings with it permission to do just about anything, but joy is a sin even the famous must not commit.

- Fun place, I said. - Get a lot of suicides in here?

- Not enough, said Phil.

He waited for them to turn away, then leaned over the low table and pulled his lunch plate toward him. He ate the way my overweight sister used to eat when we were children – hurriedly, as if to get the shameful deed over with as quickly as possible, as if committing some unspeakable crime, *And the Lord called out to Adam, saying, What have you done?*, as if he should be doing it in the dark, behind closed doors where nobody, most of all himself, could see. He forced his food down quickly, barely allowing himself a moment to chew it let alone enjoy it, then wiped his mouth with the back of his thick hand as if to rid the crime scene of evidence. My heart broke for him, as it had long ago for my sister. He didn't say this, but his mournful eyes did:

Feh.

...

- How did it go? Orli asked.

- He fell asleep, I said.

- He fell asleep?

- He fell asleep.

- Where?

- On the couch.

- When?

- While I was talking to him.

- What an asshole, she said.

- He's all right, I said. - He wants to meet again.

- How nice, she said. - Is he going to wear pajamas this time? I'll make him some milk and bloody cookies.

- He's all right, I said.

Feh knows Feh. We can sense each other; we know without a word when we have crossed paths with a fellow tortured member of our soul-murdered clan. The signs aren't what you'd expect; it's not necessarily a stubborn self-loathing (though it is with me), nor some desperate eagerness to please masquerading itself as comedy (me again). Some Feh are quiet and reserved (Peter Sellers). Some Feh will bend over backward for love (Craig). Some Feh blame themselves for everyone's pain (Hoffman). Some mask their *feh*ness behind a veil of arrogance and coldheartedness (Trump). Not all Fehs have been told the same story I was – adults don't need religion to destroy a child's self-esteem, it just helps – but the stories we were told, whatever their plots and arcs, all ended the same way: with someone we loved and whose love we desperately needed, a God or a mother, a teacher or a father, wagging a crooked finger at us and cackling, *Feh*.

- It's all my fault, I had said to Ike the week before.

- What is?

- This. This failure.

- What failure?

- This job thing. We could lose the house.

I buried my face in my hands.

- I'm in Hell, I said.

- We all have ups and downs.

- We don't all *cause* the ups and downs.

- How did you cause this? he asked. - Did you neglect your job?

- No.

- Did you sexually harass someone in the office?

- No.

- Did you get drunk at the Christmas party and say something inappropriate?

- No.

- So, what did you do?

I took a deep breath and gathered all my courage.

- I told a joke, I said.

- A joke?

- Yes.

- To who?

- People.

- At work?

- At Barnes & Noble.

- At Barnes & Noble?

It was a joke I'd made about my father, years earlier, at a reading in the Chelsea location of Barnes & Noble. It haunted me still. After the reading, it was time for questions. A woman at the back raised her hand.

- What does your father do? she asked.

- He fails, I said.

Big laughs.

I regretted it immediately. It was cruel and unfair. He had failed me as a father, that much was true, but he was fired from ITT just weeks before his pension came good; that wasn't his failure, though – it was a failure of corporate America, of capitalism, of greed. He tried, after all; he began doing menial labor for neighbors to earn what he could – fixing their toilets, cleaning their gutters, repairing their decks. He was, the neighbors joked, their *goy*.

Yiddish for *gentile*.

And my punch line.

- What was the joke? Ike asked.

- Someone asked me what my father did.

- And?

- And I said he failed.

Ike nodded.

- And that's why the new creative director of McCann Erickson fired you? he asked.

- Yes.

- He was at the reading?

- No.

- How did he hear about the joke?

- Jesus Christ, I hissed, he didn't fucking hear about the fucking joke; he fired me because God told him to fire me because I told a cruel joke, and so I deserved it!

- Oh, said Ike. - That makes much more sense.

Sunlight filled Ike's office. I wished it didn't. I wished he would close the blinds, kill the lights. I didn't want to be on his couch; I wanted to be under it. I knew he thought it a terrible joke to make, and me a terrible person for making it.

- Is it unusual for new creative directors to hire new staff? he asked.

- No.

- Is it common?

- Yes.

- But this time it's your fault?

- Yes.

- Because you told a joke?

- Right.

He tried another approach.

- Let me ask you this, he said.

- Shoot.

- Can you imagine a scenario, he asked, where you're *not* at fault?

- For what?

- Anything.

- When?

- Ever.

- No.

- You're the bad guy.

- Yes.

- Always.

- Yes.

- No matter the story, he asked, you're the antagonist.

- Yes.

There was a long silence as Ike waited for me to put the pieces together.

I did not.

- But don't the best antagonists have good reasons for doing what they're doing, he asked, even if it's wrong?

- Yes, I said. - I'm not that kind of antagonist.

- What kind are you?

- The other kind.

I told Ike about the father of one of Lux's preschool classmates, who had been playing tag one day with his son. As they ran around the dining table, the man lost his footing, fell on his son, and shattered the boy's leg. The boy needed surgery, pins, physical therapy. What surprised me was how well the father was taking it.

- I couldn't live with myself if I did that, I said to Ike.

- You said it was an accident.

- It was.

- But you don't get to have accidents, said Ike. - Everything is your fault, it always has been, from the very beginning. You are the reason for all the badness in the world, all your mother's sorrow, all your father's anger. You're the bad guy.

- That's my story, I joked, and I'm sticking with it.

Ike didn't laugh.

- No, he said. - That's *a* story. That's *their* story, the story they told you.

He fixed his eyes on mine.

- But it's just a story, he said, his contempt for the storytellers clear. - A terrible story, a story nobody should ever tell their children.

I nodded.

- But it's just a story, he said.

...

I met Phil a week later at Tiny's, his bar of choice in Tribeca, where we sat at a back table and talked for hours. We quickly discovered that we had an uncanny amount in common. He acted; I wrote. He grew up near Rochester, New York; I grew up a few hours away in Monsey, New York. We were both raised with *Feh* – he of the Irish Catholic variety, me of the Orthodox Jewish variety. Our fathers even hid their porn magazines in the same place (laundry room, downstairs, off the den, behind the boiler). We were most alike, though, in what we lacked – security, love, self-esteem – and in the psychiatrists we'd been lucky enough to have found who helped fill the emotional voids left in our souls. I joked that God was going to kill mine, I was certain of it.

At this, Phil didn't laugh. It was a long moment before he spoke.

- Mine died, he finally said.

- Your what?

- My shrink.

It happened a few years earlier. He'd received a call from him, late one night. They didn't have a session scheduled, so Phil knew it was bad news. His shrink had been diagnosed with cancer. He told Phil not to worry, assured him that he would fight it, assured him that the prognosis was good. Three months later, he was dead.

- He was my lifeline, Phil said. - He saved me. He gave me life. And then, one day, he was just . . . gone.

Phil was overseas at the time of his psychiatrist's passing, on the set of a film, and couldn't leave to attend the funeral. He asked his brother to attend in his place, to record the ceremony so that Phil could see it when he returned. Phil

came home a few weeks later, he told me, and asked his brother for the video-
tape. He hoped that watching it would give him a sense of closure. He put the
tape into the VCR and pressed *Play*.

It was porn.

His brother had taped over the funeral with porn.

At this, Phil laughed again, but this was a different laugh. It was high-
pitched, desperate, forced, the laugh of a laugher who would rather scream
in rage.

Phil ordered a second burger.

He berated himself for ordering a second burger.

He ordered a second beer.

He berated himself for ordering a second beer.

He berated himself for being a bad partner, and for being a bad father, and
for doing *Hunger Games* just for the money.

- Damn, I said. - You're even better at judging yourself than I am. And I'm
pretty fucking good.

- My mother was a judge, he said with a shrug. - I learned from the best.

The waiter brought the check.

- Split it? Phil said.

- Fuck you, *Hunger Games*, I said. - I'm not the one who ate two burgers.

He laughed – the good laugh this time. We went outside, and he gave me a
hug and said it felt as if we'd known each other our whole lives.

Feh knows Feh.

...

It was late when I got home, well past the boys' bedtime. Lux met me at the
front door wearing one of his long blonde wigs and a pair of Orli's high heels.

- It's late, buddy, I said.

- Mom said I can do a Beyoncé, he replied.

Paix, standing behind him, gave me a thumbs-up.

- He's getting really good! he said.

Every year, my friend Jason throws a Super Bowl party. We're not big football fans, but we're huge Jason fans, and it's always a great time. The year before, Lux had watched in awe as Beyoncé performed the game's halftime show. The crowd went wild, and so did he. He'd been obsessed with her ever since. Week by week, step by step, he had been watching the video of her on our iPad, teaching himself her entire fifteen-minute halftime routine – the foot stomping, the hair flips, the floor spins, the exaggerated sashaying down the runway – and every now and then, after putting together another sequence or two, he would gather us all together in the living room to show us how far he'd progressed. And so, despite the late hour, Orli, Paix, and I snuggled together on the couch while Lux pulled up the Beyoncé video on the iPad, set it on the floor, and began to dance. He matched her every move, spinning on the balls of his feet and swinging his hips and sashaying into the dining room (backstage) when the show was over, not a hint of *feh* upon him.

He was *feh*less.

He was un*feh*able.

He came back into the living room and bowed.

And the crowd went wild.

...

A few weeks later, still working with Phil on the film, I pitched a cable network an idea for a TV series. I was desperate for some security and bitter about the success of *Mad Men*, a series about the advertising industry, an industry I despised on moral, ethical, societal, cultural, philosophical, spiritual, aesthetic, literary, social, and intellectual grounds, and its glamorization in the popular television show infuriated me.

I named my series *Pigs in Shit*.

This was the first sentence of the pitch:

I have worked in the advertising industry for the past fifteen years, and so I say this with a fair degree of authority: fuck Mad Men.

Phil read the script and agreed to play the lead, an advertising executive selling fake happiness while struggling to find actual happiness. It had no basis in my real life.

The weeks and months that followed were exasperating. Network executives would phone all day, wanting to discuss the series, while Phil would phone all night, wanting to discuss his mother. Orli disliked TV, on moral, ethical, societal, cultural, philosophical, spiritual, aesthetic, literary, social, and intellectual grounds, and she was sure this wasn't the right path for me. I felt assailed from all sides – my wife needed me, my children needed me, Philip Seymour Hoffman needed me.

- Write about it, said Orli. - And *not* a bloody screenplay.

That evening, I wrote a story about a man named Mermelstein, a father and struggling writer who discovers one morning, behind the door of the laundry room of his three-bedroom, two-bath suburban home, a glory hole, from which protrudes an erect, throbbing male organ. The glory hole is, by some supernatural twist, connected to a porn shop in Times Square; a man enters a video booth on Eighth Avenue and Forty-fourth Street, twenty-five miles away, closes the door behind him, sticks his penis through the hole in the booth wall, and it emerges, needy and insistent, in Mermelstein's laundry room.

- This is a house in Yonkers, Mermelstein explains to the man whose appendage invades his split-level colonial. - You need to leave.

- Please, says the man.

- Please what?

- Relieve me.

- No.

- I'm lonely.

- Go away, says Mermelstein. - I need to write.

At last the man relents, and Mermelstein, aware that his wife will be home in a few short hours, hastily repairs the wall with some plywood and screws. But the next morning the hole has reappeared, this time behind the dryer, along with a new stranger needing his help.

- Just a little, the man begs.

- I have work to do, Mermelstein says. - This is my home.

- It will only take a minute.

- You're pathetic.

- I'm a failure.

- You disgust me.

- That's good, the man says. - Shame me. Punish me. I'm disgusting.

- Where are you? Mermelstein asks. - I'll come over.

In this way Mermelstein learns the location of the porn shop, which he travels to the following morning. Irate, he explains the situation to the store owner, who in turn scolds Mermelstein for his lack of compassion.

- These people are in need, the owner says.

- I have my own problems, says Mermelstein.

- Would it kill you to think of someone other than yourself? the owner says.

Mermelstein, defeated and conscience-stricken, heads home to find that not only is the hole behind the dryer occupied by yet another appendage, but that a second hole has appeared in his wife's sewing nook, this one connected somehow to a strip club in West Philadelphia.

The men are relentless. Mermelstein reprimands them. He tells them to go home to their wives, to their partners, to find love. The men, though, are not as fortunate as he. One says he has no wife, no companion at all, and never has. He is lonely beyond despair. The man in Philadelphia says his partner has found God and is now repulsed by him and his homosexual desire. He weeps for the love they once had.

Mermelstein upbraids himself, he who has been so lucky in love. By now it is midafternoon, and Mermelstein's wife and children will soon be home. Torn between his own needs and the needs of others, between self-expression and self-reproach, he acquiesces; he capitulates; he dons a latex glove, relieves the men of their urges, sends them on their way, washes up, seals the holes, and cheerfully greets his wife and children as they come through the front door.

That night, Mermelstein sleeps soundly, glad to have protected his family and even, perhaps, to have helped some strangers in the process. Tomorrow, at last, he will be able to write.

The next morning, though, the holes in the laundry room and sewing nook have returned, along with another above his writing desk (the shower in a Texas maximum-security prison) and a fourth in the playroom beside the foosball table (a CrossFit gym in Orange County). Mermelstein wants to write, but there are too many who need help, too many who need saving, and so he gives up writing for good and spends the rest of his days running from one glory hole to the next, pleasing everyone but himself.

The End.

Pulitzer?

National Book Award?

Nothing?

Fuck off. If Waugh can end *A Handful of Dust* with Tony Last condemned to read Dickens for eternity, I can have Mermelstein condemned to give hand jobs.

Orli read it and laughed. - Michiko is going to *love* this.

That laugh, that laugh.

...

The network executives had been excited about Phil's involvement.

- Philip Seymour Hoffman is my white whale, one of them declared.

Everyone laughed.

Phil was overweight.

But they were growing increasingly anxious. We didn't have a signed contract, Phil's lawyer was being evasive, and Phil was impossible to pin down.

Many times I took the two-hour bus ride into New York City only to receive an apologetic phone call from his producer when I got there, telling me that he had to cancel. Something had come up, or he had a doctor's appointment, or he wasn't feeling well. At last, after months of delays, the day of our latest planned meeting arrived without cancellation. Tiny's at noon. I woke early that morning to find heavy snow falling in Woodstock. Six inches had already fallen, and more was expected throughout the day.

- How can he ask you to come in during a fucking blizzard? Orli demanded.

- He didn't ask me, I said. - I asked him.

The *Pigs in Shit* negotiations were faltering. The network wanted a three-year commitment from Phil, but he would agree to sign for only one. They were at loggerheads, and the project was about to collapse. I pulled on my boots and gloves, trudged outside, cursed, put snow chains on my car tires, cursed, skidded and slid down the mountain road, cursed, waited for God to drop a pine tree on me, and drove, ten miles per hour, to the bus station. It was five a.m., and the station was deserted, a single empty bus idling roughly in the lot.

- Is this the bus to the city? I asked. - Is it running?

The bus driver nodded, his Trailways cap already crusted over with ice and snow.

- It's running, he said. - Not sure we'll get there in one piece, but we're running.

We went at a snail's pace, if the snail was dead. The New York State Thruway was riddled with auto accidents. Trucks had slid off embankments. Cars had spun out and slammed into guardrails. Sirens wailed, flares burned, emergency lights flashed. The snow fell heavier. The bus driver tried following in the path of a passing plow, but to no avail; the rear of the bus fishtailed wildly, and the usually unflappable driver called out *Whoa, whoa!* as he wrestled with the wheel. I dozed uneasily, waking in a fright every time the driver hit the brakes or swerved, then dozed again. Finally, as we grew closer to the city, the storm began to ease, and by the time we reached the George Washington

Bridge, the snow had stopped falling. There were more cars on the road, less ice, and soon, unbelievably, we were pulling into Port Authority. The driver's face was ashen. The normally two-hour trip had taken over five.

- Made it, I texted Orli.

- Great, she replied. - Let me know how it goes.

I was hurrying through Port Authority when my phone buzzed. It was Phil's producer.

- Phil's sick, she texted. - We have to reschedule. You're not on the bus yet, are you?

We'll be back with more hilarious Auslander *after these messages.*

Ike's noon patient canceled, so I stomped across town to his office, where I ranted and raved and swore I was done – with Phil, with money, with life. Ike assured me Phil's behavior wasn't personal.

- I don't care if it's personal, I said. - I need to get paid.

- You'll get paid, he said calmly.

- I owe you money, I said.

- You'll pay me, he said. - I trust you.

I owed Ike thousands of dollars, and it was on my mind. I suggested that if he forgave my debt, I could tell Hollywood to fuck off and my depression would ease.

It was his job, after all, to help me.

- Our time is up, said Ike.

Outside, the snow was falling again. Through brown puddles of slush and muck I headed back to Port Authority, stopping on the way at Lux's favorite costume shop to buy him a new wig.

- A long one, Lux had requested the evening before.

- I know, I said.

- Really long.

- Really, really long?

- Really, really, really long! he said.

Lux loved wigs. He had dozens of them, all colors and materials and lengths – blonde and blue and pink and purple, straight and curly, and short and long. The long ones were his favorite. One Sunday morning a few weeks earlier, he and I had hung them in a long row across his bedroom wall, covering it end to end. Ever since, he dreamed of finding one so long that it would reach the floor.

- That'd be like seven feet long, buddy, I said.

- Seven FEET! he exclaimed, having no idea what seven was, or feet.

I was pleased to find the costume shop open, but I was in a rush; if it took another five hours to get back to Woodstock, I wouldn't be home before his bedtime. Tracee, one of the shop employees, offered to help me, and she found a wig in the back that was six feet long.

- This is the longest one we have, she said.

It was called the Rapunzel. It wasn't the seven-footer Lux was hoping for, but he was only three feet tall.

- It will look great on you, she said.

I explained that it was for my five-year-old son.

- Good for you, she said. - My father wouldn't let me have a wig.

Something in her shyness, in the mumbling way she spoke, in her sad fake blue eyes and her insecure slouch, made me want to beat her father with a stick.

- My father caught me blow-drying my hair, I offered. - He told me I was a *feigele*.

I waited for her to ask me what that word meant. Instead, she laughed.

- That's what my father said when I came out as trans, she said. - He said I was a *feigele*.

Feh knows Feh.

- What an asshole, I said.

- Yeah, she said, and then she struck a defiant glam pose, chin up, hands on her hips. - But look at me now, am I right?

I smiled.

- Damn right, I said.

We fist-bumped, and she handed me my shopping bag.

- I hope your son likes his wig, she said.

- He will, I said. - And I hope your father hates yours.

- He will, she said.

...

- I just don't want to do two years, said Phil.

- I understand, I said.

The deal had fallen apart. The network agreed to do a two-year deal instead of its usual three, but Phil refused to sign anything more than a year. He apologized, he didn't want to be difficult, he just didn't know if he'd still be artistically interested in the project in twelve months' time. It was why he had never done TV; he wanted his work to be authentic, to come from a genuine place within himself, but TV demanded so many seasons, so many years, that he feared he would be phoning it in by season 2. The network executives were anxiously waiting for me to report that I had changed his mind. The trouble was that I agreed with him.

- Two years from now, said Phil, who knows what we'll be doing?

- I know, I said.

- Will we still want to do this? Will we want to do TV at all?

I said I doubted it.

- That's why I put Hitler in it, I said.

- Hitler?

- Yeah.

- Recurring?

I nodded.

- He's directing a Coke commercial, I said.

- Why is he doing that?

- Because Coke makes you happy, I said. - When the actors aren't happy enough, he shoots them in the head.

Phil laughed.

- Not gonna have a long run, will it? he said.

- There's no way this gets a second season. In the pilot, you fuck Ma Keebler.

- Ma Keebler?

- From the Keebler elves.

- She was hot, he said. - Why do I fuck her?

- To comfort her, I said. - In the scene before, her son blows his head off.

- Ernie?

- J. J., I said. - Ernie's the father.

He laughed.

That laugh, that laugh.

- You're right, he said. - There's no way this is going to season two.

And that was it. After months of wrangling and cajoling, Phil, confident the series would never go past season 1, agreed to sign a two-year contract. He had only one remaining condition: The series would have to be directed by John Cameron Mitchell. John was the creator, star, and book writer of *Hedwig and the Angry Inch*, a musical about the genderqueer singer of a fictional rock band. Phil had seen it many times and thought John a genuine artist, whom he admired deeply for his courage and sensitivity.

- Deal, I said.

Thus did we set out to make a TV series: a lapsed Irish Catholic actor; a fallen, excommunicated Jewish writer; and a homosexual drag queen theater director – a fabulous Feh army of the sinful and shamed, of the Feh, by the Feh, for the Feh, each of us mortally wounded before the war even began.

It could never last.

...

When I got home, Lux was crying. His school friends had been over for a playdate and saw the wigs hanging on his wall, including his new Rapunzel one, and they had teased him. When they went home, he tore all the wigs off the wall, gathered them together in a pile, and threw them in a trash bag.

Orli and I sat beside him in his bed and told him all the usual things you tell your son when his friends discover his wig collection and mock him and you weren't home to bash their fucking heads in with a sledgehammer: that his friends were just jealous, that dress-up is fun for everyone, that his friends are just too afraid to admit it, and that what other people think doesn't matter.

He didn't buy it.

- Can I have a Face? he asked.

- Of course, said Orli.

We went to the kitchen, and Orli made him the special dessert she called a Face: a dinner plate decorated with a whipped cream mouth, chocolate chip eyes, sprinkles for hair, and a Hershey's Kiss nose. As Lux ate his Face, I showed him a YouTube video of John as Hedwig, dancing and singing in a scene from the *Hedwig* movie.

- See? I said. - There's nothing wrong with dressing up.

- She has really long hair, said Lux.

- That's John, I said.

- That's John?

- Yep.

- That's a boy? he asked.

- That's John.

He smiled.

- He's a good dancer, he said.

- He is.

- And singer.

- I know.

- Is that his hair?

- No, I said. - It's a wig.

His eyes lit up.

- I want that wig! he said.

We made another Face, watched some more *Hedwig*, Googled *Hedwig wig*, found something called the MegaWig that was close enough, clicked *Order*, and went to bed. The MegaWig was mega-expensive, but the series was back on track, and we would have some stability soon.

...

- I'm sorry, said Phil.

It was late, two a.m., a few weeks later. His phone call had woken me, and I was in a half-sleep daze, trying to make sense of what he was saying, of what I was hearing, trying to put the pieces of the story together. He was supposed to be on vacation, our goal to start filming the pilot when he returned.

- I'm sorry, he said.

- What's going on? I asked. - Where are you?

- I'm really sorry.

He hadn't been on vacation, he said. He had been in rehab.

- Rehab? I asked.

While there, a patient in his group therapy sessions had secretly recorded him talking about his addictions.

- Addictions? I asked.

The man had sold the recordings to TMZ, who were threatening to release the audio online unless Phil agreed to an exclusive story about his drug abuse.

- What the fuck is TMZ? I asked.

The downside of the bubble is that you often have no idea what people are talking about. The upside is that you've never heard of TMZ.

Phil explained that this was not an uncommon occurrence. People, to use the term loosely, sign into rehab centers in the hopes of secretly recording celebrities and selling the recordings to gossip magazines and websites. Phil had no recourse; if it were just him, he wouldn't have cared about the recording, but he had his children to think about. He didn't want them to hear their father talking about his addictions, didn't want them to feel shame in school, didn't want their friends to mock them about their pathetic father. And so he had acquiesced to TMZ's demands. The interview would be posted the following morning.

I knew something of how he felt. Some years earlier, I had received an email from a *New York Times* journalist investigating a complaint that one of Ike's patients had leveled against him. When I rebuffed him, it turned ugly; he said he had access to my psychiatric records and suggested that he would reveal them if I didn't cooperate.

- Don't bullshit me, he threatened.

Fortunately, I was not a celebrity, *The New York Times* was not TMZ, and they passed on the story. But Phil was not so fortunate.

He apologized to me again and again.

I told him to focus on himself and getting better.

He emailed me later that night.

I'm deeply sorry, he wrote. *Ugh.*

What he meant was this:

Feh.

...

A few days later, at show-and-tell, Lux stood up in front of his class, put on his new wig, pulled on Orli's high-heeled boots, and performed Beyoncé's Super Bowl halftime show. I stood at the back of the classroom, tense, eyes peeled, ready to kill the first preschooler who gave him grief. If I saw the slightest hint of judgment, I was going to wedgie the whole fucking class.

Lux had no such concerns. He didn't give a good goddamn what they thought. He cranked up his music, stamped his feet, sashayed, spun, and flicked his hair, one hand on his head to keep his wig from flying off, the other on his hip. When he finished, he stood with his arms crossed in triumph with such an air of Do Not Fuck with Me that he could have been Queen Bey herself.

The children sat cross-legged on the floor, looking up at him in stunned, open-mouthed shock.

Nobody said a word.

Nobody clapped, nobody booed. Time stopped. Lux adjusted his wig, looked down at his shoes. I stepped forward, ready to mass wedgie them all, when Monty, the class bully – the hair-puller, the seesaw-stealer, the name-caller – raised his pudgy hand.

- Yes, Monty? the teacher said. - Do you have a question?

Monty's eyes were wide as he held his hands out to the side.

- How the *heck*, he asked Lux, did you *do* that???

And the crowd went wild.

Boys, girls, teachers – the questions flew at Lux like he was on the red carpet at the Grammys.

- Who taught you to dance like that?

- Where did you get that wig?

- Does it hurt to walk in those shoes?

- I tried walking in my mom's shoes, Monty said, and I couldn't even take like two steps!!!

Lux graciously answered a few questions from the fans – Practice; My dad got it for me; It hurts, but then you get used to it – but soon the superstar had had enough. He held his hand up in a perfect *No More Questions*, pulled off his wig, and sashayed offstage.

Bey needs a little me-time, y'know?

. . .

God, the ancients said, punished the Egyptians with darkness for seven days. For the first three days, the Egyptians couldn't see, but they could move about. For the next three days, the darkness was so heavy that they could not move. Those who stood could not sit; those who sat could not stand. On Day Seven, the darkness was heaviest. It was the darkness of Hell. Not only could they not see, but they could not speak or hear or even eat, and they simply laid down upon the ground in fear and hunger.

Phil came out of rehab, and we filmed the pilot. It was tense, difficult. His darkness was Day Seven. He was hounded by the press, monitored by the network. A mother at his son's school threw her arms around him and began to sob. He had no idea who she was. He was difficult on set – belligerent, moody. His body was detoxing, which caused nausea, swelling, pain. I was in full guilt mode, chastising myself for not having recognized the signs of drug abuse all along – the sleepiness, the canceled meetings, the late-night unintelligible texts. Still, over the next weeks and months, John somehow managed to film something special, something dark and funny and moving about the struggle for true happiness in a shallow, materialistic world.

A few days after completing the final cut, Phil and I met at a restaurant in SoHo. He seemed better. He had lost weight. He told me about a woman in his rehab group, a heroin addict, there because she had finally overdosed and nearly died. By way of conveying the depth of her addiction, she related that while she was in the ICU, her recently stopped heart beating once more, she looked down at the tubes running in and out of her arms, the tubes keeping her alive . . . and wished she had some heroin. How easy it would be, she thought, to inject right into the tube.

- You writers are lucky, said Phil in his grumbling, baritone voice. - You get to tell the story you need to tell, when you need to tell it. You're sick, you get the medicine. Actors, though – we have to sit around, mute, waiting for a script to come along that somehow, if we're lucky, tells the story we need to tell.

Soon it was time for the restaurant to close. Phil and I went outside and stood on the street corner, going over the upcoming production schedule if the show got green-lit, and figuring out when we could meet again to go over scripts. Then he hugged me and told me he loved me, and I hugged him back and said, for some reason:

- Don't die on me.

He threw his head back and laughed, and that laugh caused the shop signs overhead to swing, and it set off all the car alarms, and it filled the streets of SoHo, and it traveled up to Midtown and it shook the windows of the buildings there, and it shook the city, and it shook the world, and I was sure that if I could laugh like that, even once in my life, I might never cry again.

That was Thursday.

On Friday, the series was green-lit. The network was going to produce ten episodes.

Saturday night, Orli and I celebrated. We sat side by side at our favorite bar in nearby Kingston, not worrying for once about how much the cocktails cost and imagining how happy American Express was going to be to hear the news about the series. She laughed – oh, that laugh, that laugh, jade-eyed and blue-skied and butterflied, so sinful and celebratory – and then we drove to my office in an old warehouse down the road, where we locked the steel doors, turned up the space heaters, smoked a joint, and made love.

The next morning was Super Bowl Sunday. The boys were excited for Jason's party and were looking forward to helping Orli make her special guacamole. I rose early, went to the local coffee shop, took out my laptop, and opened a new Word document.

Episode Two, I wrote at the top.

I smiled.

The phone rang.

It was the network executive.

She was crying.

- Phil's dead, she said.

...

Jason's Super Bowl party was scheduled to begin at two o'clock that afternoon. He phoned me at noon, having heard the news about Phil, and asked me to come despite it.

- It will be good for you, he said.

Jason had recently lost his wife, Lisa, to cancer. He knew about sorrow. He knew about darkness.

- Come out, he said, hang with some friends. You can mourn tomorrow.

I had spent the past few hours in a grief-stricken rage, too furious to cry, pacing back and forth in the living room, searching for a target for my anger and frustration. Yes, I admit – I was angry that my plans were for naught, that I was back where I started. I was worried about my career and about money, and Phil was supposed to be the answer to both those things. It was selfish and it was petty, and it felt good to be selfish and petty, because there was something darker, something more ominous, that was cutting me deeply about his death, something that frightened me, something that felt like a threat, a warning, something I didn't want to acknowledge. And so I directed my rage at Phil, at his mother, at his brother, at the piece of shit who recorded him in rehab, at TMZ, at the heroin dealers, at myself, then back at Phil.

- We should go to the party, Orli said.

- Why?

- The boys love it, she said. - They look forward to it. It's a chance to teach them.

- About heroin?

- That life goes on. Don't let Phil's story ruin yours.

She hugged me.

I wondered if she thought I was fat.

Two hours later, we went to the Super Bowl party. I had some gin. I had some more gin. After that, I had some gin. I was managing well, allowing myself to get caught up in the drama of the game, but the celebrity-filled commercials did me in. Phil often joked about doing *Hunger Games* only for the money, but he drew the line at commercials.

- I'm a piece of shit, but at least I never did commercials, he said.

To a man who made commercials for a living.

Watching them, I felt my anger return. Maybe it was the thought that the last actor with any integrity had just passed away. Maybe it was because Phil and I had spent so much time trying to deal with our feelings of *feh* that I couldn't bear the spectacle of millionaire celebrities earning even more millions to make nonmillionaires feel *feh* – convincing them that Hyundais (Jeff Bridges) and Kias (Laurence Fishburne) and Chryslers (Bob motherfucking Dylan) were what they needed to like themselves. Worse still, no one at the party, no one in the world, seemed at all bothered that this hideous whoring was going on; on the contrary, they were excited for the commercials, didn't see anything wrong with a woman who probably never touched a SodaStream (Scarlett Johansson), lying, fellating a drinking straw, for money, and saying that she had. It wasn't even whoring, I thought; at least whores make people feel better.

- I have to go, I said to Jason.

- You okay?

- I have to go.

- You sure?

- I have to go.

The boys were done anyway. Seattle was up twenty-two points at the half, Paix was bored with the game, and Lux was disappointed with the Bruno Mars halftime show. He couldn't understand why Beyoncé didn't do it every year.

It was a cold night in early February, and the frozen snow crunched under our feet as we hiked up the road from Jason's house to our own, the bright moon lighting our way.

- Are you sad, Dad? Paix asked.

I nodded.

- Why? he asked.

I took his hand in mine.

- Because your friend died? he asked.

- Yes, I said.

Paix had met Phil on set. They had discussed superhero comics.

- He was nice, said Paix.

- He was a good man, I said. - He didn't know he was a good man, though. He thought he was bad.

- Why?

- Because someone told him he was.

He looked up at me, confused.

- Why would they do that? he asked.

- That's a good question, I said.

And at last, for the first time since I'd heard the news, I cried. We walked the rest of the way home in silence, owls hooting in the pines overhead and coyotes howling in the distance. When we got inside, Orli made hot chocolate.

- I know what will cheer you up, Lux said to me.

He ran to his bedroom, while the rest of us went to the living room and snuggled together on the couch. Lux came running in a moment later, wearing his new MegaWig and the sparkly purple dress that we'd bought him for Chanukah. He set the iPad on the floor, pressed *Play*, and performed his latest dance number, "Not Fair," a song by Lily Allen.

- *It's not fair*, he sang as he danced and twirled, his dress fanning out as he flicked his hair from side to side. - *I think you're really mean.*

- Is this a song about God? I whispered to Orli.

- It's about getting fucked, she whispered back. - So yeah, kind of.

Lux stamped, spun, and flicked his hair. When he finished, he stood with his arms crossed in triumph, with the same air of Do Not Fuck with Me that he'd had at school.

The kid was *feh*less.

He was utterly un*feh*able.

With a final flourish, Lux kicked off Orli's shoes and bowed.

And the crowd went wild.

16.

*A*nd *Moses stretched forth his hand toward Heaven; and there was a thick darkness in all the land of Egypt.*

Exodus 10:22.

Rashi, the eleventh-century French Torah commentator, asks regarding this verse:

- Why did God bring darkness upon them?

It's an odd question for him to ask. After all, Rashi digs God. Rashi and God are tight. And as Avivah Gottlieb Zornberg points out in *The Particulars of Rapture: Reflections on Exodus*, with none of the other plagues does Rashi have any issue or ask such a question — not with frogs, not with blood, not with locusts, not even with the death of the firstborn. So why ask it here?

Her answer:

Because there is nothing quite so monstrous as blinding.

There is something about the plague of darkness, she writes, *about the way it reduces the human being to a blind and paralyzed vulnerability, that defies rational or moral explanation.*

Even Rashi thought blinding unconscionable.

There is no possible response, Zornberg concludes, *to the terror of such a condition.*

17.

- That was a bit harsh, says Gabriel.

- What? asks God.

- Killing Phil.

- Since when do you give a shit about Auslander?

- I don't, says Gabriel. - I give a shit about Hoffman.

- Did you see the look on Auslander's face when he heard? God laughs.
- That was *classic*.

But Gabriel isn't so sure.

Lately, something about God has been troubling Gabriel. The night before, he had gone to his room, taken out his Bible, and began reading. He read
it, and read it again, and read it again. And then, after that, he read *The Art
of Fiction*, and he read *The Art of the Novel*, and he read *Aspects of the Novel*,
and when he was finished, he read the Bible one more time. And he thought,
Uh-oh.

He thought, *Oh, fuck*.

Because something was very wrong with the Bible story. Narratively. Fun-
damentally. Essentially. Something about this foundational story that has so
shaped mankind's history seemed, well, off. Something about the characters,
about the structure. Something didn't add up.

So Gabriel put on a pot of coffee and read it all again, and it wasn't long before he identified what it was — it was right there, in fact, in the story's very first sentence.

And when he did, a deathly chill ran down what would have been his spine . . .

18.

People Also Hate You

Once upon a time there was a nation called Canaan. The people who lived in Canaan were known as Canaanites. All you need to know about the Canaanites is this: They hated you. Why? Who knows. God had His reasons for hating you; the Canaanites had theirs. You could say it was the Canaanites' problem – haters gonna hate and all that – but don't kid yourself because they weren't the only ones. After them came the Midianites, and they hated you too, probably for the same reason the Kenizzites hated you after them, which was no doubt why the Kadmonites hated you after the Kenizzites. The Kadmonites were a violent bunch, but they were nothing compared to the Hittites, who really despised you. What the fuck did you do to the Hittites? Something bad. Something very bad. Hittites were brutal, but they had nothing on the Perizzites, who dreamed of nothing more than raping and killing you. You must have pissed the Perizzites off but good. This wasn't some simple You Left the Toilet Seat Up anger; this was rage and fury. Thankfully, the whole Periz-zites thing doesn't last very long, but don't get too comfort-able because the Rephaim hate you next, and if you think the Rephaim are bad, wait till the Amorites show up. You might survive the Amorites, but don't pop the champagne yet, kid, because the Hivites are coming, and Hivites don't fuck around. Neither do the Jebusites – the Jebusites come *heavy.* Get your ass to the Fertile Crescent ER and stop the bleeding, stat, because the Amalekites are on the way, and those sons of bitches are furious. They hate you so much they want to wipe you off the face of the earth. Why? Frankly, buddy, at this point the why doesn't even matter. *Is it over?* you wonder when the Amalekites have gone. *Has the hatred toward me ceased?* No, it has not. You must be as awful as God said you are, because just as you're finishing burying your loved ones from the whole Amalek throw-down, the Ammonites show up, and Ammonites want blood. Still, at least they're not Egyptians, praise God (or don't; it doesn't seem to be helping). Egyptians enslave you, kill your babies, and use their corpses as building material for their pyra-mids. Because you control Hollywood? Because you control the banks? Because you control the media? Who knows? Who cares? It's gotta be something. By now you're battered. You're bruised. You're wondering, *Can things possibly get any worse?* The answer is yes. Much worse. Freedom rings, you escape from Egypt, and you head straight into the Edomites, who hate you even more than the Egyptians did. *Who the fuck are the Edomites?* you wonder, but don't wonder too long, Son, because right behind them are Moabites. *Fuck me,* you think, *is there anyone on Earth, in all of history, who doesn't hate me?* Maybe, but it's not the Greeks. And it isn't the Romans. And it sure as fuck isn't the Spanish. Or the French. Or the Muslims. Or the Christians. And we haven't even mentioned Germans or the Polish or Russians or White Nationalists or Kanye West yet.

Who all hate you too.

The End

19

Saturday afternoons, my friends and I would walk to the nearby Spook Rock Golf Course to kill some time until Shabbos ended. Golf was forbidden on Shabbos, as were most things, but at least walking was permitted. One day, as we walked along the neatly manicured golf course in our bright yarmulkes and dark Shabbos clothes, some men began hitting golf balls at us. Like rockets from Lebanon they rained down upon us, and we ran. We ran and we ran, hands pressing our yarmulkes to our heads so they wouldn't fly off, our Shabbos shoes slipping on the black asphalt as we did.

- What happened? my mother asked as we rushed inside my house and locked the door behind us.

- We were attacked! I cried.

- Attacked? she gasped. - By who?

- Antisemites! said Meyer.

- A lot of them! said Zalman.

Her face went white, her eyes filled with rage.

- We were at the golf course, Yoel said, still trying to catch his breath. - We were just walking there . . . minding our own business . . . and these guys . . . started hitting GOLF balls at us . . . hard!

Zalman and Meyer chimed in, giving her the terrifying details: the balls raining down, whizzing past us, fast and hard and relentless, missing us by inches. But as they retold the story, and as I reimagined it in my mind, I slowly realized the terrible truth:

We'd been walking on the driving range.

They weren't hitting balls at us. They were just hitting balls.

- No-good Nazis, my mother hissed, shaking her head.

It was my fault, I knew — my friends had only rarely been to the golf course, living as they did a long walk away, but I had been many times.

My mother was livid at the attack, and so were my friends. She knew the story of *People Also Hate You*, and so did they.

- You think they would have hit those balls, she huffed, if you weren't wearing yarmulkes?

- No! said Zalman.

- Of course not! said Yoel.

- *Antisemitin*, said my mother.

Yiddish for *antisemites*.

I couldn't admit my mistake, and besides, I told myself, they all seemed rather excited to have been attacked. And so, for the next few months, my friends and I talked about the time we had been attacked by a horde of anti-semites in white pants and polo shirts, armed with deadly nine irons and an arsenal of Titleist golf balls.

- Hate and more hate and more hate, said my mother. - Nothing changes.

That was forty-five years ago. The men who were hitting those balls are dead or close to it. And yet to this day, when I drive past golf courses, no matter where they are, this is what I think:

No-good antisemites.

Stories are powerful things.

20.

Okay, so here's where the story gets weird:

The night Phil died, Orli and I were celebrating the series pickup in my office. We'd lit candles, and we'd put on music, and we'd made love on the bean-bag chair I kept in the corner. Afterward, we lay together, holding each other's hands and catching our breath. It was then that I felt someone's hand pat my shoulder – a heavy hand, a warm hand, a thick hand. I yelped, jumped, spun around – but nobody was there.

- You okay? Orli had asked.

- Yeah, I had said. - Fine, fine.

This was around one or two a.m., roughly the time, I would find out the next morning, that Phil passed away.

It's ridiculous, I know. It's superstitious, it's malarkey, it's hocus-pocus. Richard Dawkins would be horrified. But I haven't been able to shake it. I know what I felt, and I felt it before I knew he had died.

Sometimes I think back to that night and try to figure out what kind of pat it was. Apologetic? Remorseful? And at those times when the darkness engulfs me, when I can't take another minute of the judgment and the judging, I remember his hand, and I feel it still patting my shoulder, and this is what I imagine it says:

Hang in there, my fellow Feh, hang in there. This shit will all be over soon.

21.

Jeffrey Moskowitz had a bad reputation among the religious adults of Monsey, but they didn't know him like I did. Jeff was my only real friend — loyal, clever, funny, a sensitive soul beneath his rebellious gelled-up hair, and possessed of a genuinely caring heart. Our yeshiva was in Washington Heights, at the northern tip of Manhattan in the shadow of the George Washington Bridge, a blessed hour away from Monsey. Every morning, Jeff and I sat together on the school bus and talked about how much we hated everyone. One afternoon, Rabbi Fink called me to his office.

- He's beneath you, said Rabbi Fink.

He was talking about Jeff.

I left and hurried up the stairway to the roof of the four-story yeshiva, where I knew Jeff would be waiting for me. It was our usual meeting time, just after Rabbi Cohen's Talmud class and right before Rabbi Seigel's Jewish History class. Ours was a long day, from morning prayers to evening prayers; there were classes mandated by God (Torah, Prophets, Talmud) and classes mandated by the state (math, science, English), and so sometimes Jeff and I met on the roof twice a day or more, a brief respite from the world below, to vent and to sin and to laugh. Rain or shine, snow or ice, there we stood at the edge of the roof, overlooking the Harlem River and the Bronx, wishing death upon Rabbi Fink, smoking cigarettes and dreaming of the day we would leave this place forever.

- You have to come over, Jeff said that day, and see the new TV.

Jeff's family was wealthy. He wore designer jeans and expensive sneakers. He had a card that he could put into a machine at the mall and cash would come out. Saturday nights, after Shabbos, he would drive us to the local non-kosher pizza shop in his father's Mercedes, a car so expensive that I was afraid to sit in it. The Moskowitzes had cable TV, video game consoles, and VCRs. It was the mid-1980s, the beginning of what would later be referred to as the home video revolution. VCRs were becoming more common every day, but they were financially out of reach for my parents. And just last week, the Moskowitzes had purchased a device even more rare and expensive than a VCR: a giant-screen projection TV.

- You have to see it, he said. - It's amazing.

He picked me up the following Sunday afternoon. His parents were going to be away for the night; I would sleep over, and he would drive us to yeshiva Monday morning.

The TV took up the entire wall of their living room. Three colored lights – one red, one blue, one green – projected lifelike images onto a screen taller than I was, with a VCR built right into the console. At home I had a small black-and-white TV in my bedroom, which I took over from my parents after they splurged on a color set for themselves.

- Check this out, said Jeff.

He went to the bookshelf, reached behind some books, and pulled out a videocassette.

- What's that? I asked.

- My dad's, he laughed.

He fed the cassette into the VCR and pressed *Play*. After a moment, life-size, full-color, moving images of naked nurses fellating their well-endowed patient filled the screen, their moans filling the room from the giant TV's powerful speakers.

And behold Moses's face was radiant, for he had seen God.

Jeff laughed and pressed *Stop.*

- Let's watch a movie, he said.

- That was a movie.

- A real movie, he said.

But the seeds of my destruction had been planted. VCR-less as my family was, I was forced to rely upon pornographic magazines – soundless, motionless – to relieve my unrelievable desires. As we sat on the couch and Jeff flipped through the TV channels, I seethed. The Moskowitzes were masturbating their way into the future, and here I was, still jerking off in the past. Why should the rich get large-screen TVs and VCRs? Didn't the poor need relief more than the rich? Why shouldn't the working class enjoy the same onanistic opportunities as the wealthy? I was becoming something of a revolutionary masturbatory Marxist, and that night, as Jeff slept, I ransacked his house. I wasn't looking for anything in particular; I just wanted to violate his parents, to hurt these rich people with their luxury cars and big-screen projection TVs and VCRs. I searched the den, I searched the kitchen, I searched the garage, I searched the closets. And then, in the top drawer of his parents' dresser, I found a VCR, all its cords and remotes and wires wrapped around it, not even being used.

Shabbos afternoons, after synagogue, my family sat around the lunch table and judged our wealthy neighbors.

- What'd he pay for that Town Car?

- An arm and a leg.

- And a head.

Laughter.

- Bet they never even use that pool.

- Good luck heating it.

- A tennis court, they have. *Noch besser.*

Yiddish for *Even better.*

- Then they go away for vacation!

Laughter.

I carried the VCR down to the kitchen, careful not to make a sound, where I stuffed it in a black trash bag I found below the sink, then lashed it across with some packing tape I had found in a kitchen drawer. I crept silently out to the driveway, placed it in the back seat of Jeff's father's car, and gently pressed the door closed before hurrying back inside.

A night of bitter self-reproach followed. A thousand times I thought to creep back outside, grab the VCR, and return it to the dresser drawer, and a thousand times I didn't. At last dawn broke, but it brought no relief. The bastard sun rose and trapped me in its harsh, accusing light. I tried to avoid my reflection in the bathroom mirror. I rolled down the car window so as not to have to see myself.

Gonif, I thought.

- What's that? Jeff asked regarding the strange package in the back seat as he backed out of the driveway.

- What?

- That.

- That? That's my package.

- What package?

- The one I had yesterday.

- You had that yesterday?

- I put it in when you picked me up.

- You did?

- Yeah.

- Oh. Right. What is it?

- Some stuff I ordered, I said. - I don't want my parents to see it; they'll kill me.

- What stuff?

- Books.

- Oh, said Jeff.

Literature is always a good conversation stopper.

...

Video Preview Booths, read the sign in the porn shop window. *Sixty-four Channels*.

With the Moskowitzes' VCR securely hidden at the back of my bedroom closet, a whole new world of pornography opened to me. I cut Talmud class, walked a few blocks to the A-train station, and took the subway down to Times Square. The shelves of the porn shop were filled with thousands of video-cassettes, organized by perversion – Oral, Anal, Bondage, S&M – and arranged in order of ascending depravity (blow jobs at the front of the store, bondage at the back). The images on their brightly colored boxes provided tantalizing glimpses of the degeneracy inside, but the tapes were expensive – twenty to thirty dollars each for a new release – and I couldn't afford more than one. I cursed the system again, and the heartless capitalists who ran it. Jeff's father could walk in here and purchase the whole Gang Bang section without batting an eye, and here I was faced with the impossible task of choosing between *Let Me Tell Ya 'Bout White Chicks* and *Let Me Tell Ya 'Bout Black Chicks*. Let me tell ya 'bout democracy, okay? Was this what our Founding Fathers intended? Was this the equality they fought and died for? Fortunately, this inequity was so pervasive that at the back of the shop was a row of what the neon pink sign above it called *Fantasy Preview Booths*. Inside the three-foot-by-three-foot booth was a small TV screen, built into the booth wall; below it was a slot for dollar bills, and below that were two illuminated yellow buttons, one labeled *Channel Up*, the other *Channel Down*. Here the undecided poor could preview the films before deciding on which one to buy with their meager week's pay; here the wretched VCR-less could masturbate to films whose required technology they couldn't afford.

$1 for 2 minutes, explained the yellow placard above the TV.

Two minutes? I thought as I locked the door behind me. *Lousy capitalists. That won't be enough time.*

I began at channel 1.

I was done by channel 3.

I had only spent a dollar.

Feh.

I went to the counter, grateful at least that I didn't have to actually say the title of the video to the cashier – Rump Humpers 2, *my good man, and a bottle of your finest lube* – and that I could simply lower my head, avoid eye contact, and mumble *Channel 3.*

I stuffed the videocassette into my backpack and hurried outside, anxious to get away from the porn shop and excited to get back home. Alas, the only way back to Monsey from Midtown Manhattan was via something called the Monsey Bus, an overcrowded, backfiring, smoke-belching *shtetl* on bald, under-inflated tires, the outside covered in soot and the inside filled with raucous Hasidim, boisterous bearded men on one side of the aisle, subdued shaven-headed women wearing bad wigs on the other, divided by a moth-eaten curtain that ran down the center of the bus to keep the genders apart. At the back of the bus hung a small Holy Ark, complete with a small Torah, which swung precariously back and forth as the bus weaved through traffic. In the morning, the bus pulled over, everyone got out, and they prayed the Morning Service. In the afternoon, the bus pulled over, everyone got out, and they prayed the Afternoon Service. In the evening, the bus pulled over, everyone got out, and they prayed the Evening Service. They might not ever have gotten anywhere at all were it not for the devout driver, who, when not praying on the side of the New Jersey Turnpike, drove as only someone with a strong belief in the afterlife would.

I hurried to Forty-sixth Street, between Fifth and Sixth Avenues, where the Chus Bus, as it was affectionately known – short for *Chussid*, Yiddish for *Hasidic* – picked up its brusque, bearded, black-hatted passengers. The bus was late that day, though, and I had to wait uncomfortably on the sidewalk with the Hasidim.

They eyed me suspiciously.

What's in the backpack? I imagined one of them asking in Yiddish.

Oh, you know, I would reply. *A Talmud. My phylacteries.* Rump Humpers.

Rump Humpers eins, they would ask, *oder* Rump Humpers drei?

Yiddish for *Rump Humpers 1* or *Rump Humpers 2?*

As it happened, the Chus Bus picked up right in front of a venerable NYC bookstore called Gotham Book Mart, where some months earlier the bookseller had introduced me to Kafka and *The Metamorphosis*. Kafka had made me laugh at my own shame and self-loathing. He had made me feel better about myself. It wasn't just that Gregor Samsa turned into a bug. It wasn't just that his father killed him. It's that his hateful family are happy when he dies. I felt Kafka knew me. I returned some weeks later to buy more of this Kafka fellow's books. I had no idea he was an important literary figure; I just thought he was funny, and funny was my salvation. When I had read all I could of Kafka, I returned again to the bookstore.

- What's funny? I asked the bookseller again.

He led me down a different narrow aisle and pulled out a play called *Waiting for Godot*, by someone named Samuel Beckett.

- What's it about? I asked.

- It's about two guys standing around waiting for someone to show up.

- And?

- And he doesn't.

- And?

- And they decide to kill themselves. One of them tries to hang himself with his belt.

- And?

- And his pants fall down.

- That's not funny, I said. - That's my life.

- That's why it's funny, he said.

Now, anxious about the porn hidden in my backpack, I decided to wait inside Gotham, away from the Hasidim. The bookseller already knew my penchant for humor, and after a quick hello, he led me down a narrow aisle and handed me *Gulliver's Travels* by a man named Jonathan Swift.

- What's it about? I asked.

- It's about a guy who travels to distant lands, he said.

- What's funny about traveling to distant lands? I asked.

- Everywhere he goes, he said, people suck.

At last the bus arrived and I grabbed a seat in the last row, between the Holy Ark and the bathroom, and began reading *Gulliver's Travels*. In yeshiva, we read the Old Testament. We read Prophets and Psalms. We read *Night*, by Elie Wiesel, and we read *The Diary of Anne Frank*. Basically, we read *Feh*. That was why I had so taken to Kafka; in story after story, he laughed at shame, he mocked his accusers. He rejected, through his writing, the parents, institutions, and systems that had rejected him. Critics and commentators claimed he was attacking bureaucracy or government or the justice system, but I knew he wasn't. He was attacking *feh*. Kafka was the inmate in the cell beside mine, tapping on our shared wall, letting me know I wasn't alone. *This*, I had thought, *is writing. This is the secular, the free, the accepting.*

But Swift was none of those things. Maybe it was the porn hidden in my backpack, maybe it was the stolen VCR hidden in my closet, maybe it was my lying to my only real friend in the world and stealing from his parents, but Swift was not what I needed. Swift was harsh, scornful, condemnatory. All men were violent, according to Swift, all women repulsive, all of mankind wicked and foolish and detestable. I had been hoping for something funny. I had been hoping for someone who would make me feel better, or at least laugh at my feelings of awfulness. What I got in Swift, though, was something much more biblical. Swift was as disgusted with mankind as Yahweh, as judgmental as Jeremiah, as disapproving as Isaiah. At least God paid lip service to the possibility of forgiveness, of redemption. Swift allowed for none. For Swift, there was no atoning for being human.

Swift was not what I needed.

The bus pulled over. It was time for the Afternoon Service. The bearded men stood, stepped off the bus, and began to pray, loudly beseeching God to enter them unto Heaven, while I sat inside with Jonathan Swift, who whispered bitterly in my ear that we all deserved Hell.

...

I had first tried cannabis the previous summer in Jerusalem, where I had attended a four-week art program at Hebrew University. There I met a girl named Betty, who flirted with the older college students so they would give her drugs. One night, as we sat on the grassy hill outside the dormitory, she filled a small wooden pipe with some brown, waxy hashish and offered me a hit. Thinking it might lead to sex, I accepted. She took a hit, then I took a hit, and then she stood and took my hand, and my heart filled with hope, and she led me to the bathroom and asked me to watch her pee.

- Pee?

- Pee, she said with a devilish grin. - And then, who knows?

She winked as she pulled down her panties.

- Anything can happen! she sang.

Anything turned out to be nothing. She urinated, wiped, flushed, stood up too quickly, got dizzy from the hashish, felt nauseous, asked me to help her to her dorm room, collapsed in her bed, and fell asleep.

We'll be right back with more hilarious Auslander.

Back in New York, I decided to give cannabis another chance. The hashish had given me a mild sense of euphoria, and I wondered what actual pot would do. I purchased a dime bag from a street dealer down the road from the yeshiva, and a small wooden pipe from the bodega nearby. That night, when everyone had gone to sleep, I opened my bedroom window, took a hit, and left. I left my room, I left the world, I left myself. With one simple puff, the voices of judgment in my mind, those bitter constant companions of condemnation and consternation, were silenced. I took another hit and another and another. How far could I leave myself? I wondered. If I smoked enough, would I never come back? Could I leave this hideous Me forever? Sadly, I could not. Eventually, the weed wore off. But even a short break from being me was a gift.

Two hours of the Chus Bus and Jonathan Swift had depressed me. I didn't want to be me, I didn't want to be human. I didn't want to be. That evening, while my parents slept, I locked my bedroom door, dug the VCR out of my closet, and connected it to my small TV. I put *Rump Humpers 2* in, pressed *Play*, took my pot stash out of my phylacteries bag, opened the window, and took a hit. I took another hit, and another. I left. I was gone. I smoked until my throat burned and my lungs ached, each puff disappearing Me until at last I faded completely away. This was why, in Genesis, God created plants before mankind; He knew we'd need the weed.

I returned to myself some hours later. The pot was wearing off, the high was coming down, *Rump Humpers 2* had ended, and the VCR had shut itself off. It was three a.m. I was covered in sin and shivering from the cold night air coming through the wide-open window. Naked and hideous, I stuffed the pot back in my phylacteries bag, buried the VCR at the back of my closet, and hid *Rump Humpers 2* at the back of my desk drawer, trying as I did to avoid my reflection in the bedroom window or in the blackened TV screen or in the mirror behind my closet door.

It was no use.

I was everywhere.

Feh.

Said the king of Brobdingnag to Gulliver:

- *I cannot but conclude the bulk of your natives to be the most pernicious race of little odious vermin that nature ever suffered to crawl upon the surface of the earth.*

Said Gulliver:

- *No shit.*

Swift was not what I needed.

...

- We were robbed, said Jeff, taking a nervous drag of his cigarette. We were on the roof of the yeshiva, the first time since my crime. Jeff was a cool, unruffled sort, but now he looked anxious, shaken.

- What? I asked.

- Someone broke in, he said. - To my house.

- No way!

- They stole my parents' VCR.

- Holy shit, when?

He wasn't sure. His parents hadn't used the VCR since getting the big-screen TV. But who would break in just to steal a VCR? And how would they know it was there?

His parents were furious. They were certain it happened the night they were away. They had questioned him, grilled him, accused him of leaving the doors unlocked. They demanded to know if he'd had anyone over. He swore that he hadn't. They grounded him and revoked his driving privileges.

- Did you hear anything? he asked me.

- When?

- That night.

- What night?

- The night you came over, he said. - Did you hear anyone come in?

- No, I said, lighting another cigarette. - Not a thing.

...

I was back in the preview booth that afternoon, back where I belonged, with the perverts and the criminals and the odious vermin. The higher the channel, I discovered, the more extreme the deviance. By channel 20, British women were getting caned. By channel 30, Japanese women were being violated with eels. By channel 40, Germans were defecating on each other.

How sick was I? I wondered. Was I channel 50 sick? Was I channel 60 sick? If channel 40 was defecation, what the *fuck* was happening on channel 64?

I left the booth, waited for the other customers to leave, and then approached the register.

- Channel 45, I mumbled to the cashier.

- *Extreme Sklavin?* he asked.

German for *Extreme Slave.*

I nodded. On the cover, a naked woman was tied to the stone wall of a dark dungeon. I noticed that the cashier was wearing blue latex gloves. Had he been wearing them before? Was he wearing them just for me, just for the reprehensible channel 45ers?

- Boxes? he asked.

- No, I said.

Odious vermin know to leave the video boxes at the store. Boxes are evidence, boxes can be found. He pulled the videocassettes from the boxes, slid them into a brown paper bag, taped the paper bag shut, then put that bag inside a black plastic bag, and that plastic bag inside another black plastic bag.

He handed it to me with his gloved hand.

- You're a good customer, he said.

It was nice to be good at something.

...

Jeff stopped taking the bus. He avoided me at lunch. Every day after Talmud class, I hurried up to the roof, but he was never there. I stood alone on the roof, smoked cigarettes, peered over the roof's edge, and thought about jumping. It was becoming obvious that this whole life thing just wasn't my sport. Some people are good at basketball, some people are good at soccer, some people are good at life. I wasn't. Why continue to play a game I had no talent for, a game I hated playing, a game I never signed up for?

I passed Jeff one afternoon after school.

- How's it going? I asked.

- Okay, he said without stopping.

Rabbi Fink pulled me aside. He had noticed of late that Jeff and I weren't spending as much time together.

- Good for you, he said. - He's a *no-goodnik.*

Yiddish for *lowlife*.

Here's the narrative trick Swift pulled in book 2:

We first meet Gulliver, the beleaguered protagonist, in book 1 – a good guy, a surgeon, happily married. The story is told in the first person; we are in his mind, and he is in ours. We are one. We are him.

Gulliver travels to Lilliput. The Lilliputians are petty, mean, and bellicose. *Despicable*, Gulliver thinks.

We like Gulliver. We are Gulliver. And so we agree: Fuck those despicable Lilliputians.

Book 2 now. Gulliver travels to a place called Brobdingnag. The Brobding-nagians are moral, ethical, upstanding, rational. In contrast to the Lilliputians, the Brobdingnagians are better than Gulliver, better than the nation he comes from, better than all of us. And so Gulliver has a terrible realization:

I'm *the despicable one*, he thinks. *Me. I'm the worst. I'm a* no-goodnik.

And we, being Gulliver, agree.

Yes, we think. *You are a* no-goodnik.

And so we are no-goodniks.

And so I am a no-goodnik.

The End.

...

Jeff stopped me outside school a few days later.

\- They called the police, he whispered.

\- Who?

\- My parents, he said.

My legs went weak.

\- The police? I asked. - Why?

\- The VCR, he said. - They're coming over today to look around.

\- Look around?

\- Investigate, he said. - Fingerprints, whatever. Just so you know.

He turned and walked away.

I'd lie. I'd deny it. I'd blame Jeff. I'd say he told me I could take it. They weren't going to come after me. The cops had better things to do. Fingerprints? Now? A week later? Ridiculous. He was trying to scare me. His parents were trying to scare him. I'd hide it in the shed. I'd toss it in a neighbor's trash bin. They weren't going to come after me. For a VCR? Don't be ridiculous. I'd lie. I'd deny it. I'd blame Jeff.

Rabbi Fink, having seen me talking to Jeff, wagged a finger in my face.

- When you lie down with dogs, he said, you get up with fleas.

But I knew who the real dog was.

The bell rang. It was time for Talmud class. I crept out the back door of the yeshiva, walked to the A-train station, traveled downtown to Times Square, and went to the porn shop.

God was right about me.

Swift was right about me.

The cashier smiled to see me as I entered and waved his latex-covered hand.

- Welcome back, he said.

Back to the sewer.

Back where you belong.

I browsed the shelves, at home among the shamefaced, the shifty-eyed, the trench-coated. What shall it be tonight, oh Most Odious of Odious Vermin? Shall we sail to the Land of Fisting, to the Kingdom of Whipping, to the Forbidden Isle of Transsexuals?

I went to the back, but the booths were occupied. At last, one of the booth doors swung open and out stepped a Hasidic man with a long black beard, wearing a long black coat, the brim of his big black fedora pulled low to hide his face, his *peyis* flapping behind him as he hurried out the front door.

I went inside the booth.

His video was still playing.

A woman was fellating a horse.

Channel 64.

In the final part of *Gulliver's Travels*, Gulliver discovers a land that is a dark inversion of our own: The humans are ignorant beasts, the horses are wise and peaceful and good. The horses speak English, but so noble are they that they have no words for *crime* or *lie* or *steal* or *VCR*. So good are they that when Gulliver tries to touch one, it recoils in disgust.

He probably should have been wearing blue latex gloves.

When I got home, my videocassettes were gone. All of them. I sank into a dark sea of terror. Had my mother discovered them? My father? What would they do, what would they say? Maybe the police had been over, maybe the police had found them. Maybe Jeff had told them I stayed over, and they had searched my bedroom. Maybe they'd found the weed too.

I tried to calm myself down.

I was high when I watched them last – maybe I misplaced them?

Maybe I'd put them somewhere else?

- Dinner, my mother called from the kitchen.

- Coming, I said.

I tried to interpret her tone – angry? sad? disgusted? I couldn't tell. I searched the den, the laundry hamper, the bathroom, the cabinets. The VCR was still buried at the back of my closet, which was a good sign. The weed was still in my phylacteries bag. That was a good sign too. If the police had searched my room and found the videocassettes, then surely they would have found the VCR too; so if they didn't find the VCR, then they probably didn't find the videocassettes. But then who had?

My father called.

- Shalom, he said flatly.

Angry.

Monotone.

Threatening.

I went upstairs and sat at the table, trying not to meet their eyes, wishing I could leave myself forever. The idea of suicide was growing on me. One less human, one less me, a return to the blessed Nothing before the catastrophe of my birth, before that wretched day of this sickening, sudden Something.

Dinner passed without a word. Not about VCRs, not about police, not about anything. This is all that was said:

- The kugel's dry, said my father.

- I made it the way I always make it, said my mother.

- It's always dry, said my father.

Later that night, after they had gone to sleep, I crept into the garage and quietly lifted a small hand shovel from the pegboard above my father's workbench. I took it and the VCR, and all its cords and remotes and cables, outside to the dark woods behind our house. Once I was deep in the black forest, I knelt down, took out the shovel, and began to dig. It was late fall; winter was coming and the earth was stiff. By the time I'd carved out a pit big enough for the VCR, my hands were raw. I placed the VCR in its grave, covered it with dirt, dead leaves, pine cones, and broken branches. In a thousand years, after humankind had died off and noble horses had taken our place, they would unearth this VCR, and they would study it and try to understand what it was. Eventually, they would put it on display in their museum and call the mysterious object *The Shalom*.

- We think, the horse guide would tell the curious horse visitors, they used it for masturbation. To be *Shalom*, she would explain, meant to be vile.

Days passed.

The videocassettes never showed up.

The police never came.

And Jeff never spoke to me again.

Throughout *Gulliver's Travels*, Gulliver hates. He hates lawyers and judges, he hates war and warriors, he hates politics and politicians. In the end, though, when he returns home for the last time, he hates none so much as his own self:

When I happened to behold the reflection of my own form in a lake or fountain, I turned away my face in horror and detestation of myself.

The End.

22.

One Monday morning, Bobo, an ordinary chimp residing in the Monkey House of the Bronx Zoo, achieves total conscious self-awareness. He understands, in a flash of terrible cognition, that just as he was one day born, so too one day must he die. Unsolvable mysteries plague his newly evolved mind. Where did he come from? Why is he here? Assailed by the unknown, he questions his purpose; he wonders about meaning. Most of all, though, he feels shame. He is ashamed of his fellow monkeys, ashamed of himself. He grows anxious and depressed. The zookeepers prescribe him Prozac, but it has little effect. Bobo turns to art. He begins to paint, first with his own feces, then with artist paints provided by his keepers – oils, acrylics, watercolors. Word of the painting chimp begins to spread. The zoo profits handsomely off his sudden fame. They raise their Monkey House entrance fees and sell his dark, impressionistic canvases for exorbitant sums. They are pleased, but fame and success offer no relief to Bobo from the terminal affliction of Being. When his aching heart is broken by one of the female chimps (she goes for the alpha, not the artist), he strides into the wading pool, knowing full well that he cannot swim, and takes his own life.

As Ike read my story, I sat on his couch reading him, trying to gauge his reaction, hoping for validation. He frowned as he reached the ending.

- Not coming soon, I joked, to a theater near you.

I had written the story some years earlier but had returned to it recently. I thought there might be a novel in it. There wasn't.

- Do you think Phil killed himself? Ike asked.

It had been a year since Phil's death, but the streets of New York City were still haunted by his presence. I would swear I saw him at a Starbucks or buying a pack of cigarettes at some corner bodega. My mind was plagued by hope. He'd faked his death, the clever bastard. He wasn't dead at all. He was living on the sly, watching his partner and children from afar.

Ike's suggestion infuriated me.

- Killed himself? I snapped. - He fucking *overdosed*.

- Do you think he wanted to? he asked.

I tried not to look at Ike's hands. He was getting older. I'd been seeing him for years, and lately I'd noticed that his hands were beginning to tremble. I was afraid to ask him why. Parkinson's? Worse? Phil had lost his surrogate father, and it had destroyed him. I didn't think I could survive losing mine.

- I don't know, I said. - Do you?

- There are different types of suicides, he said.

He didn't think Phil had sat down that evening with the intention of dying, no. But he compared drug abuse to walking along the icy ledge of a tall building. It wasn't suicide, he said, but it was reckless.

- People who want to live, he said, tend to avoid icy ledges.

I snatched my pages from his hands.

- Phil didn't want to die, I said.

Ike nodded.

- But did he want to live? he asked.

It was a rebuke, I knew, but not of Phil.

We both knew I'd walked an icy ledge or two myself.

23.

Hell is not a dark wood. Dante was way off.

Hell is a swimming pool.

Hell is an endless swimming pool in an endless summer, a pool surrounded by elegant lounge chairs and pristine white umbrellas, a dream house oasis that stretches for eternity, where there is but one single, inviolable rule, a terrible rule inscribed on the heavy stone archway that welcomes the condemned to their eternal awkward doom:

No Shirts.

No tees, no tanks, no robes, no nothing. Women are permitted to wear bikinis, but nothing more. Men are permitted only Speedos. The revolting rest – the flabby bellies, the chest fat, the love handles, the stretch marks – all must be ingloriously exposed. The pool is surrounded by a twenty-foot-tall mirrored wall, ensuring that the wretched denizens of this ghastly School have no way to escape their appalling selves. *No Running*, reads the sign on the wall, but who would? If I know God like I think I know God, He is saving the diving board for me, upon which I will be condemned to bounce, shirtless and jiggling, until the end of time.

There is one enclosed cabana.

It is empty.

But it is booked.

Forever.

I was twenty-five years old, and the bastard season of summer had arrived. Summer, the interminable season of bare skin and tight clothes, the season of no reasonable excuse for my beloved overcoat; summer, the season Fehs dread more than a high school locker room, more than a fluorescent-lit fitting room, more than the infernal barber's chair where you are forced to consider your hideous reflection without respite until the damned haircut is over; summer, the time of year when a young wife named Orli sits on a lounge chair by the pool and looks over to her young husband and says, Aren't you hot in that T-shirt? and he says, Yes, I am, and she says, Then why don't you take it off, and he says No, and she says, It's ninety degrees, and he says, I'm not busting your fucking balls about what you're wearing, why are you busting mine? and the whole goddamned day is ruined because she agreed to go to some stupid neighbor's stupid fucking pool party.

Which is Hell.

Please join us for a pool party this Sunday. There will be music, beer, awkwardness, flab, thigh pimples, hairy backs, and a kidney-shaped hole in the ground filled with a revolting stew of sloughed skin, pubic hair, and snot.

Bring Your Own Penicillin.

Later that evening, the tension of the pool party abated by time and marijuana, Orli climbed into bed, cuddled up beside me, and rested her head on my chest.

- I'm sorry, she said. - About the T-shirt thing.

- It's okay, I said.

Still wearing the T-shirt.

I hated subjecting her to me – to my body, my insecurities, my moods, my pathology. She deserved better. She deserved a proud man, a confident man, a tall man, a tan man, a man with abs and pecs and quads and glutes, a man who didn't require the complete absence of light in order to have sex.

And darkness was on the face of the earth.

Perfect.

And God said, Let there be light.

Schmuck.

Orli looked up at me, inexplicable love in her eyes, and kissed my cheek. She kissed my chin. She kissed my neck.

- I love this body, she whispered.

It was a ludicrous thing to say, we both knew it. My neck is too short and too narrow and only serves to accentuate my oddly shaped skull. Orli fake moaned with fake desire as she forced herself to kiss her way down my chest, which isn't really a chest at all, just a vast, featureless landscape that connects my too-wide shoulders to my too-pronounced abdomen. The southern end of my sternum collapses downward, *pectus excavatum*, creating a hollow in the center my chest; when I lie in a tub, water gathers there like a woodland pond, and the children who live in the villages atop my too-puffy nipples run down to splash and play.

Be careful! Mom calls after them. *And don't go climbing Mount Potbelly, it's too steep!*

- I'm tired, I said, shifting away from Orli's touch.

- I wish you could see yourself, she said, the way I see you.

The following afternoon, back in New York City, back in the blessed land of black shirts and black pants and no pool parties, I told Orli I was going to the bookstore, then got on the subway and hurried uptown to Health n' Vitamin Best Price Best Selection.

Like geese heading south for the winter seeking warmth, Fehs head to vitamin shops for the summer seeking self-esteem. We head to General Nutrition Center and to Vitamin City and to Vitamin World and to Nutrition Warehouse. We go for pills and capsules, for shakes and powders, for creatine and for

Xenadrine, for fat burners and myostatin inhibitors and appetite suppressants, for androstenedione and dibencozide and ornithine alpha-ketoglutarate, for whatever unregulated chemicals and foul concoctions we can force down our throats that might have even the slightest chance of making the reflection in our mirror something we can like, or at least abhor slightly less.

My need that day was particularly acute. Five years into our marriage, Orli was growing more beautiful every day. Her eyes seemed to glow greener, ablaze with life, and the light for which she is named glowed ever brighter, sunlike, warming all around her. I was growing uglier, inside and out, smoking cigarettes during the day, drinking gin with dinner, and taking a hit of marijuana before bed. I thought often of the engagement ring I had given her, that ominous stone, its flaw a presage, a warning, an omen of inevitable act 3 heartbreak. Ike had put me on antidepressants, but I didn't want to be antidepressed. I wanted to be joyful. Orli deserved someone joyful. She deserved a genial, winsome man who smiled as often as I frowned, who stopped to pet puppies and told people he passed on the street to have a wonderful day.

Not a *nice* day.

A *wonderful* day.

You know who I'm talking about.

That guy.

And so, as I perused the shelves at Health n' Vitamin Best Price Best Selection, my heart leaped when I spotted a product I had never seen before: *RenewTrient.*

For Fehs, a new pill or potion is cause for celebration. The possibility of transformation, a bottle of UnFeh. But RenewTrient promised a promise I had never been promised before:

Mood elevation.

I wanted mood elevation. Mood elevation sounded pretty damn good. *RenewTrient* also promised fat loss, increased muscle mass, better sleep, and increased libido. For fifty bucks, it was a bargain.

I bought two bottles and decided to go to a bookstore to look for books about writing. I had taken Orli's advice and had been trying to write of late, but it wasn't going well. I hated everything I wrote. I read and reread Kafka – his short stories, his novels, his letters. So many of his stories seemed to be about me. One was called *The Foolish Man Who Shouldn't Have Bothered*. Here's how it goes:

The Foolish Man Who Shouldn't Have Bothered

Once upon a time there was a man who was an artist. His art was the art of starvation. Every day he would get into his cage at the circus and starve himself. For a little while, people liked it. Then, soon, they didn't. Suffering wasn't interesting. Suffering was a downer.

- Boo, said the people.

The artist died.

The circus owner bought a panther.

- Yay, said the people.

The End

I examined his narratives, I analyzed his structures, I studied his style. I took his stories apart and put them back together. I wanted to know how he did it, how he had taken his pain and turned it into art. But the more I looked for an answer, the further away it seemed to get, as if the looking itself was my problem. I was stuck. I was lost. I didn't know what to write. - You can write anything you want, said Orli, but she also said *I love you* and *You're sexy*, so what the fuck did she know? On the rare occasion I managed to put down something I liked, I was certain Michiko Kakutani would hate it, and what was the point of writing something if Michiko Kakutani wasn't going to like it? I pored through her book reviews to try to figure out what she wanted, determined to give it to her, but they only confused me further. Of the recent *Infinite Jest*, she had written:

It's Thomas Wolfe without Maxwell Perkins, done in the hallucinogenic style of Terry Gilliam and Ralph Steadman.

Of a new collection of Nabokov she had written:

All can be found in these pages, pushed, prodded and honed into a variety of shapes, into whimsical fables, old-fashioned character sketches, Poe-like exercises in the macabre, and clever, Postmodernist confections.

Confections?

What the fuck was she talking about?

And who the fuck was Maxwell fucking Perkins?

Just tell me, Michiko, I silently begged, my head in my hands as I sank into another failed midnight. *Just tell me what you want to read, and I'll write it. Whimsical fables? Fine. You want whimsical fables, I'll give you whimsical fables. Or maybe you're whimsical-fabled out? Maybe you're sick of whimsical fables. Do you want non-whimsical fables? Just tell me, please, Michiko.*

But like all gods, she never responded, and so I dragged myself to bookstore after bookstore – to Barnes & Noble and to Shakespeare & Co. and to the Strand – to the shameful, ignominious Writing Reference section, that exclamation-pointed leper colony where self-respect goes to die.

Start That Novel!

101 Plots

No Plot? No Problem!

For those of you not cursed with the need to write, Writing Reference is the bookstore equivalent of the Golden Showers section in porn shops – the lowest of the low, way in the back where only the most desperate dare to tread.

- Jesus Christ, the otherwise unsuspecting patrons gasp, having strolled too far back and spotted *Golden Guzzlers 17* on the shelf. - What sickos are into *this* shit?

Writing Reference, too, is located at the back, usually between Literary Criticism and the toilet. Here we frustrated writers loiter, pretending to look for encyclopedias and grammar guides until the line for the restroom clears and we can grab a copy of *How to Write a Damn Good Novel* without anyone seeing. My technique? I would grab a few writing books – quickly, randomly, the titles didn't matter, they're all the same – then carry them over to Philosophy or some other more respectable section and read them there, pretending *There's a Novel in You!* was Kant or Schopenhauer.

I was as nondiscerning as only a desperate hunger artist can be. I read every book on writing I could find, from the respectable classics by Ray Bradbury and Milan Kundera to the syphilitic crack-whore desperations of *How to Write a Novel in 21 Days* and *Secrets of a Best-Selling Author!* The books left me feeling empty and ashamed, but the possibility of an answer to my frustration was too appealing to resist. Hope is the thing with feathers that you just backed over in the driveway, and I refused to believe that there wasn't an answer – in the pills for my repulsive body, in the books for my mediocre mind – and hoped that one blessed day I would stumble on the book/pill that would transform me at last into the person I most wanted to be: someone else.

Discovering RenewTrient made me feel optimistic, so I made my way over to Coliseum Books on Fifty-seventh Street, not far from Health n' Vitamin Best Price Best Selection, where I grabbed *20 Master Plots* and a copy of *So You Want to Write a Novel*, tried to avoid eye contact with the cashier as I paid, stuffed them in my bag with the bottles of RenewTrient, and hurried home (if only booksellers wrapped my shameful purchases the way porn sellers did; I dreamed of a bookstore with the same sort of Preview Booths that porn shops have, where I could simply mumble *Book Number Three* to the cashier instead of handing her *Ready, Set, Write!*). Orli was working as a DJ at a radio station on Long Island at the time and was never home before midnight. When I got home, I locked the front door, went straight to the kitchen, and poured myself a capful of yellow-green RenewTrient. It smelled awful and tasted worse, but a few moments after forcing it down, I felt a delicious warmth growing in my belly, a warmth that quickly rose through my torso to my face, to my lips, to my fingers, to my soul. The room began to spin, and I thought I might fall, and I reached for the wall to steady myself, and I stumbled to the living room, and I aimed for the couch, and I fell, and I fell, and I fell.

And I smiled.

Note: I hate my smile. I'm not a big fan of my face in general, but smiling only makes a bad situation worse. I have too much face, that's the problem. When I smile, there's nowhere for all that extra face to go, so it just spills over wherever it can, like sewage backing up through a drainpipe.

But face.

Now, though, I smiled. I smiled so widely and for so long that my cheeks hurt.

RenewTrient wasn't like pot. It wasn't a numbing or a masking; I didn't feel heavy or drugged or disconnected. Pot made me leave myself, which was enjoyable – but RenewTrient made me like myself, which was inconceivable.

Reader, I danced.

I stood in the living room of our West Village apartment, and I danced.

Note: I hate dancing even more than I hate my face. I hate dance clubs and I hate dance music. If I'm wrong and Hell isn't a pool, then it's a dance club. No lakes of fire, no boiling cauldrons, none needed; just a disco ball, a dance floor that stretches across the firmament, and some hyperenthusiastic DJ cranking out shitty bass-thumping dance music who exhorts me to *Get on out there!* and *Don't be shy!*

For eternity.

And yet, after just a single capful of RenewTrient, I was dancing.

And I liked it.

I liked the way my hips moved; I liked the way I spun and swiveled and shook. I wished Orli could see me. Orli loves dancing, but no matter how strenuously she implored me to join her, even in the privacy of our own home, I refused. Her dancing is exuberant, ecstatic; she begins slowly, amorously, stripteasingly, but it doesn't last — joy quickly overwhelms lust and she goes berserk, dancing frantic versions of the twist or the hully gully like an *American Bandstand* dancer on meth. She dances like she doesn't care who is watching. Because she doesn't. It's very annoying.

I couldn't wait for her to come home — to see me smiling, to see me dancing, to see the Better Me she deserved. I was overcome with desire; I wanted to fuck, and I wanted to be fucked; I wanted to be a man, and I wanted to be a woman; I wanted to be a top, and I wanted to be a bottom. I masturbated until I could masturbate no more, and collapsed in a self-liking, noncritical mass of spent desire. I closed my eyes and light washed over me, and I felt, for the first time in my life, what it was like to exist for a moment without shame, without judgment, without condemnation. I felt, at last, alive.

I woke sometime later near death. I couldn't breathe. I was cold, shivering, gasping for air. It felt as though someone had forced a plastic bag over my head and cinched it tight around my neck; the more I tried to fill my lungs, the deeper I sank into a cold black sea. I tried to call out for Orli, forgetting in my terror that she wasn't home, but so short was my breath that I couldn't even manage a whisper. I was alone, and I was dying.

Months later, after people began dropping dead from the chemicals in Renew-Trient, I would learn that physicians referred to what I was experiencing as a G coma. RenewTrient's main ingredient was an industrial solvent called 1,4-butanediol (BDO), most commonly used in floor strippers and nail polish removers. On its own, BDO is of no practical use to the Feh. Once ingested, however, BDO metabolizes in the stomach and becomes gamma hydroxybutyrate (GHB), otherwise known as liquid ecstasy or the fabled date-rape drug, a drug whose sedative effect is so powerful in higher doses that it not only suppresses Feh, it suppresses the respiratory system itself and causes coma or death.

I managed to roll over onto my hands and knees and crawled to the living room window, yanking it open with the last of my strength; in great heaving breaths I drew the frigid night air into my lungs, shivering, teeth chattering, legs weak. Breath by shallow breath, I filled my lungs. As Death departed disappointed, I turned from the window to take stock of my inglorious situation: I was covered in perspiration, shivering and sweating at the same time; my nose was bleeding; pornography was playing on the VCR, and *So You Want to Write a Novel* was lying on the living room floor in a puddle of sex lube. Asphyxia became nausea, sudden, overwhelming, and I ran for the bathroom; cold and naked, I vomited, then vomited again, wondering if the neighbors could hear me, wondering what they thought of me, wondering how they judged me — *Sicko, Drunk, Failure*. Thank goodness they didn't know about the writing books.

When I could vomit no more, I stumbled to the kitchen, splashed some water on my face, and poured myself another capful of RenewTrient.

I was liking myself again before the vomit on my shirt had even dried.

For fifty bucks, it was a bargain.

...

Having read all I could about how to write, I began to wonder if perhaps it wasn't the how I was struggling with, but rather the how-to-not-hate-what-I-had-written. None of the writing guides covered that; they talked about structure and character and subtext; they all told the old Early-Man-Telling-Stories-Around-the-Campfire story, but none ever told the Early-Man-Afraid-to-Share-His-Story-Around-the-Campfire-Because-He-Thinks-It-Sucks-and-So-He-Wants-to-Throw-Himself-into-the-Campfire story.

How, I wondered, did Kafka write a story about a hunger artist and not throw the pages in the trash? How did he write a story about a man who wakes up as a bug, or about a man hounded by two mysterious bouncing balls, or about a country mouse who could sing but whom nobody loved? Who told him that was allowed? Who gave him permission? Who told Voltaire the grim horrors of existence could be funny, that tragedy could be laughed at, philosophers mocked? Who told Beckett he could write about two tramps waiting for someone who never came, or Cervantes that he could write about an optimist who gets his ass kicked for a thousand pages, or García Márquez that he could write about an angel of the Lord who appears on a beach only to be beaten by the believers who discover him? Their strengths began to seem more about courage than about craft. They seemed to have a confidence I lacked. And so, a few days later, I enrolled in a writing workshop.

- A what? Orli asked.

- A writing workshop.

- Why?

- To help me write, I said. - To give me confidence.

Orli doesn't like instruction. As a rule, she doesn't like rules. Perhaps this stems from her childhood in a strict patriarchal community, but she will accept no guidance, consider no instruction. This Emersonian self-reliance sounds admirable in theory, but practically speaking, it has some drawbacks.

- The fucking blender doesn't work, Orli would say.

- Did you read the instruction manual? I would ask.

- No, I did not read the fucking instruction manual.

- Why not?

- IT'S A BLENDER! YOU PRESS *BLEND*!

She grabs the blender by its neck.

- BLEND! she shouts. - BLEND, YOU PIECE OF SHIT!

I believe I mentioned her Middle Eastern descent.

The only guides she reads are about the human brain, and of those she reads them all. Books about the brain line her shelves and are stacked on the floor beside her bed. She didn't like my workshop idea.

- Wouldn't *not* going to a workshop give you confidence? she asked.

- How would not going to a workshop give me confidence?

- Because then you wouldn't think you need it to have confidence, she said.
- It's a brain thing. The more writing instruction you get, the more your brain decides you need that instruction, because if it didn't, you wouldn't be getting it, so the less it trusts itself without the instruction. It's a vicious cycle.

- Are you high? I asked.

- Yes, she said.

I didn't blame her. If I had to live with me, I'd be stoned too. And suspicious of brains.

The workshop was held once a week in a loft on Lafayette Street in Greenwich Village. It was founded by a respected poet who never came to class. His name was Edgar. The instructors spoke of him as my rabbis had spoken of God.

- Edgar, the instructor said, is a genius.

- Edgar, the other instructor said, is my guide and mentor.

- Edgar, said a third instructor, will show you the way.

- Will Edgar be coming to classes? I asked.

- Edgar will not be coming to classes, the instructor said.

Each class began with the instructor handing out copies of a highly regarded short story, which we would read in silence and then discuss. Then we would go home and write stories in a similar vein, and the following week, read them aloud. The story we read on the first day was by a man named Raymond Carver, whom I had never heard of before. The name of the story was *Splat*. This is how it goes:

SPLAT

Once upon a time there was a little boy. His birthday was coming up, so his mother planned a party. She ordered him a cake. Everyone was very excited.

The morning of his birthday, the little boy got T-boned by a car.

Splat.

The End

- Amazing, said one student.

- So good, said another.

- Who can tell me, the instructor asked, what this story is about?

The woman beside me raised her hand.

- It's about a boy who gets hit by a car, she said.

- No, said the instructor.

- It isn't?

- No, said the instructor with great self-satisfaction. - It's about the person *telling the story* about a boy who gets hit by a car!

- Ooooh, the woman said.

She wrote that down.

I raised my hand.

- I think I'm missing a page, I said.

The story on my pages ended abruptly, just as the mother was getting home from visiting her comatose son. She runs herself a bath, and as she does, the phone rings.

- Is this about my son? she asks.

- It is, says the man on the other end of the line.

The End.

I held my pages out to the instructor.

- And that's all I got, I said. - That's where it cuts off.

- That's all there is, the instructor said with a beatific smile. - It's ambiguous, isn't it?

- No, I said, the GHB high beginning to wane. - It's *un*ambiguous. A kid got flattened on his birthday. He's dead. It sucks, but it's not ambiguous.

- I was referring to the ending, she said.

- There is no ending.

- That's what makes it ambiguous.

- That's not ambiguous, I said. - That's unfinished.

- I think Raymond Carver knows when a story is finished, she said. Everyone laughed.

- Will Edgar be coming to classes? I asked.

- Edgar will not be coming to classes, she said.

...

I began taking GHB every night when I came home from my advertising job, and again every morning before I went to it. But the high wore off by noon, and when it did, a frightful darkness followed, a darkness even darker than the one that preceded it. Asked to create a campaign for Duracell, I presented a series of commercials of batteries who wanted to die but couldn't because they were Duracell.

- Will we *ever* die, Papa? Child Battery sobs.

- I don't know, Son, Father Battery replies. - Not for a very long time.

They weep.

Logo.

Duracell didn't like the suicide angle. I assured them it was a growing market. They went with *Trusted Everywhere*.

Probably a good move.

The following workshop, we put our chairs in a circle, and the instructor asked us to read our versions of *Splat*. A dull parade of predictable tragedy followed: There were stories about dead newborns, dead kittens, dead roommates, dead spouses, and dead parents; there were stories about heart attacks and cancer; there were stories about drunk drivers and plane crashes and train wrecks. My story was about two young boys who, one sunny summer after-noon, decided to surprise their father by barbecuing dinner. I think you know how it ends.

- Excellent, said the instructor.

It wasn't. I had stolen it from the Bible. The original is in Leviticus 10:1–3. It's called *The Barbecuing Children Who Got Barbecued by God*. Here's how it goes:

THE BARBECUING CHILDREN WHO GOT BARBECUED BY GOD

Once upon a time, a man named Aaron escaped from Egypt. He had two sons. With the help of God, they survived a year in the brutal desert, and so, to honor Him, they built a temple. One day, Aaron's sons, grateful for all that God had done for them, decided to make a burnt offering to God.

They did it wrong.

- Feh, said God.

And so He made the fire leap from the altar, onto Aaron's sons, and they both burned to death.

The End

- I like how they were doing something good when they died, said the instructor.

- It's ironic, said one student.

- It's ambiguous, said another.

- It is, I said.

It wasn't.

I excused myself, went to the bathroom, had a shot of RenewTrient, and returned.

Orli, unaware of my growing reliance on RenewTrient, was pleased with the change in my personality. She liked my new lightheartedness. At night we danced – danced! – and we made love in the kitchen, on the couch, on the living room floor, often in harsh, broad daylight. But dosing RenewTrient was a delicate affair: Not enough and nothing happened; too much and I was vomiting; way too much and I was dead. One evening we passed out in each other's arms, and I woke sometime later with a start, blue and shivering, gasping for air, my nose bleeding.

- What's wrong, Shal? Orli cried. - Should I call someone? Shal, what's wrong?

- Window, I panted. - Open . . .

It was allergies, I assured her, nothing more.

- It's not allergies, she said.

- It is.

- What's going on?

- It's allergies, I said. - I'll see a doctor.

She helped me to bed, cuddled up beside me, and held me in her arms. A half hour earlier I wanted to be enveloped in her: in her arms, her legs, her hair, her breath; now, coming down, I cringed even to be touched.

Second to coma, the biggest problem with GHB was sleep. GHB sleep wasn't real sleep, and it left me exhausted, struggling to keep my eyes open. I fell asleep on subways, on buses, at Starbucks. I capfulled my way through two bottles in as many weeks, and stumbled half-asleep to Health n' Vitamin Best Price Best Selection to buy some more.

- A hundred bucks? I asked the shop owner. - Fuck you, it was fifty last week.

- Best price, he said. - Very popular. For make happy.

I was too sleepy to argue.

- This is good, too, he said, holding up a bottle of pills called Dymetadrine 25 with one hand while patting his distended belly with the other.

- For make skinny, he said.

I bought two bottles of RenewTrient, a bottle of Dymetadrine 25, and a tub of something called Hot Stuff Anabolic Steroid Alternative.

- For make muscle, he said as he took my credit card. - Three hundred dollars.

This liking myself shit was costing me a fortune.

...

- I'm worried about you, said Ike.

I avoided taking GHB before our sessions. Ike knew me well enough to be suspicious of any uncharacteristic joy. Without GHB, though, I was despairing and sullen, even more so than usual, and so instead of his being concerned about my uncharacteristic positivity, he was now concerned about my worsening negativity.

- Have you been writing? he asked.

- No, I said, fighting to keep my eyes open. - But I've been reading *about* writing. Does that count?

- No. Have you been drinking?

- No.

- Smoking?

- No.

- No pot?

- Oh pot, I said. - Yes.

He explained, yet again, the rebound effect – that while drugs may work in the short term, the brain fights to reestablish its chemical balance, and the depression after can be worse than the depression before. I assured him I wasn't on anything and blamed my mood on Raymond Carver.

- The writer?

- Yeah, I said. - Bit of a bleak worldview, to be honest.

I had just come from another workshop, where we had read a second Carver story. This one was called *Split*. It was a lot like *Splat*. This is how it goes:

SPLIT

Once upon a time there was a baby. The baby's parents were having a fight.

- I want the baby, said the father, grabbing the baby.
- I want the baby, said the mother, grabbing the baby.

They tugged and tugged until they tore the baby in half.

The End

- Must be nice to be wanted, I said.
- Didn't Solomon write that story? Ike asked.
- Yes, I said. - But this one won a National Book Award.

I asked him if he'd ever read Kafka's *Hunger Artist*.

- It's about an artist, I told him. - His art is starving. He works in a circus, but nobody likes his art. He dies and they replace him with a panther.
- Does he die happy? Ike asked.
- Who?
- The artist, he said.
- Happy?

It wasn't a question I had considered.

- To have done the art he wanted, Ike continued, public adulation or not.

I didn't know. I supposed that since he never changed his art, since he never quit and started writing Marvel screenplays, I guessed he was happy doing it. I guessed it was the only art he could do.

- So maybe the story isn't the story of a failure, Ike offered, but of victory on one's own terms.
- Great, I said. - Now I feel even worse about myself.

Ike began to sing Frank Sinatra's "My Way."

- There's no way I'm paying for this session, I said.

I left, stopped in his lobby bathroom, took a quick shot of GHB, and headed home.

...

The ephedra in the Dymetadrine 25 was making me anxious and giving me vertigo. Whatever was in Hot Stuff was giving me heart palpitations. The GHB was making it hard to get hard and impossible to orgasm. I ran out of it as quickly as I could buy it, and soon I was out of it again. Health n' Vitamin Best Price Best Selection had upped the price to $150 a bottle, and I just couldn't afford it. I considered sipping nail polish remover, which was only $10 a bottle. Floor stripper was $10 a gallon. Darkness descended. Asked to create a campaign for a life insurance company, I presented a series of commercials featuring a forty-foot-tall desktop fan at the top of a remote hill overlooking a valley.

- Somewhere, the announcer said, there is a fan. And sooner or later, the shit is going to hit it.

Logo.

They went with *We're on Your Side*.

Probably a good move.

- I'm worried about you, said Orli. - You're not yourself.

- I wish, I answered.

- What if I'm not here when it happens? she said. - What if you stop breathing when I'm away, when I'm at work?

I scoffed.

- God isn't going to cancel His favorite comedy, I said.

At the next workshop, we put our chairs in a circle and read our *Split*-inspired stories about dysfunctional relationships. Couples yelled, cried, pulled out guns, set fire to their apartments. Men beat women, women murdered men. The instructor, noticing me nodding off, asked me to read mine. I did my best to sit upright.

- Sure, I said.

I had written the story the night before, late, in a furious rush. It had been sometime after midnight, and I was frustrated, hopeless, and out of Renew-Trient. I didn't give a fuck about the workshop or about Carver or about Edgar. I didn't give a fuck about anyone.

- Good, Orli had said. - Now write.

The story concerned a Jewish man named Goldfarb who dies and goes to Heaven, where he discovers to his dismay that God is a big, forty-foot-tall chicken. Goldfarb is overcome with terror, recalling all the chickens he'd eaten in his life, all the omelets, all the hot wings, to say nothing of all the chicken soup he'd served his children on Shabbos night, who would now surely burn in Hell with their father. Goldfarb falls on his knees and begs Chicken to let him return to Earth, please, oh Lord, to reveal to his beloved children who (and what) God really is, to allow them to repent for their terrible but entirely inadvertent sins. Chicken grants Goldfarb's request. Back in the hospital room on Earth, his family cheers as Goldfarb's heart miraculously begins to beat again. They hug and kiss, and Goldfarb decides to tell them all about Chicken that Friday at Shabbos dinner. But when the evening comes, and his wife lights the elegant white Shabbos candles, and he sees his children enjoying God's holy day, he can't bring himself to tell them the truth. It would destroy their happiness and upend their joyous traditions.

To hell with Chicken, he thinks. *Happiness is more important.*

His children sing. All is warmth and joy. His wife brings out the soup: Chicken.

The End.

The workshoppers stared at me blankly.

- What kind of story is that? one asked.

- It's a fable, I grumbled.

- A fable?

- Yeah, a fable.

- What kind of fable?

- A whimsical fable.

- Tell me something, the instructor said. - How does the person *telling* the story about the chicken *feel* about the chicken?

- The chicken?

- Does the teller like the chicken or dislike the chicken?

- It's not really about the chicken, I said. - The chicken's beside the point. He chooses happiness.

- What if it was a tiger? she asked.

- What if what was a tiger?

- The chicken.

- If the chicken was a tiger?

- Yes.

- Then the chicken soup wouldn't matter. It would have to be tiger soup.

- But if it was a tiger, she said, and there was tiger soup, would the person telling the story *like* the tiger?

My head ached. I didn't see where this was going.

- Is Edgar coming? I asked.

- He is not, said the instructor.

She was pleased to announce, though, that they were now selling cassettes of Edgar's instructor-level classes, which she strongly urged us to buy.

For twenty bucks, she said, they were a bargain.

. . .

Sunday afternoon, I climbed into a cab and headed uptown to Health n' Vitamin Best Price Best Selection. I was miserable and gloomy. Whatever the cost of RenewTrient, I would pay it.

- No more, said the man at the counter.

- No more?

- No more.

- What do you mean *no more*?

- I mean all gone.

- When does it come in?

He shook his head and told me people had died from taking it.

- Died?

- Idiots, he said. - They take too much, can't breathe, die. Put it in girl's drink, rape her when she sleeps. Animals. Now good customers can't have. You're a good customer.

He glanced down the aisles to make certain the shop was empty of other customers, reached beneath the counter, and produced a bottle of yellow-green liquid.

Video Head Cleaner, read the label.

Toxic.

Not for Human Consumption.

- One hundred fifty, he said. - Cash.

I was confused.

- It's for VCRs, I said.

- Yes.

- I'm not a VCR.

- Same as other, he said. - Same chemical. Cheap.

- How is a hundred and fifty cheap? I asked. - It's the same price as Renew-Trient.

- If I had RenewTrient now, he said, it would be two hundred. You're a good customer.

I stopped at Coliseum Books, bought two books about narrative structure, another about the history of the novel, and a new, lube-free copy of *So You Want to Write a Novel.*

- It's for my wife, I said to the cashier.

- Mm-hmm, said the cashier.

That evening, Orli, working late at the radio station, decided to sleep over on Long Island. I got home, drank some video-head cleaner, and waited to like myself. But video-head cleaner was a fair degree stronger than Renew-

Trient, the dosing more delicate. I took too much, skipped right over euphoria, and went straight to coma. A bottomless pit opened in the living room floor beneath me, and I tumbled into the dark abyss. I lay on the living room floor, gasping for air, the window too far away to reach, to open. The light around me began to fade, and all the world went dark and silent. Down, down, down I fell; I tried to call for help, but no sound came out. As death approached, I closed my eyes, and all I could hear in my last precious moments on Earth was Edgar, on my cassette player, discussing Raymond Carver and persona narrators.

Splat.

I woke the next morning, the too-bright sun assailing me, our dog Duke licking my face, whining to go out. It was ten a.m. Harley, our other dog, had already shat in the kitchen.

I'm worried about you, I said to myself.

I needed to be away – from people, from the city, from Raymond Carver, and from Health n' Vitamin Best Price Best Selection. When I could stand without needing a wall for assistance, I showered, cleaned up, and walked the dogs, half asleep in a video-head cleaner fog that was even heavier than RenewTrient's.

Duke refused to shit.

- Come on, buddy, I said. - Hurry up.

There was no negotiating with Duke when it came to shitting. He refused to shit in the city. He refused to shit on pavement. He preferred being in the woods, shitting on soil the way Dog God intended. From Monday to Friday, the days we spent in New York City, Duke refused to shit. By Thursdays he was a trembling, whining nuisance, asking to go out every hour but refusing to shit once he got there.

- Hurry up, buddy, I begged him that morning. - Let's go, come on.

Nothing.

I admired him. He didn't care what anyone wanted or needed or expected. He did it his way. He was a shit artist.

When I got back inside, I phoned the workshop and left a message on their answering machine, telling them that I was quitting.

- I'm sorry, I said. - I just need to hear my own self.

Some say Kafka's *Hunger Artist* is an allegory for Christ. Others say it is about the rejection of religion by the panther of secularism. Still others say it is an examination of the ethereal artist contrasted with the corporeal beast. Academics are weird. Much more important to me was that he was able to write it at all; and he was able to write it, I decided, because he didn't give a fuck what anyone thought about it. He couldn't have, or he wouldn't have written it. I'm sure, like any human being, Franz worried about acceptance when he sat down to write his stories, and again when he had finished them; but right then, in the moment, in the act of writing, Franz didn't give a fuck. Cervantes didn't give a fuck, and Beckett didn't give a fuck. Twenty-three hours a day, sure – Kafka wanted Michiko to like him, Cervantes wanted Edgar's approval. But I was beginning to suspect that every story or novel I'd ever loved, from *The Trial* to *Candide* to *Don Quixote*, represented the collective, blessed, strung-together few moments the writer was strong enough, defiant enough, Duke enough, to just write their souls – that their permission came from deciding, at long last, that they didn't need anyone's goddamned permission. Perhaps they just had to get to a place where they were so tired of being silenced by themselves that they finally screamed, a place where the need to speak overwhelms the need for approval, where the desire to be heard overwhelms the desire to be loved, where the voice whispering *Speak!* becomes louder than the one shouting *Feh*.

- Wait, please, Kafka's hunger artist never begs the circus owner. - You want panther, I can give you panther. What kind of panther do you want? You want a whimsical panther? I did a whole Panther Workshop in the West Village . . .

I packed my laptop and some clothes, leashed the dogs, got us all in the truck, and emailed Orli that I was heading up to Woodstock.

- Good idea, she responded.

I never made it.

I had been fighting the GHB grogginess all morning, and it only grew worse the farther I drove. Twice my eyes had closed, but I'd caught myself before veering off the road. Halfway there, I was forced to pull over at a highway rest stop for a nap and a coffee. But caffeine is no match for industrial solvent; I was ten miles from our house when I finally fell asleep at the wheel, out cold, doing fifty miles an hour in a thirty-mile-per-hour zone on a four-lane highway in a three-ton pickup truck.

The impact woke me. The crunching of steel, the death groan of metal crushing metal. The force slammed me against the steering wheel. I was disoriented, unaware of where I was or how I had gotten there. The dogs were sailing across the cabin, legs flailing, trying to find some purchase. I looked out over the hood of the truck and beheld an impossible sight: the steel guardrail, which I was accustomed to seeing to my side as I drove, was now passing directly underneath me, and I realized that we were sliding along the top of it, skateboarder-style.

Only at fifty miles an hour.

With a sixty-foot cliff on the other side of the rail.

I began frantically twisting the steering wheel, stomping on the brakes, but the wheels of the truck were off the ground, lifted by the rail, and my desperate actions had no effect. A witness coming the other way told the police that I was doing at least sixty; I must have fallen asleep with my foot on the gas. In hindsight, the police officer said, it was a good thing I had been going that speed; any slower, and the truck might have tipped off the rail and tumbled down the cliff. But the speed provided enough momentum for the truck to slide the entire length of the guardrail, right off the tucked end forty feet away, so that the truck came to rest, miraculously, upright at the side of the highway, without flipping or spinning or striking another vehicle. I got out, amazed to be alive. Behind the truck, strewn across the roadway, were the disemboweled organs of the truck's underside – exhaust, muffler, transmission – like the entrails of a gutted fish. *I'll gut you like a fish*, Kafka's father used to say to him. The police officers arrived and asked my name, and asked my address, and asked me if I had been drinking. They searched the truck, they searched the glove compartment, they searched under the seats, they searched my backpack. All they found were two terrified dogs, a book about how to write a novel in an unreasonably short amount of time, and a half-empty bottle of video-head cleaner.

- It's for my wife, I said about the book.

- You're lucky to be alive, said the officer, peering into the ravine below.

They drove me home, where I sat on the front porch, chain-smoking cigarettes and trying to stop my hands from shaking. I poured the remaining video-head cleaner into the soil behind the garage. I flushed the Dymetadrine 25 pills down the toilet and dumped the Hot Stuff Anabolic Steroid Alternative powder into the trash, along with the androstenedione and the dibencozide and the ornithine alpha-ketoglutarate and something called Ultimate Orange Pre-Workout Energy Drink, which was later revealed to contain clenbuterol, an illegal fat-burning substance chemically similar to methamphetamine.

- For less self-hate, I imagined the man at Health n' Vitamin Best Price Best Selection saying.

My phone rang.

- Hey, I said, expecting it to be Orli. - I'm here.

It was Edgar. And he was livid. He demanded to know why I was leaving the workshop, told me I was lazy, called me a quitter, declared I was not a real writer, and swore to me that if I left his workshop I would never be published.

- Never! he shouted.

I told him he wouldn't be either, so at least we had that in common, and then I hung up.

Note: That has not happened.

He's doing great.

He won a Pulitzer.

I phoned Orli. I told her I had fallen asleep at the wheel, that the truck was totaled, that I needed to be more careful, and that I needed to start writing again.

- I'm worried about you, she said.

On the plus side, I said, Edgar had phoned and I had quit the workshop.

- What did he say? she asked.

- He said what they all say, I told her. - He said *Feh*.

24

It was Gordon Lish, Raymond Carver's editor, who chopped the end off Carver's dead kid story and titled it *The Bath*. Printed in its original form in a later collection, the story ended not with an ambiguous phone call as the boy's mother ran her bath, but rather with the shattered, grieving parents, heartbroken, communing with the baker of the boy's birthday cake, sitting together after hours in his bakery, nibbling from pastries and accepting that life goes on, maybe even sweetly, despite the pain and loss.

Lish cut that ending off.

The story wasn't ambiguous.

It was butchered.

Carver had begged him not to:

If the book were to be published as it is in its present edited form, he wrote to Lish, *I may never write another story, that's how closely, God Forbid, some of those stories are to my sense of regaining my health and mental well-being.*

Carver wanted to tell a story about getting through the darkness, about seeing the good in life and each other.

He had called his story *A Small, Good Thing*.

Lish wanted to tell a darker story. A story called *Life Sucks and People Suck, So What's the Point?*, a story we all, living and dead, Eastern and Western, have been told a thousand thousand times, in a thousand thousand forms, a cancer-like story we have internalized as a species and believe without question. A story called *Feh*.

25

Five-sixths of human beings, wrote the German philosopher Arthur Schopenhauer, are worth only contempt.

I first read Schopenhauer in my early twenties.

I was pretty sure he was being optimistic.

...

Every year, the members of the Woodstock Day School LGBTQ+ Club make a film. It is a small club, no more than a handful of students, for whom the films are a vehicle to express themselves, to be heard by the rest of the student body. Paix was not LGBTQ+, but his friend Eve was in the club, and he had joined as an ally. One evening, he asked me if I would help them with their movie.

- We have a good idea, Paix said. - We really need your help.

In previous years, he explained, the films focused on how different the club members were from other students. This year, though, they wanted to do something I thought beautiful and radical: They wanted to make a film showing just how *alike* all people were – gay and straight, black and white, he, she, or they.

The idea appealed to me. After so many years in the ad business saying how great every brand was – Ford was number one, Xbox was number one, Burger King was number one – I appreciated the counterintuitive strategy of *We're Ordinary*. Some years earlier, I had been asked to come up with a slogan for the US Army. Among the armed services, they wanted to be number one. Unfortunately for them, it was widely agreed that the Marines were number one, and had been for some time. The Navy was number two, the Air Force was third, and the Army was a very, very distant fourth. I suggested the Army embrace their position. After all, what good was being number one? What did being number one do for a Marine? It got him sent into war first, that's what it got him. It got him sent home in a body bag. Marines may be number one, I argued, but they were idiots. *The Few, the Proud, the Dead.*

- *The US Army*, I proposed. - *Because the Marines Go in First.*

The agency didn't like it.

They went with *Army Strong*.

Probably a good move.

I felt buoyed to have Paix ask me for help. I had been feeling particularly *feh* of late, and I wanted him to admire me. Career, money, finances – everything seemed to be failing, mostly me.

- *What does your father do?*

- *He fails.*

Big laughs.

Orli insisted the boys admired me already, but I shrugged off her opinion.

- You love me, I said.

- So?

- So, your opinion isn't valid.

- Fuck you.

- It's valid, I backpedaled, it's just biased.

- Why wouldn't they admire you?

- Because I'm a failure.

- In what?

- Name it. Life. Career.

- Because we're not rich?

- No.

- You're a published author.

- So?

- Your books are published, she said again, slower this time. - They're in bookstores.

- Not airport bookstores, I said.

- Airport bookstores?

- Yeah, airport bookstores.

- How do you know they're not in airport bookstores?

- Because I check, I said. - They're never there. It pisses me off. All these shitty books are there but not mine.

- Because it's an airport bookstore, she said. - They sell shitty books.

- I know, I said. - But they don't sell mine.

- So, you know they only sell shitty books, but you want them to sell your book?

- Yes.

There was a long silence as she waited for me to put the pieces together.

I did not.

- But if they sold your book, she said, it would mean it was a shitty book.

- Yes, I said. - But it would be for sale.

- You should really see a psychiatrist, she said.

I did. That afternoon. Ike suggested that perhaps I was unable to accept love because I didn't believe I deserved it. He asked me to put aside my own feelings about myself for a moment and answer his next question as objectively as I could:

- Do you think Orli and the boys love you?

I thought about it a moment.

- Probably, I said. - But they know me.

- So?

- So, it doesn't count.

- Why doesn't it count?

- Because they're my family.

- And that doesn't count?

- No.

- What could count more than the love of your family?

- The love of strangers.

- The love of strangers?

- Yes.

- Why?

- Because they don't know me.

- You should really see a psychiatrist, he said.

Love or not, we were in serious financial trouble, and my plan to take over Hollywood was going nowhere. Orli knew it, and the boys knew it. A year after Phil's death, we filmed *Pigs in Shit* with a new title – *Happyish* – and a new cast, but it had been canceled after just ten episodes.

- What's *canceled* mean? Paix had asked.

- It means they're not going to make it anymore.

- How come?

- I don't know.

- Was it good?

- I liked it.

- Did other people like it?

- I don't know.

- People like video games! he offered.

- I know.

- *Minecraft* has like a million players!

- I know.

- They make a lot of money!

- I know.

- You should write video games! he said.

I explained to him that money wasn't the only reason to do something; that for me, writing was a way to know myself, to see myself in a new light, to grow.

- Like Stephen King?

- No.

- People like Stephen King.

- They do.

- He sells like a million books.

- He does.

- Like J. K. Rowling?

- No.

- She sells a lot too.

- She does.

- Like who then?

- Like Kafka.

- Who's that?

- A writer.

- Do people like him?

- They do now.

- Why?

- Because he's dead.

- Did they like him when he was alive?

- No.

- Oh.

And so I decided, somewhat self-interestedly, to help with the LGBTQ+ Club film. Disaffected preadolescents! Gender issues! Identity struggles! It might not win the Oscar for Best Documentary, but it would sure as hell be nominated. If I could cram a Holocaust survivor in there, that fucking statue was mine.

I met with the club a few days later in the sun-filled, cheerful school library and immediately felt for them. They bit their fingers, they slouched in their seats, they nervously tapped their feet. They were the oddballs, the weirdos, the strange, the awkward. There was a sadness within them, a sadness I remembered from my own troubled adolescence. They were trying to find themselves, to be themselves, whoever those selves might be. Harriet, formerly Leslie, was now a They, their hair cropped close, their clothes as androgynous as possible. Jet, once Sally, was now a He. Sophia struggled with crippling social anxiety, Sky's parents were going through a difficult divorce, and Eve, who didn't show up to the meeting, was burdened with overwhelming depression. You might expect, as I did, to find a certain camaraderie between these societal outcasts, a sense of unity, aligned as they were against the world and its petty, hateful judgments.

You would be wrong.

Like any marginalized group, they fought most savagely among themselves. And with me.

- Paix explained the theme of the film, I began, and I love it. It really moved me. But what are we going to actually see?

- Have you ever even *made* a film? asked Harriet.

- I had a TV series.

- What's it called?

- It's not on anymore.

They laughed.

- But I've written books, I said, and I can tell you that when it comes to . . .

- What books? Harriet demanded.

- Book books, I said.

- What kind of books?

- The kind with pages.

- Are they in here?

- No.

- Why not?

- Because these books are for kids, I said. - And kids are fucking stupid.

They laughed.

Harriet: 1, Shalom: 1.

- So, what are we going to see in this film? I continued, trying to get the discussion back on track.

- It's simple, Harriet said. - We're going to spend a day on campus, interviewing students about how they're the same. I've compiled a list of locations with high visual interest, along with a second list of interview methods by which we can engage students on their –

- That's stupid, Jet interrupted.

- Let her finish, I said.

- Them, Sky corrected me.

- Why is it stupid? Harriet asked Jet.

- How do you ask someone how they're the *same?* Jet asked.

- You point your camera at them, Harriet snapped, and ask them how they're the same.

- *How are you the same?* Jet asked. - What does that even mean? The same as what?

- We agreed on this approach at the last meeting, Harriet said firmly. - The meeting, I might add, *you* missed.

- I was sick! said Jet.

- You were vaping!

- I was sick because I was vaping!

I was quickly losing control of the meeting.

- I think it's a good idea, I said, I do. But I wonder if there's something . . . larger we could do.

- What do you mean *larger?* Harriet asked.

Their basic notion of our essential sameness, I said, of our common humanity, was such a beautiful and important one that perhaps we could include people other than students – people from outside the school. Woodstock was a wealthy, white community, and the student body reflected that. What if we were to go into nearby Kingston, which was neither wealthy nor white, and ask people there, people from other demographics and races and backgrounds, what it was that they thought people had in common? I had driven past Motel 28 that morning, I told them, the decrepit fleabag motel beside the New York State Thruway, and I thought it could be a good place to interview people; we could find businesspeople stopping over on their way to the city, truck drivers catching some sleep, drifters drifting, not to mention the staff – the chain-smoking woman at the front desk, the Hispanic housekeeper, the elderly African American maintenance man. It would, I suggested, make for a more rounded film.

- That's exploitive, said Harriet.

- It's what? I asked.

- It's exploitive, Harriet said. - Using poor black people to make our film is exploitive.

- Well, I said, I'm not sure that's what I inten –

- Everything's exploitive to you, snapped Jet. - Do you even know what that word means?

- It means to exploit, said Harriet.

- You can't use the word you're defining in the definition of that word, said Sky.

- Says who? demanded Harriet.

- Says *Webster's Dictionary*, mumbled Sophia.

Sophia was the eldest of the group, a tall Latina with a remarkable singing voice, the type who you might expect to be the leader of the group but who rarely spoke because of her anxiety.

- Male, Harriet said to Sophia. - Miriam Webster was a male, so don't even.

- Merriam, I corrected them.

- Miriam's a girl's name, said Sky.

- There's no such thing as a girl's name, said Harriet. - That's genderist.

- I thought it was a good idea, said Paix.

- What a surprise, said Harriet. - White male.

- I'm not white, Paix said, I'm fucking Jewish.

Paix is defiant and strong-willed, open-minded but never afraid to defend himself. He gets that from Orli. From me he gets allergies and nosebleeds.

- I'm feeling very attacked right now, Harriet said.

- *You* attacked *me*! said Paix.

- Where's Eve? I asked, trying to de-escalate the situation.

I didn't really give a fuck where she was — God knows I didn't need another lunatic to deal with — but I was beginning to regret committing to this project. I thought I could use Eve's absence to reschedule the meeting and then come up with a reason to quit.

- She's in the Crying Room, said Sophia. - With Robin.

- In the what? I asked.

- The Crying Room, she said, pointing to a closed door at the far end of the library that I had assumed was a storage closet.

- The Crying Room? I asked.

Robin was the school librarian, a kindly, gentle woman whom the students loved and trusted beyond all others. Robin loved books, and she loved reading, and she loved the children who came to her library, wide-eyed and chattering about the stories they had read and about the stories they were waiting to read. She organized the annual book fair, the highlight of the year for students and parents alike, during which she transformed the dull steel gymnasium into a wonderland filled with paper dragons and fairies and mermaids and cakes and cookies and long lines of children, their arms filled with hardcover books and paperback books and comic books and graphic novels. The library was a paradise of Robin's creation, too, a place where students came to hang out, laugh, chat, and occasionally, it turned out, cry. When students were sad or lonely or angry or hurt, Sophia explained, they would go to the library, and Robin would see their faces and know without a word that they needed to talk, and she would take them to that small room, and she would close the door, and there they would open their hearts, confiding, revealing, crying. It came to be known as the Crying Room. The members of the LGBTQ+ Club spent more time in the Crying Room than others.

- And Eve's in there now? I asked.

Paix nodded.

- She's been going a lot lately, he said, heavy with worry.

Harriet nudged him with their foot, as if he shouldn't have revealed anything to this outsider. I glanced at the closed door of the Crying Room, and any thoughts I had about backing out of the project disappeared.

- Why don't we make a film about that? I said.

- About what? asked Sophia.

- About the Crying Room, I said.

It would be beautiful, I explained, and make the point that we *are* the same – that we all feel, that we're all afraid, that we all hurt. That we all cry.

They looked from one to the other.

Jet nodded.

Sky and Paix did too.

- Yes, Harriet proclaimed. - Yes, let's do it!

Sophia shrugged, which was taken as a vote in favor of the idea. Paix said he would clear it with Eve later, and for once, they all agreed.

It was the first film idea I'd sold in years.

...

I leaned forward on Ike's couch and buried my face in my hands.

- *Homo homini lupus*, I said. - *Man is wolf to man*.

Ike wrote something on my chart.

Pretentious, I assumed.

- I've been reading Schopenhauer again, I said.

- You don't say, said Ike.

Arthur Schopenhauer was an influential German pessimist. In his defense, he lived in Germany in the early 1800s, which was probably a tough time to be an optimist. Jonathan Swift may have claimed man was contemptible, but mere claiming wasn't enough for Schopenhauer; he developed an entire theory *proving* we're contemptible and explaining why we always would be. We're contemptible, he said, because of what he referred to as the Will – the endless striving, wanting, desiring that is at the center of all Being. We're born want-ing, we die wanting, in between we fuck and fight and kill to get what we want. *The End.* I had read him when I was younger and remembered liking him, thinking him brave to state the truths that others denied. I had returned to him recently in my darkness, for company, for validation. Schopenhauer, I told Ike, said that life was a gift that anyone in their right mind would have declined. I was beginning to think he had a point. Maybe, I said, that was what Phil thought that tragic night. Maybe Phil had been right too.

Ike asked me what had changed in recent days that might account for my depression. I didn't know. I wondered if it was the students in Paix's club. I remembered being that age, I said, and feeling such agony at being me. But it wasn't the pain alone – it was the feeling that nobody else understood, that nobody cared. Sometimes it seemed, even today, that I was the only one feel-ing anything at all.

- Why don't you write about it? asked Ike.

- About what?

- Pain.

- That's the best you can come up with? Write about it?

- Man is wolf to man, said Ike.

- I'm not paying for this session, I said.

- Our time is up, said Ike.

...

OUCH

Hannah, a young woman in her early twenties, lives in a modern-day metropolis much like our own – loud traffic, cramped apartments, careening taxis – except for one critical difference: Nobody in her world feels pain. There are bumps and bruises, but

with a simple Tom and Jerry cartoon—style shake of the head,
they disappear and the fighting resumes. It is, consequently, a
casually violent world: Falling anvils, giant mallets, all the
hideous weaponry of Saturday-morning cartoons come to terrible
life. Hannah reluctantly plays her part in this rote violence, as
everyone does — she's quite good at it, in fact — until one night
when she is attacked and beaten so viciously that when she wakes
the next morning, she feels something strange:
　Pain.
　Blinding, excruciating pain.
　And the gash on her forehead, no matter how hard she shakes
her head, won't disappear.
　She runs to her bathroom, locks the door. She shakes her head
again. Nothing. Again, harder. Nothing. She's bleeding, sick
with fear. Is it a virus? A curse? Dread fills her heart, as she re-
alizes that she is the only one in the world who feels.
　If her sensitivity is discovered, her family will reject her. If she
can't fight, her enemies will harm her. If she doesn't find a solu-
tion, fast, she will never survive.

- It's autobiographical, I said to Henry.

Henry laughed.

It was important that Henry laughed.

It was evening, and we were in the kitchen of his renovated 1800s farm-
house at the center of his sprawling Dutchess County estate. Henry was a senior executive of a global media empire known for its searing documentaries
about the poor and downtrodden – starving African children, Namibian diamond miners, Thai sex workers, all the wretched rubblestone of modern humanity. If you ever find yourself feeling even remotely optimistic about being
alive, Henry's company has a documentary that will make you wish you were
dead. His company was moving into scripted – Hollywood for *fiction*. I had

been watching some old Looney Tunes cartoons with Lux a few months earlier, and that, combined with Ike's suggestion and the pain the students in the LGBTQ+ Club seemed to be suffering, had given me an idea for a story about pain: the story of a young woman in a non-cartoon world that was blighted by cartoonlike violence, violence without agony or consequence – a bump on the head, a quick shake, and all is over but the fighting – who suddenly, inexplicably, begins to feel pain. I wrote it up, hoping to have it made into a film. Henry had read it and asked if we could discuss it.

- Come on, he said, let me show you around.

Henry was a passionate, intelligent, well-read man, and his house was magnificent; I felt less *feh* just being there. The marble tiles in the bathroom had been imported from Somewhere, the counters in the kitchen had been made in Wherever, the furniture in the den had been made by Someone in Someplace to match the look of Something that Henry had seen Somewhere Else.

And Orli didn't want to be rich.

Idiot.

There were various barns (which Henry called *structures*) on the property (which Henry called *the Property*). He led me outside to the first barn, which he'd had converted into a music studio/dance club, complete with massive speakers, turntable, sound system, dance floor, and disco ball. At the far end of the property stood another barn, this one even larger than the first. He opened the door, revealing a pristine garage filled with classic Ferraris.

- What do you think? he asked.

- I think those movies about starving Africans are really paying off, I said.

- You should see my partner's house in LA, he said. - Twenty million.

- That's a lot of Africans.

Henry laughed and led me back to the main house.

- We're making your movie, Henry said.

I tried my best not to let him see my excitement. *I* wanted a renovated farmhouse. *I* wanted tiles from Somewhere and counters from Somewhere Else. *I* wanted a barn full of Ferraris.

- Let me ask you a question, Henry said, slapping my back.

Uh-oh.

Writers in Hollywood perform a sort of reverse prostitution, in which they have sex first and only afterward do the clients decide if they want to pay. *I really liked your blow job*, the network executive says as he zips up his Hugo Boss pants, *but I was looking for something different. Try sucking Frank's dick over at HBO; I think he'll like it.*

- Do you think it works as TV? Henry asked.

I didn't.

- Of course, I said. - TV. Even better.

- Great, he said. - Hour-long episodes, that's what they're buying now.

- Really?

- Oh yeah, he said. - The half-hour is dead.

. . .

The Realtor was optimistic about our finding a buyer for our house, but the process was taking time and we needed to cut costs quickly. We decided to check out the towns surrounding Woodstock — Red Hook, Kingston, Olive — which were more affordable. They were more rural and more blue-collar. Less concrete countertops, more concrete mixers. Less floating in pools, more drowning in debt.

A week later, we decided to have Paix spend a day at the Greenville Public School to see if he liked it. While he sat in class with the other students, Orli and I sat in the main office with the principal.

- And in senior year, he said to us, we take them on a trip to Europe.

- Wow, we said.

- They talk about it for the rest of their lives, he said.

- Of course, we said.

- After all, he said, most of them will never leave again.

- Leave where? we asked.

- America, he said.

- The country? I asked.

- Most will never even leave this *town*, he said.

He did his best by his students, he explained, and many of them had great minds and generous hearts. But for most of them, high school was the end of their story. There were no great adventures ahead, no journeys, no worlds they were going to conquer. Few would go to college; most would join their father's landscaping business, or take jobs as excavators digging out in-ground pools for people in Woodstock, or work at Home Depot or Walmart. They were good jobs, he said, and honorable, but he believed they could do so much more. He tried to encourage them to think beyond their small town, but he was fighting against parents who told them they had to stay, that to leave town would be disloyal, shameful.

- Small towns, he said with a sigh.

- We know, we said.

- Paix is a very bright boy, he said.

- We know, we said.

- This isn't the place for him.

- We know, we said.

We met Paix out front and walked to the car.

- How was it? we asked.

- Okay, he said.

- Were the kids nice? we asked.

- They're dead inside, he said.

- We know, we said.

That night, I lay in bed reading Schopenhauer.

- *For to the man who knows,* I read aloud to Orli, *children may at times appear to be like innocent delinquents who are condemned, not to death, but to life.*

- What's that from? Orli asked.

- *Studies in Pessimism,* I said. - *Volume Two.*

Orli has no patience for pessimism. She thinks it too easy to declare the world and all that is in it to be shit. She's no optimist, not by a long shot, but she can't countenance resignation.

- You should pitch it to Henry as a series, she said. - Every week the entire cast kills themselves.

Schopenhauer would no doubt attribute it to my relentless will, but I thought that was a pretty good idea.

...

One summer, when Arthur Schopenhauer was a child, his parents decided to take him on a fun-filled trip across Europe. They went to England, they went to Amsterdam, they went to France. It was a grand time. Then one day, Mr. Schopenhauer had a kooky idea.

- Hey, Mr. Schopenhauer said, y'know what would be fun? Visiting a gruesome penal colony!

- That *does* sound like fun! said Mrs. Schopenhauer.

The Bagne of Toulon, as the prison was known, held over four thousand prisoners, every one of them wretched, starved, diseased. It was a hell on Earth equal to the hulls of slave ships or the death camps of Germany. Young Schopenhauer was appalled by the prison and by the terrible anguish and misery he witnessed there. It wasn't the last suffering Schopenhauer would behold on this earth, and the more he saw, the more he began to suspect that the world itself was a *bagne*.

The penal colony wasn't in Toulon, young Schopenhauer decided.

Toulon was in the penal colony.

...

Robin refused to appear in the student film. She was camera-shy, reluctant, and had already turned me down once, but I wasn't sure we had a film about the Crying Room without the woman at its center. I was on my way to the school library to try to convince her when Sophia hurried over in a terrible panic.

- Do I have to be in it? she asked.

- In what?

- The movie.

- Of course not, I said. - It's up to you.

- There's just . . . she said, struggling to find courage. She was troubled, wary. - I don't . . . I mean, I want to . . . it's just . . .

- Sophia, I said calmly, it's just a movie. There are no prizes for being in it, and there's no shame for not. There's plenty of other things you can help with — like keeping Harriet away from me.

She smiled but only for a moment.

- It's like, she said, I mean, I want . . . I want to say something . . . I just, I don't know if I should . . .

I told her there was no need for her to decide just yet. The plan was for us to set up a camera in the Crying Room and interview the students there, where they would be safe and protected. Any questions they didn't want to answer, they could simply pass on. In fact, she could decide on the day. Sophia nodded but seemed terribly conflicted, ashamed of whatever it was she was keeping inside, and ashamed of not being able to let it out.

- It's not easy, is it? I said. - This whole feeling thing.

She shook her head. A tear ran down her cheek. I told her I was working on a TV series about a girl who suddenly feels pain.

- The rest of the world doesn't feel anything, I told her. - She's the only one. And she doesn't want anyone in town to find out. It's her terrible secret.

- What happens? she asked.

- They find out.

- What does she do?

- She runs away, I said, and finds a bunch of other people who feel pain, too, living in a tunnel outside town. They form a community of feelers, and she joins them.

- That's a TV series?

- Yes.

She shrugged.

- Sounds more like a film, she said.

I met Robin a few moments later, and she took me into the Crying Room. It was tiny, with barely enough space for two small chairs and Robin's coffee maker. The window overlooking the schoolyard was draped with a curtain for added privacy.

- So, I said. - This is the Crying Room.

- It's more of a Whining Room, Robin said with a smile. - They are teenagers, after all. Everything hurts at that age.

- What age doesn't it?

She laughed, and as she did, I recalled the first time I met Ike.

- Doctor Herschkopf? I had asked.

- Call me Ike, he had said. - Come in, come in . . .

He was wearing a Mickey Mouse T-shirt and a yarmulke.

I could forgive the Mickey Mouse shirt.

- So, he had said when I sat down. - What hurts?

It had taken every ounce of my being not to burst into tears.

Robin offered me some coffee. She admitted to offering coffee to the older students too; she wasn't supposed to, but it told them that she saw them as adults and that they could trust her.

- They're taking much worse things nowadays anyway, she said.

She pulled the window curtain aside. Outside, on the school lawn, students were taking selfies.

- It's so strange, she said. - They spend all day taking pictures of themselves. Why do they do that?

- Because they're psychotic, I said.

- But they *hate* themselves, she said. - They come in here and tell me they're awful and fat and ugly and stupid and failures . . . and then they go outside and take photos of themselves.

- My shrink says we aren't born hating ourselves, I offered. - That we're taught to by fathers, mothers, teachers.

- The stuff these parents tell them, she said. - It's awful. One girl's father literally said to her, *Why can't you get an A for once, you idiot?*

- *My spirit will not contend with mankind forever*, I said.

- Who said that?

- God.

- He may have had a point, she said.

- So? I asked. - Will you be in the film? We need you, it's your Crying Room.

She shook her head.

- Not a chance, she said. - Find another psychotic.

There was a gentle knock on the door, barely audible. Robin opened the door to find a young girl, no older than ten, looking up at her with desperate, tear-filled eyes.

- Julie, Robin said, her voice tender with concern. - Come in, come in . . .

. . .

Hannah is forced to flee her hometown. It has become too dangerous. Her father doesn't understand her pain, her mother resents it, her friends deny it, and she can no longer take part in her world's endless cycle of violence and revenge. One night, filled with shame and fear, she steals into the woods where she stumbles upon an abandoned train tunnel. Inside, she discovers a community of others who have also begun to feel. They are bandaged, bruised, frightened. Some have turned to art to express their fear and suffering; others have turned to drugs; others have turned to God.

I liked the idea of a community of outcasts, rejected because they feel, hiding out in an abandoned railway tunnel. I liked that they had varied responses to the pain itself, from painting to praying to handguns and cleavers. But could we sell a TV series that takes place in a tunnel?

I phoned Henry.

- The tunnel is very important to me, I said.

- Lose the tunnel, he said.

The evening before, I had Googled Henry's partner's house in Los Angeles. His house had a name – Villa Something. Something Villa. Palm Villa Something. Villa Palm Something. It had thirteen bedrooms. It had twelve bathrooms. It had a seventy-five-foot infinity pool. It had citrus groves and a Japanese-style soaking tub and a pizza oven.

Every individual, wrote Schopenhauer, *makes himself the center of the world, and considers his own existence and well-being before everything else. In fact, from the natural standpoint, he is ready for this to sacrifice everything else; he is ready to annihilate the world, in order to maintain his own self, that drop in the ocean, a little longer.*

No shit, Arthur.

I wanted a Japanese-style soaking tub. I wanted an infinity pool. I wanted a house with a name. If I had a Japanese-style soaking tub and an infinity pool and a house with a name, I would never feel *feh* again.

I got rid of the tunnel and replaced it with a cartoon weapon megastore. Violence was commonplace in their world, as commonplace as food or electronics in ours, so in place of the tunnel of sufferers, I had Hannah work in a big-box violence supply store, sort of a Best Buy for psychopaths, full of two-by-fours, cleavers, and anvils. There Hannah would have friends, coworkers, an asshole boss – all of whom she would have to hide her pain from.

- I love it, said Henry. - It's a workplace comedy.

- Great, I said.

- Let me ask you a question.

Uh-oh.

- Do you think it works as a half-hour?

- I thought you said half-hours were dead.

- Yes, but now this is comedy, he said. - Comedies are half-hours.

- Sure, I said. - Half-hour. Even better.

. . .

The following LGBTQ+ Club meeting was even more contentious than the first. We were scheduled to film in two weeks, but the club members were having trouble finding anyone who would agree to appear in it. Robin had flatly refused, as had Sky. Jet agreed, mostly out of guilt, but Sophia was still undecided, and Paix had made it clear from the beginning that he was more of a behind-the-camera kind of guy. As for Eve, she once again didn't show, and nobody had been able to reach her; we didn't know if she'd take part in the film or not. Harriet had hung flyers around the school, inviting students to participate, but none had come forward. The film was falling apart, and the club knew it.

- I'm feeling very disenfranchised, said Harriet.

- Disenfranchised? Paix asked. - How are you feeling disenfranchised?

- Because Sophia won't be in the film!

- What does that have to do with *you* feeling disenfranchised? Paix asked.

- Because the film is ruined, said Harriet, and I feel like my vote to make it didn't matter!

- Disenfranchised isn't a feeling, said Paix.

- Yes, it is.

- No, it isn't. It's an organized system designed to deny someone their rights.

- Sophia can do what she likes, Harriet, I said. - You should respect her decision.

- *Their* decision, Harriet sneered.

- I'm not a They, Sophia said.

- You're not? asked Harriet.

- I'm a She/Her, she said. - Jesus, Harriet.

- I don't want to be in it either, Jet added.

- What? snapped Harriet. - This is ridiculous, why not?

- I just don't! Jet shouted.

Harriet got to their feet and raised their hand.

- I hereby vote that we return to my original film concept and just walk around with cameras, asking people what makes them the same. All in favor say *Aye*.

- Aye, grumbled Sky.

- Aye, grumbled Jet.

- Whatever, grumbled Paix.

The film was dead.

It wouldn't be my last.

...

Soon after, I flew to Los Angeles. Henry and I were scheduled to pitch the pain series to HBO. Orli came along, sick as she was of the cold in New York, of the miserable gray and the suffocating clouds.

- It's a workplace comedy, I said to the executives.

- We love it, said one.

- It's perfect for us, said another.

My heart leaped. I began to imagine the home we would buy, how happy we would be once we did, with an infinity pool and a citrus grove and a pizza oven.

- Let me ask you a question, said the first executive.

Uh-oh.

- Does it work as a film? he asked.

We'll be back with more hilarious Auslander *after these messages.*

Henry and I went for a drink afterward. I was depressed. He was undaunted.

- That's the game, he said. - It takes more than one pitch. It could take dozens. It could take months. Can you be in LA next week? We'll try some others. We'll try Showtime. We'll try FX. We'll try Apple. That's the game.

- Will you cover my hotel and airfare? I asked.

- I will not, said Henry.

The following morning, Orli and I decided to go for a walk along Ocean Avenue, the café-lined street overlooking the Pacific Ocean. Orli grew up in London's East End, hating the dark skies and the endless rain; she had never been a fan of the cold Northeastern climate and had never intended to stay there. Here in the LA sun, she looked so happy, so joyful, that I castigated myself for the years of gray I had condemned her to. Everyone here looked happy, everyone here looked joyful. It reminded me of somewhere, somewhere long gone, somewhere warm and happy and peaceful, and soon I remembered where it was:

Penthousia.

Los Angeles *was* Penthousia, that mythic paradise of my youth where all was pleasure and joy and acceptance, from the beachgoers in their skimpy bathing suits, to the café-goers in their form-fitting clothes. And like Penthousia, it wasn't just what LA had; it was what it didn't: shame.

Here, nobody felt bad.

Here, nobody hid themselves.

Here, nobody said *Feh*.

I wanted to live there.

Orli stopped to smell the roses.

- Smell them, she said.

And I did.

I sneezed. Later I would take some Claritin. My nose would bleed. But a plan began to form in my mind, a new plan, inspired in part by the noble Penthousians and in part by the brave story-seekers of the LGBTQ+ Club, wondering what their own stories might be, where their own journeys might end:

We would move to Penthousia.

Why not sun? Why not joy? Why not, at long last, peace? Orli could smell the roses all year long, the boys could get out of their small town, and I could pitch network executives whenever Henry wanted to.

For the first time in months, I began to feel excited. I began to feel good. We turned up Wilshire Boulevard and headed east toward the Third Street

Promenade, a charming pedestrian thoroughfare lined with shops and restaurants. Orli took my hand in hers. I looked at her and we smiled. Maybe, I thought, this romance could be salvaged. Maybe it didn't have to end in tragedy. I was determined to do whatever I had to: I would write half-hours and hours and hour-and-a-halfs; I would write car chase scenes, and fight scenes, and sex scenes; and soon we would have a house in Central Penthousia, a house with a name and citrus groves and an infinity pool. We turned onto the peaceful Third Street Promenade, with its gentle fountains and elegant palm trees and cheerful street performers, and so lovely was it, so positively Edenic, that I didn't notice the homeless man lurching toward me until it was too late. He stopped, looked at me a moment, reared back, and punched me square in the face.

This, in storytelling terminology, is known as foreshadowing.

...

It was a glum, dispirited LGBTQ+ Club that gathered the following week to prepare for the shoot of the film they didn't like and didn't want to make.

- Welcome to Hollywood, I said.

Nobody laughed.

Harriet half-heartedly read a list of questions she had prepared to prompt the students to discuss how they were the same, but nobody really cared. Eve entered the library, went straight to the Crying Room, and closed the door behind her.

- I don't want to do this, said Jet.

- Me neither, said Sky.

- I'm out, grumbled Paix.

Everyone stood to leave.

- Wait! Sophia called out.

All turned, surprised to hear Sophia speak, let alone loudly. She seemed on the edge of panic, wide-eyed and trembling. She took a deep breath, lowered her head, and tried to stop her hands from shaking; when they wouldn't, she sat on them, and then she took another deep breath.

- I'm . . . autistic, she said.

The club members were shocked. It was clear this was the first they had ever heard of it. She had been diagnosed a few months ago, she explained, and hadn't told anyone. She had been lying to her friends and teachers about her poor grades, trying to cover her social anxieties, which were so overwhelming at times that she would run from class to the Crying Room, where Robin comforted her and promised to keep her secret. She was beside herself with fear; she didn't know what the diagnosis meant for her future, for her life, for her story. She had decided, the previous evening, to use the film of the Crying Room as a way of revealing her condition to her friends and schoolmates. She begged the club members to reconsider their decision.

- But nobody will be in it, said Harriet. - It will be stupid with just a few kids in it.

- I know, said Sophia.

Jet bit his fingertips.

Sky pulled at her hair.

- Then fuck them, I said.

They looked at me, as shocked as they had been by Sophia.

- Fuck them, I said. - Seriously. We don't need them. Let's do this. If it's just Harriet and Sophia, fine. It will be worth it. More than worth it. This is an important thing to do, guys. We should do it. We really should.

Sophia wiped a tear from her face.

- Who's in? I asked, raising my hand.

They looked from one to the other.

- I'm in, said Paix, raising his hand.

- Me too, said Sky.

- Me too, said Jet.

Sophia looked up and nodded.

- I'll do it, she said. - I will. I'll do it.

Everyone smiled but Harriet.

- What now? I asked.

- You shouldn't use that term.

- What term?

- *Guys*, said Harriet. - It's male-centric.

- I apologize, I said. - How about *lunatics*? This is an important thing to do, *lunatics*. Does that work for everyone?

Paix smiled.

- Works for me, he said.

...

Schopenhauer never recovered from his childhood experience at the Bagne of Toulon. Many years later, in one of his final notebooks, he wrote:

When I was seventeen, without any proper schooling, I was affected by the misery and wretchedness of life, as was the Buddha when in his youth he caught sight of sickness, old age, pain, and death . . . The destiny of suffering is written all over human existence.

Stories are powerful things.

...

We began filming at nine a.m. A couple of friends of mine had volunteered to assist, one to run camera, one to cover sound. We figured since we were recording only a few students, we would be finished by eleven.

It didn't work out that way.

The sight of filmmaking equipment on campus – microphones, lights, tripods – sparked the curiosity of the other students, who came by the library to see what was going on and asked if they could stay and watch.

- Sure, I said.

But the production quickly ran into a problem. The Crying Room was small, so small that once Robin and the student were inside it, there was no room for the tripod and camera. We tried moving the table out, tried re-arranging the chairs, but there was just no way to film the interviews with the door closed – as I had promised the club we would.

I sat them down and explained the situation: In order to film them in the Crying Room, the door would have to be left open. And, since we were film-ing during regular school hours, the library would have to remain open to other students, coming and going as the club members bared their souls. I told them that if they wanted to change their minds, if they wanted to back out, I totally understood.

Not one of them did.

- Let's do it, said Sophia.

One after another they came in, sat down, and told their stories. They told stories about sadness and worry and fear. They told stories about guilt and shame and hiding.

- I'm really lonely, Sky said to the camera.

- My parents are getting divorced, said Jet. - It makes it really hard to talk to them.

- You wake up, said Paix, and you're like, *Damn, why am I in this mood?*

Sophia came in and talked about her diagnosis and about the shame that had come with it – the feeling that she had done something wrong, that it was her fault, that she deserved it. After each interview, Robin clapped and cheered, and she and the student hugged. We went through a lot of tissues. At last we finished, and I switched off the camera.

- I'm so proud of you guys, I said to them. - *Lunatics*, I'm so proud of you *lunatics*.

Harriet smiled.

A first.

We were beginning to take down the lights and tripods when some of the students who had come to watch approached us.

- Could we be in it? they asked.

- In the film? I asked.

We turned the camera back on and moved the setup into the main library. Nobody minded. Lower schoolers. Middle schoolers. High schoolers. They all wanted a chance to talk.

- I feel like I don't fit in, said Markus.

- I just feel guilty for everything, said Sherry.

- Everyone's changing, said Liam. - It's scary.

- I've been having a lot of panic attacks, said Stella.

They fidgeted while they spoke, or picked at their fingertips, or fiddled with their pencils, or gripped the edges of their chair as if they might fall should they let go. They spoke of their fears of leaving town, of not leaving town, of going to college, of not going to college.

- I don't know about a lot of things in my life right now, said Lula.

- I've been questioning the way I'm going to go, said Nathan. - I thought I knew, but I don't know anymore.

They talked and they shared, and Robin listened and nodded, and they cried and they laughed. We recorded until late in the afternoon, and still the students kept coming. Parents, teachers, all wanted a chance to speak, to unload, to un*feh* themselves by telling a story where for once they weren't the antagonists. When the last of the students had finished their recordings, Robin turned to me and said, - I guess it's my turn.

- You sure? I asked.

- If they can do it, she said, so can I.

She took a seat in the Crying Room. The students gathered to watch.

- Sometimes I feel like I'm a bartender, Robin said. - I'm sort of this other person.

Adolescence was change, she said, and change was difficult. A new story was beginning for these young people, and it was only natural that they were fearful of what type of story that would be. Would they be happy? Loved? Loathed? She wondered if that was why the students spoke to her, why they felt so safe in the library of all places – because the library was a heaven of stories, a kingdom of possibilities, some funny, some tragic, but stories they could imagine themselves in, flourishing, happy, accepted, and alive.

She dabbed at her eyes with a tissue and motioned for us to stop recording.

- Cut, she said. - Cut.

- We love you, Robin! the students called.

- I love you too, she called back.

I watched in awe. Schopenhauer, I knew, would surely attribute all this hugging and weeping to just so much hideous Will in action. What is telling your story but your will to survive?

Fools! he would grumble. *All stories end in the grave!*

Years ago, when I first read Schopenhauer, he sounded like a prophet. *You tell 'em, Arthur*, I thought. But now it seemed he was telling the same accursed story Rabbi Hammer had.

Said God:

Cursed is the ground because of you.

Said Schopenhauer:

The truth is that we ought to be wretched, and are so.

God:

The Lord saw how great man's wickedness on Earth had become, and that his every inclination was evil all the time.

Schopenhauer:

Nothing else can be stated as the aim of our existence except the knowledge that it would be better for us not to exist.

God:

The Lord was grieved that he had made man on Earth, and his heart was filled with pain.

Schopenhauer:

The chief source of the most serious evils affecting humanity is human beings.

I was beginning to wonder if Schopenhauer, that fiercest of atheists, had any idea what a hideously religious story he was telling.

Some weeks later, the entire school gathered in the auditorium – students, teachers, parents – to view the final film. I was in Los Angeles at the time, looking for apartments for us to rent. But I imagined that as the film played back in New York, the members of the Woodstock Day School LGBTQ+ Club sat a little taller in their seats, and bit their fingers a bit less, seeing themselves at last as protagonists – flawed, imperfect, struggling, sometimes failing, sometimes succeeding – and not as the unwanted antagonists the world had been telling them they were.

26.

Nigerian novelist Chimamanda Ngozi Adichie speaks about the dangers of having a single story. Stories, she says – how they are told, who tells them, when they're told – are dependent on power. Power is the ability not just to tell the story of another person but to make it the definitive story of that person. It is a way, she says, of destroying a people, of reducing them, of dehumanizing them.

Adichie was talking about the story one group of people tells about another, about the stories others had been told about her and the stories she had been told about others.

I've been wondering lately, though, about the single story we tell about ourselves, about our species, about humanity as a whole. A hateful story of dirtmen and sinners and violent predators, of criminals and fools and despoilers. A single story, forever changeable but never changing, a single story told by humans, to humans, that dehumanizes us all.

27.

One evening, not long after we married, Orli came home to find me curled up on the floor in the fetal position beside the bathroom sink. We lived on Second Avenue, in a fifth-floor walk-up railroad apartment with a slanted floor, and the bathroom was the farthest distance away from the window I had been planning to throw myself out of. Suicide is forbidden by Jewish law, but what were they going to do to me if I committed it? Kill me? They can send you to Hell, sure, but Hell was a step up from Earth. At least in Hell, everyone acknowledges that it's Hell. In Hell, when you say, *I'm in Hell*, nobody says, *You're such a pessimist*. Nobody says *Turn that frown upside down*. Nobody says *You're as happy as you want to be*. At least in Hell, you know you're in Hell.

Orli knelt beside the sink and held me. She begged me to see someone, and I figured I owed her at least that much for putting up with me thus far. I found a psychiatrist named Ike and arranged to meet with him. I sat on his couch, and he asked me what hurt. This is what I said to him:

- I'm in Hell.

- If only, he said. - At least in Hell *everyone's* in pain.

Over the years, he became my father, my guide, my mentor. I learned from him, grew from him, began at last to see through the fog of darkness that had so long entombed me. It worried me. It made me nervous. He helped me so much I couldn't sleep. Because as every writer knows, at some point, in every story, like it or not, the mentor dies.

...

I sat in Ike's office, days before our move to Los Angeles, trying to commit his office to memory: the diplomas on the wall, the plants by the window, the small model of Lucy Van Pelt in her psychiatrist booth he kept on his desk.

The stupid fucking Mickey Mouse shirt.

I tried to remind myself that he wasn't dying, that I was merely moving to Los Angeles, that he would be just a phone call away. But he could see the foreboding on my face.

- If you miss me, he joked, you can always listen to the podcast.

The journalist pursuing the patient complaint about him had moved on to Bloomberg, and they were going to produce a podcast about Ike. Over his forty-year career, Ike had treated thousands of patients; this had been the only complaint. But he was concerned that if the podcast did well, the publicity might force the Department of Health, which had previously dismissed the patient's complaint, to act. There was a possibility, he had explained, that his license would be revoked.

- And? I had asked.

- And I could no longer treat you, he had said.

He was my lifeline, Phil had said. *And then, one day, he was just . . . gone.*

- It's just a possibility, he had assured me. - I don't want you to worry, but I wanted you to know.

I tried to smile at his podcast joke, tried not to look at his trembling hands.

- On second thought, he laughed, maybe don't listen to the podcast.

I stood, slung my bag over my shoulder. He came to face me and reminded me of the first time we met, of all the progress I had made, of all the changes I had made.

- You'll do great out there, he said.

We hugged.

I wondered if he thought I was fat.

I tried not to cry. It helped to think of the thousands of dollars in unpaid bills I owed him.

- If you're wrong, I said, I don't have to pay you, right?

Ike smiled.

- Our time is up, he said.

28.

We arrived in Penthousia on a bright, sunshiny afternoon. As we made our way from Los Angeles International Airport to our new apartment, we took a brief detour down the famous Ocean Avenue, with its elegant outdoor cafés on one side, the magnificent Pacific Ocean on the other.

- Look, kids! Orli gasped, pointing to the miles of pristine sandy beach. - Can you believe we live here?

Orli's skin turns deep golden brown with the briefest touch of sunlight, making the green of her eyes glow even brighter. She was already in love with our new home, and so was I. Every palm tree seemed to me a celebration, a firework of foliage bursting with joy beneath a sky of such radiant blue that even this avowed hater of God wanted to sing praise to the artist who brought it forth into being.

We settled quickly into Eden. In the mornings, Orli walked. She walked down the avenues; she walked along the bluffs overlooking the ocean; she stopped to smell the flowers. Lux went to the nearby playground to play handball with his new friends, Paix went to the nearby park and played basketball with the local teens and adults, and I woke early and went to write in the various coffee shops on Wilshire Boulevard. Back in New York I'd rented a small office in town, but to help ease the boys' transition to LA, we had

splurged on a nice apartment. Renting an additional workspace wasn't financially feasible, so cafés and coffee shops became my rent-free office. Every
morning I headed out, passing runners, walkers, joggers, cyclists, in tank
tops and tights and yoga pants, full of pride – pride! – stopping at red lights to
admire – admire! – their reflections in storefront windows. Some mornings I
passed a group of fit men and women marching down the sidewalk holding
heavy kettlebells over their heads.

- It's the Go Show, baby! their trainer yelled as they marched, huffing and
puffing, back to the door of their CrossFit gym. - Go go go!

Maybe, I thought, it was time for *me* to join a gym! Doctor Superior had
advised me to live clean, to avoid booze and smoking. A gym was just what I
needed. Yes! I thought. I will join a gym!

I found the Penthousians a friendly people, who smiled and said *Good
morning* and *What a beautiful day.* Our neighbors were friendly, too, despite
Flynn's trying to kill them, and it wasn't long before Yasmin, who lived in the
apartment next door, invited us over for dessert and drinks.

- It's just so beautiful here, said Orli as Yasmin opened a bottle of rosé. - You
must feel so lucky to live here.

- Yeah, Yasmin scoffed. - If you like rape and murder, it's perfect.

Yasmin had three small children and a thousand terrifying stories about life
in our new city: break-ins, assaults, rapes, shootings. And she told us them all.

- It's a hellhole, she said. - More wine?

Orli and I exchanged confused glances. There was no doubt Los Angeles
suffered the usual modern urban blights – homelessness, income disparity,
terrible bass blasting from overpowered sports cars – but a hellhole? Had she
been outside? Were we talking about the same city? Yasmin reminded me of
Ida, the old lady in the hospital, insisting the brightest day was the darkest
night.

- The homeless are everywhere, she said. - Sorry, sorry, she added, I mean
the unhoused. They'll kill you for a dollar.

The more she railed, the more I began to worry for her safety – not from criminals, but from Orli. I could see the storm clouds gathering in her eyes. Orli was happy here in LA and didn't like her new homeland coming under attack. I imagined her grabbing Yasmin by the throat and slamming her against the wall.

Are we going to have trouble here? Orli asks. *Because if you want trouble, I can give you trouble . . .*

- Well, Orli managed to say with a forced smile. - I'm sure it's not all bad.

- Are you on Nextdoor? Yasmin asked.

- What's Nextdoor? I asked.

- You should go on Nextdoor, said Yasmin.

. . .

The first thing Orli does when we check into a hotel room is jump on the bed. She jumps and kicks her legs and bounces on her butt and jumps some more. She jumps like she doesn't care who's watching. Because she doesn't. It's very annoying. Meanwhile, I check the nightstands for Bibles before hurriedly unpacking, worried that my Pepto-Bismol has leaked, whereupon I realize I forgot my Imodium, call down to inquire about the nearest pharmacy, search the room for hidden cameras, and try to guess how much the bed frame is going to cost us to replace when she breaks it.

- Fuck them, she laughs as she jumps. - They have enough money to fix it!

- Is that what you're going to say when they hand us the bill? I ask. - *Fuck them?*

- No! she shouts with glee. - I'm going to say *Fuck you*, since I'll be addressing them directly.

This time, though, I joined her.

I climbed onto the bed, and I jumped.

The move had been stressful, and we'd decided to leave the kids with a sitter for the night and have some alone time. We checked into the Oasis, a nearby hotel we couldn't afford, but *Zoo*, an animated series I had written, was getting some traction; George Clooney's company had signed on to produce it, together with Dan Harmon. Dan and I had been getting together to work on the script, and signs were looking good.

So I joined her.

I jumped on the bed.

We jumped and held hands and laughed and fell onto the bed in a riot of laughter. She had brought candles and lingerie; I had brought chocolates and sex toys. And Pepto-Bismol. And Imodium. Then we showered, and we jumped some more, and then we kissed, and then we held each other, and then, after I closed the blinds, drew the curtains, had a drink, dimmed the lights, had a hit of weed, dimmed the lights some more, turned them off completely, had another drink, and made certain I couldn't see the bed in the mirror or reflected in the TV screen, we made love. Afterward, as we lay in bed, Orli took my hand in hers and smiled.

- I'm going to like it here, she said.

- Me too, I said.

- It's so peaceful, she said.

A police siren screamed by.

Then another.

Fehs don't do well in paradise. Joy makes us uneasy. Contentment gives us indigestion. Because we know we don't deserve it. We can't possibly. We're *feh*. So we do what we can to destroy the paradise we shouldn't have, before we get the punishment we know we've got coming for enjoying it. We won't enjoy the torments of Hell, but we'll sleep better than we will in the glory of Heaven. Glory keeps us up at night. Glory's a problem.

I heard Yasmin in my mind, talking about hellholes and crime.

More sirens joined the first two.

- Gonna have to get used to that, I said to Orli.

But Orli was already asleep, a peaceful smile upon her face.

...

THE VERY BAD PEOPLE IN
THE VERY BAD CITY

Once upon a time, God came down to Earth, stopped over in Sodom, and decided to wipe it off the face of the earth.

- I'm going to destroy the Sodomites, God said to Abraham.

- All of them? asked Abraham.

- All of them.

- Why?

- They're awful.

- All of them?

- All of them.

- They can't all be awful.

- They are.

- What if I find fifty good people in Sodom? Abraham said. - Will you spare the city then?

- You won't find fifty good people, said God.

- I will.

- You won't find twenty.

- You don't think I'll find twenty good people? asked Abraham. - In all of Sodom?

- I don't think you'll find ten, hippie.

- Bet? said Abraham.

- Bet, said God.

And God destroyed Sodom.

The End

Yasmin's damnations grew like a cancer in my mind.

- You got this! the trainer shouted at the kettlebellers. - All you, baby!

I couldn't believe they were exercising. Did they not hear the constant sirens? Did they not see the woman on the corner, begging for food?

- We got this! one kettlebeller shouted.

He was wearing a T-shirt that featured the words *Under Construction* superimposed over a cartoon illustration of an exaggerated male bodybuilder wearing a tank top and a hard hat doing bicep curls.

- It's the Go Show, baby! shouted another.

This one was wearing a T-shirt that featured the words *Beast Mode* superimposed over a cartoon illustration of a grimacing muscular horned beast of some sort wearing a tank top and doing bicep curls.

I have a problem with T-shirts that say things. Someday, perhaps, I will achieve nirvana, some elevated state of perfect equanimity, and I will not want to push people wearing statement shirts in front of passing buses, and I will not picture the wearer at home that morning, standing before his closet, deciding which juvenile sentiment most accurately expresses his adolescent worldview.

I just don't know, the jacked jackass ponders between sips of Red Bull. *Should I go with* Beast Mode *or* Under Construction? *I enjoy the semiotic subversiveness of* Under Construction, *referring as it usually does to decidedly nonhuman construction, that is, for example, of roadways and shelters.*

- It's the Go Show! the trainer yelled.

- Let's go! the kettlebellers yelled in response.

But I'm also quite fond of the directness of Beast Mode, *of how it doesn't attempt to employ wit to garner favor with the audience, which to me always smacks of a certain undershirtian desperation.*

It was then that I spotted, coming the opposite way, a man of such wretchedness and despair that I gasped. This, shuffling toward me, was neither unhoused nor homeless. This was tormented. This was godforsaken. His clothes were in tatters, his feet bare, blue-black and swollen. With one hand he held up his soiled trousers, with the other he carried an enormous black trash bag over his shoulder, a burden so heavy that despite his powerful build he was bent over with its weight.

The kettlebellers never broke stride. They kept their eyes fixed on the horizon behind him and determinedly CrossFitted their way around him, twisting their shoulders so as not to touch him, turning their heads so as not to breathe the same air. They never looked at him, never acknowledged his existence, never for a moment seemed even remotely aware of the devastating indictment of humanity in which they had just participated.

- All you! the trainer shouted again.

The man stopped to adjust the load on his back, sweat pouring down his face. The kettlebellers huffed and puffed past him, trying their best to pretend he wasn't there, and marched their way back into the gym.

Ezekiel – holy prophet to Jews and Muslims, revered saint to Christians – disagrees with Rabbi Scold. Ezekiel does not lay the blame for the destruction of Sodom on *feigeles*. In fact, in Ezekiel 16:49, he says that Sodom was destroyed because people were unkind.

This was the guilt of your sister Sodom, he proclaims. *She and her daughters had pride, excess of food, and prosperous ease, but did not aid the poor and needy.*

Ezekiel doesn't mention homosexuals at all. He doesn't hold up a *God Hates Fags* placard, or recommend conversion camp.

It wasn't the gays, says Ezekiel.

It was the cruels.

- How cruel were the people of Sodom? the ancient scholars asked.

- So cruel, the ancient scholars answered, that they lured strangers to their city by giving them gold and silver but no bread. In Sodom, they said, it was forbidden to give strangers bread. In this way, the stranger soon died of starvation. Once he died, the Sodomites took back the gold and silver they had given him, and they took all his clothes and all his money, and they divided it among themselves before burying the stranger naked in a shallow grave.

The destitute man tightened his grip on his waistband and resumed his journey. As he walked toward me, I determined to not look away. I would look at him, see him, acknowledge him as a human being.

- Good morning, I said as he passed by.

The man stopped, shocked that I had spoken to him, shocked that I had seen him, shocked that I had treated him with basic human dignity. He looked at me, his eyes red with suffering and anguish.

- Suck my dick, faggot, he said.

- I . . .

- SUCK MY DICK, FAGGOT!

The pedestrians behind me crossed the street.

The kettlebellers hurried inside.

The trainer double-locked the door behind them.

The man followed me down Wilshire, shouting after me until at the next corner he lost interest and began shouting at passing cars instead. As he did, I watched, and I hated. I hated the kettlebellers, I hated the trainer, I hated Los Angeles, and I hated the drivers passing by, slowing down to laugh and gawk at the destitute wretch shouting at them from the side of the road, so full as he was of pathetic, impotent rage.

. . .

- How was your day? Orli asked later that evening. - Did you write?

She was glowing, her cheeks sun-kissed after taking the boys to a nearby park for a picnic.

- A homeless guy told me to suck his dick, I said.

- Why did he do that?

- I'm not sure. Then he called me a faggot.

- He sounds conflicted, Orli said.

She had seen the homeless at the park too. The boys, having lived their lives in a small rural town with little more than the local drunk, had never seen so many homeless. She had to try to explain to them why people were sleeping on benches and sidewalks, why they were picking through trash cans for food and shouting at passing cars. She told them that some were mentally ill, that some had chemical dependencies, that some were former soldiers suffering from PTSD and neglected by their nation. She thought the experience invaluable for them; they had been sheltered in Woodstock, and she believed it was important for them to see the reality of the world, to learn compassion for the less fortunate. They, in turn, had insisted on giving every homeless person they passed a dollar.

- Such sweethearts, she said of them.

Yasmin disagreed.

- You shouldn't give them money, she said. - They'll just spend it on alcohol and drugs. More wine?

She told us there had been a home invasion the night before. She'd read about it on Nextdoor. An old woman, she said, in a house up the road. They broke in, tied her up, beat her, stole all her jewelry.

- Animals, she said. - Lock them all up, that's what I say.

I was relieved the children were out of earshot, downstairs playing handball in the garage, which Yasmin only permitted them to do during daylight, and only then because of the heavy steel security gate that kept the criminals out.

- We really should install cameras down there, she said. - The police will give you the Amazon ones for free.

- Free? I asked.

- Yup. All you have to do is share your footage with them.

- With who?

- The police, she said. - And Amazon, I guess.

- How nice of them, I said.

I added that I had always found Huxley's *Brave New World* darker than Orwell's *1984*, because while the authoritarianism in Orwell was imposed, in Huxley the people welcomed it.

Orli kicked me under the table and continued to politely push back against Yasmin's bleak view of our new home. The city seemed peaceful to her, she insisted, neither as hectic as London nor as crowded as Manhattan, and thus far everyone had been quite nice. After all, it had taken months of living in Woodstock before we met the neighbors, while here in LA we were having dinner with them after just a few weeks.

Yasmin was unconvinced.

- You should check out Nextdoor, Yasmin said. - Have you been on Nextdoor?

...

Get the most out of your neighborhood with Nextdoor! It's where communities come together to greet newcomers, exchange recommendations, and read the latest local news! Welcome, neighbor!

The upbeat Nextdoor welcome page belied the grotesque horrorscape that lurked behind it, the usual *Arbeit macht frei* (German for *Work sets you free*) of social media. We didn't have Nextdoor in Woodstock, but I was in a new city, with my wife and children, and Yasmin's stories had me concerned. That night, as Orli slept, I went on Nextdoor.

It was, by all accounts, a collection of paranoid lunatics, peeking through their venetian blinds and convinced the end-times were upon us. I laughed at their fears and condemnations. Nextdoor seemed to be mostly white people concerned about the black people in their upscale neighborhoods, mixed in with the occasional desperate notice about a lost Labradoodle. I thought they should rename the app Found Black Man, Lost White Dog.

- I saw a black man in a sweatshirt walking down the street, wrote Kathy R. - He was walking VERY slowly!

- Did anyone else hear gunshots??? asked James T.

- I heard them, replied Sophia M. - I can't live like this anymore!

- Arm up, people, wrote Trevor L. - The war is coming, and the police are on the side of the criminals.

- Has anyone seen my Labradoodle? asked Vinnie Z.

- People are stealing *dogs* now, Trevor L. said. - Probably Hunter Biden LOL.

Maniacs, I thought.

Crackpots.

Nutjobs.

But the more stories I read – stories about theft and violence, about break-ins and beatings, about riots and protests and failed Liberal policies and the breakdown of law and order and the end of America and a world gone mad – the more the stories began to take hold.

They couldn't *all* be crazy.

There had to be *something* going on.

- What's with all the helicopters overhead? Ginger P. posted.

- They've been there for hours, said Harriet A.

- They're flying really low, said Tony M. - Like, low low.

- Probably after someone, said Trevor L. - Lock your doors, America.

- I've lost my cat, said Mark W.

- Aww, Ginger P. replied, followed by a crying emoji. - So sad!

They could have been describing Aleppo or Kabul or Detroit. Was this really the place I had just brought my wife and children, some postapocalyptic nightmare straight out of Cormac McCarthy's *The Road*, a novel I found lazily despairing, fashionably pessimistic, and shocking in the least shocking way imaginable? I was certain it marked the end of McCarthy's career.

Note: That didn't happen.

The Road won the Pulitzer.

- I also saw a black man, Leah K. replied to Kathy R. - Was he wearing a sweatshirt?

- Yes, that's him, said Kathy R.

- He was getting into a car, said Leah K., but I don't think it was his.

- Why? asked Phillip B. - Because he was black? Black people can't have cars?

- HE WAS FIDDLING WITH THE DOOR HANDLE! Leah shouted.

Said Ginger P.: - Maybe that's what the helicopters are about?

Trevor L. said: - Even if they catch him, he'll be back on the street in ten minutes. Thank a Liberal.

I closed my laptop, turned off the bedside lamp, and closed my eyes.

Lunatics, I thought.

Paranoids.

Cranks.

A helicopter passed overhead.

Seemed low.

Another one followed it.

I went downstairs, dead-bolted the front door, checked that the garage gate was closed, locked the windows in the boys' bedrooms, and fell, a long while later, asleep.

...

Finally, from so little sleeping and so much reading, his brain dried up and he went completely out of his mind. – Cervantes, *Don Quixote*.

- I'll drive Paix to school, I said.

- He can walk, said Orli.

- It's okay, I said. - I'll drive him.

- It will be good for him to be independent.

- I'm going that way anyway, I said.

I wasn't.

- You've been reading that Nextdoor shit, haven't you? she asked.

- No, I said. - There was a home invasion ten blocks away.

- That's very helpful.

- You can't live with your head in the sand, I said.

She was irritated by my growing negativity. I was shocked by her naive positivity. I implored her to stay on the busier streets during her morning walks, to avoid the drug-riddled parks, to stay out of the alleyways. I'd have preferred that she stopped going for walks alone at all, and I texted her incessantly when she did to make sure she was okay.

- I'm being raped, she replied. - I'll get back to you.

I went for walks, too, trying to find the same peace she had, but Sodom is no place for a stroll. One morning I passed a seemingly sane young man who, apropos of nothing, began shouting at me with sudden fury.

- D'FUCK YOU LOOKING AT? he shouted.

Utterly placid a moment before, he was now suddenly afire, his fists clenched at his sides, looking to fight. Only then did I notice his frayed jacket, his soiled pants.

- D'FUCK YOU FUCKIN' LOOKING AT? he shouted again.

The pedestrians behind me crossed the street. I crossed with them.

- Everyone has a gun these days, Phil R. on Nextdoor had written. - They'll kill you just for looking at them.

I reached the other side of the street and turned to see if D'Fuck You Looking At was following. He had stopped at the side of the road and was now shouting at a terrified elderly woman who had just passed him going the other way.

- D'FUCK YOU LOOKING AT? he shouted at her.

She crossed the street.

That afternoon, I bought pepper spray for Orli. It was the same formula used by the Los Angeles Police Department. It was guaranteed to knock down a full-size male. It came with a pink leather holder.

- What's this for? she asked.

- It's perfume. What do you think it's for?

- I'll take my chances with Natasha, she said.

Natasha was our Rhodesian Ridgeback. Though the males of the breed are renowned for hunting lions, it is the females who stayed back to guard the tribe that are especially protective.

- Just take it with you, I said.

- Why?

- Why not?

- I hate pink, she said.

- You hate pink?

- Yes, I hate pink.

- You hate pink more than you hate rape? Is that what you're telling me?

- Are those my only options?

I gave her the blue one.

- You bought two? she asked.

- There are dangerous people out there, I said.

- There are, she said, tossing the pepper sprays into a drawer and slamming it shut. - But they're all on Nextdoor, so it should be easy to round them up.

...

Paix flopped down on my bed in a funk. He pulled out his phone and showed me some YouTube videos of other middle-school basketball players. Paix loved basketball, and he worked hard on his game, but the kids in the videos were six feet tall in sixth grade, dropping threes in seventh, and dunking in eighth.

- Everyone's so much better than me, he sighed.

It was easy to tell when he had been on his phone, because afterward, this preternaturally confident boy was always utterly miserable – depressed, defeated, insecure. The story these screens tell today is the same story Rabbi Hammer told me years ago: *You Suck*. Everyone is better than you – more talented, more popular, more interesting – and you, therefore, are worse than everyone. *The End*.

I asked him how many players he thought he had watched.

- In total? he asked.

- In total, I said.

- Dunno, he said - A hundred?

I pointed out that even if it was ten times as many as that – a hundred times, a thousand – it still represented a tiny fraction of the people in the world. I explained that social media presents a deliberately skewed image of the world, a world of basketball with the missed threes edited out, of adolescence with the acne Photoshopped away, a world on Reddit and 4chan of violence and hate where everyone has a gun and every stranger wants to cut your throat.

- But that's not reality, I said.

I was thinking about our talk the following morning when I passed a homeless man sitting cross-legged on the sidewalk outside the local market. He asked me if I would buy him some food, and he asked with such humility and desperation that I felt sickened by what Nextdoor had been doing to me. He held a drawing pad in his lap and a broken pencil in his hand, and he offered to draw a picture of me as payment.

- That's okay, I said. - What would you like?

- Peaches! he said. - Peaches are my favorite.

I bought him three peaches, a turkey sandwich, and, because it was a brutally hot day, a bottle of water and an ice-cream sandwich.

- Ice-cream sandwiches! Peaches shouted when he opened the bag. - I love ice-cream sandwiches! Thank you!

I smiled.

- Have a good day, he called after me.

- You too! I called back.

Fuck Nextdoor, I thought.

That afternoon, we were robbed. The thieves had forced the garage gate open and stolen all our bicycles, even Lux's beloved old kick scooter. Power tools, luggage – they took it all. They had gotten into Yasmin's garage, too, and made off with her deceased mother's wedding dress.

- It's not even *worth* anything! she wept.

The police came, eventually, and suggested we install cameras.

- Will that help? I asked.

- No, they said. - But it might make them go to a different garage.

Lux was frightened and asked to sleep in our room that night.

- Why the fuck don't they have cameras down there? I whispered to Orli when he'd fallen asleep. - Everyone has a gun these days. They'll kill you just for looking at them.

Orli was angry too, the angriest I had seen her since the move. She was angry at the cheap garage door, angry at the useless police, angry at the thieves – but she was angriest at me and my Nextdoorian attitude.

- It's easy to focus on the bad, she said. - It doesn't make you clever; it just makes you lazy.

- People suck, I said.

- No, she snapped, *thieves* suck. What the fuck does this have to do with *people?*

...

The home invasion wasn't. A homeless man had broken into an elderly woman's house and had been found asleep on the couch when she returned – frightening, to be sure, but there was no invasion, no tying up, no theft. It didn't matter. The story had already been told.

I woke early the next morning to write. It was warm and sunny, and Orli and the boys were going to spend the day at the beach. She was in the kitchen making avocado sandwiches when I left, filling plastic containers with chips and cookies.

- Have fun, she called after me.

I locked the front door behind me, secured the dead bolt, checked the security gate. Out back, in the alley, I noticed two scruffy men loitering around our garage. They saw me watching them, pretended to be looking at their phones, and walked off.

Scumbags, I thought.

A car pulled alongside me, slowed, then drove away. I made note of its license plate.

Casing the street, I thought. *Piece of shit.*

What a toilet. Dog shit, human shit, rotting food, anger, fear. D'Fuck You Looking At was sitting at a bus stop on the corner of Wilshire.

- D'FUCK YOU LOOKING AT? he shouted at me.

I kept my hand in my pocket, clenching my pink mace. I crossed to the gas station to buy cigarettes.

- Live clean, Doctor Superior had warned me. - Don't drink, don't smoke.

But Doctor Superior wasn't living in *The Road*.

An orange Lamborghini was parked at the pump. An elderly homeless woman approached and asked the driver for a dollar. The driver said he didn't have one. The homeless woman slumped away. I stopped at the grocery store for something to eat. Peaches was sitting outside with his pad and pen. I went in, bought myself a sandwich, and got him some more peaches and an ice-cream sandwich. I came outside and handed him the bag.

- What the fuck is this? he asked.

- Peaches, I said.

- I don't need your fucking peaches, he said.

- You said they were your favorite.

- Don't tell me what I said! he snapped. - I'll shove those faggot peaches up your ass!

I crossed the street. There was shit on the pavement, trash in the gutter, rats in the alley, and a corpse-gray sky overhead.

Animals, I thought. *Lock them all up.*

Eventually, God, disgusted by the cruel people of Sodom, decided to destroy the entire city. Abraham begged Him not to. He got God to agree to spare the city if he found fifty good people there, then forty, then thirty. Abraham haggled God all the way down to ten.

- Why, the ancient scholars asked, did Abraham stop haggling with God when he reached the number ten? Why not haggle God down to five or even one?

- Because, the ancient scholars answered, Abraham already knew he had

ten good people: Lot and his wife, their four daughters, and their four hus-
bands. He had found ten good people, and the city would be spared.

- But if Abraham found ten good people, the ancient scholars asked, why
did God destroy Sodom?

- Ah, the ancient scholars said. - Because in Sodom, even the good people
were bad.

Feh.

29.

There are, then, two versions of the Sodom story: version one, the Rabbi Scold version, and version two, the Prophet Ezekiel version.

Version one is a tale of sordid homosexuals, of *feigeles* run amok, of a God so disgusted by mankind that He destroys an entire city.

Version two of the Sodom story is the tale of a God so disgusted by a city's cruelness to strangers that He destroys the entire city.

In the first version, God is cruel.

In the second version, God can't abide cruelness.

The two versions are incompatible. Version two makes historical sense: Many ancient cultures at the time abided by the concept of *hospitium*, the belief that hospitality was the divine right of guests and strangers. Visitors were clothed and fed and presented with gifts. Hosts who violated this rule would face the wrath of the gods. The mythology of the time is filled with such tales: Birkat Ram, a volcano crater in Northern Galilee, is said by the local Arabs to be the site of a city destroyed because of its unhospitable residents; Ovid tells of a couple who were hospitable to Zeus, and so avoided the destruction he brought on their unwelcoming neighbors. Be kind, held the ancients, or be gone.

Version one makes less sense: Homosexuality was unremarkable at the time of the writing of Genesis. It was only Philo of Alexandria, writing fifteen hundred years later, who canonized the idea that Sodom's sin was same-sex sexuality.

The two angels arrived at Sodom in the evening, and Lot was sitting in the gateway of the city. Genesis 19:1. He invites them to his house to wash up (19:2), cooks them dinner (19:3), and gives them a place to sleep (19:4).

- Why, the ancient scholars asked, did a cruel Sodomite like Lot invite the strangers into his house?

- Because although Lot lived in Sodom, the ancient scholars said, he was raised in Abraham's house, where he learned to be kind to strangers.

One story.

Two versions.

Version one promotes hate.

Version two promotes kindness.

Version one says love is a sin.

Version two says hate is a sin.

And for some reason, for thousands of years, we have been telling the version that teaches hate.

30.

Schopenhauer wasn't the first philosopher to judge mankind as harshly as God. Thomas Hobbes and Jean-Jacques Rousseau are considered by many to be the two central pillars of Western philosophy.

Said Rousseau about man:

Once we were good. Now we are awful.

Hobbes was more specific:

We're awful when we're free, he said. *When we're controlled, we're merely reprehensible.*

And so, concerning mankind, the two pillars of Western philosophy agree on this:

Feh.

31.

- I worry more about your success, Ike once said, than about your failure.

- Why is that?

- Because you think you deserve failure, he said. - Success tends to result in self-destruction.

- Self-destruction's my whole thing, I said.

I wonder sometimes if that was what tortured Phil. Told he was *feh*, believing he was *feh*, all his success – his career, the love of his partner, his adoring children – paradoxically drew him closer to the roof's icy edge.

Shortly before we met, he'd completed a run of Arthur Miller's *Death of a Salesman* on Broadway. Some nights, he told me, after the performance, he would slip out the back door and go to a nearby McDonald's, hat pulled low to hide his face, and just force those shitty burgers down his throat until he felt sick. His therapist had suggested that perhaps he was poisoning himself because he didn't believe he deserved acclaim. I told Phil that was why I write – in my writing, I could be a better me, funnier, wiser, bolder. Phil understood. He played dark characters, he said, to find the goodness within them – something he couldn't do with himself.

We sighed and ordered another round.

- We're Asian porn, I said. - All the good stuff is blurred out.

Phil threw his head back and laughed.

That laugh, that laugh.

32

- You seem down, Elijah says to Gabriel.

- I'm in a bar, says Gabriel. - I'm supposed to be down.

Gabriel signals the bartender for another drink. He hasn't slept. He's been up all night, three nights in a row now, watching *Auslander*. He's been watching *O'Malley* too, and *Smith* and *Rodriguez* and *Abebe* and *Ng* and *Ashwari* and *Kumar*. He's been watching all of God's favorite comedies, and all of God's favorite tragedies.

- And? asks Elijah.

Gabriel checks over his shoulder, makes sure no one is around, drops his voice to a whisper.

- And what if we have it backward? he asks.

Elijah eyes him. Gabe's been acting weird lately.

- Have what backward? asks Elijah.

Gabriel is nervous, jumpy. He has a theory, a theory he is terrified to think, let alone voice. But after binge-watching mankind for so long now, one story after the next, it's begun to dawn on him that what God deems entertaining, Gabriel thinks cruel.

- Remember what you said when God first created Man? Gabriel asks.

- No.

- You said *Meh*, says Gabriel. - And you were right. Not great, not awful. Sometimes lowly, sometimes noble. Sometimes evil, sometimes heroic.

- So?

The bartender brings Gabriel's drink. Gabriel waits for him to head back down the bar before continuing.

- So, what if God isn't the protagonist? Gabriel whispers. - What if He's the antagonist?

- God?

- Yes. What if mankind is the hero, and God is the bad guy? What if it's God who is *feh*?

- I don't think we should be talking about this, says Elijah.

- You like Voltaire, right? says Gabriel.

- Yeah, says Elijah. - I mean, for a Frenchman.

- Voltaire said that God is a comedian telling jokes to a room full of people who are too afraid to laugh. But what if He isn't? What if Voltaire was wrong? What if God's the asshole at the back of the club shouting, *You suck!* and ruining everyone's good time?

Elijah signals the bartender for another drink.

- I don't think we should be talking about this, he says.

33.

If you ever find yourself thinking, *You know, maybe my wife is right, maybe I'm not a worthless failure, maybe I shouldn't be judging myself and others so harshly, and certainly not by the twisted standards of a corrupt neoliberal kleptocratic form of capitalism that places more value on the material than the spiritual,* I recommend you stay the fuck away from Zillow.

This magnificent one-of-a-kind home features three large bedrooms, a Sub-Zero refrigerator, and two and a half baths. The half bath is larger than your whole bath. The refrigerator costs more than your car. This is the perfect home for people who aren't you.

For the second time in as many years, we had to move. We could no longer afford the rent on our apartment, and the response I was getting to *Zoo*, the animated series I was trying to sell, was not exactly filling me with hope. Clooney couldn't help. Harmon couldn't help. The major streaming services had already passed, and so once again our apartment was filled with moving boxes and packing tape. We needed something smaller, cheaper. More failure-y.

Orli pretended to be happy about the move.

- Something smaller, she said. - Cheaper, less stress.

It was as ludicrous as saying I was sexy.

- Bullshit, I grumbled as I scrolled through Zillow. - Who doesn't want to live in a nice place?

- You don't want nice, she said, you want magnificent. Wouldn't you rather live in a place we can afford without your having to work for bloody Hollywood?

Orli had been even more skeptical of Hollywood than she had been of advertising. She didn't trust them. She thought their praises empty, their promises shallow, the executives phony, the actors not worth their dysfunctions. Some years earlier, Showtime flew us out to Los Angeles for a *Pigs in Shit* meeting. They put us in the top floor of a luxury hotel on Ocean Avenue, a grand suite with multiple bedrooms, bathrooms, a living room, and a private patio overlooking the Pacific.

- Look at this place! I said, looking out from our magnificent room to the magnificent blue ocean across the magnificent street.

Orli came outside and stood beside me.

- They are going to *fuck* you, she said.

- What?

- There's no way they put you in this room today, she said, and don't fuck you silly tomorrow.

This spectacular town house is a must-see.

But not by you.

I was on the couch, deep in yet another Zillow depression, when Lux came bounding in, bright with joy, a great green glob of gooey slime in his hands.

- Guess what! he exclaimed. - Karina Garcia just passed nine million subscribers!

Karina Garcia makes slime.

- Mm-hmm, I said.

- Nine *million*! he said.

I didn't give a fuck.

- She's a *millionaire*, said Lux.

To be a parent on present-day Earth is to be assailed by one's children on a regular basis with information about how many millions of dollars various other people earn. Paix, a basketball fan, would tell me about how much LeBron James earned, and how many houses LeBron James had, and what cars LeBron James drove. Lux, a slime fan, told me about Karina Garcia. To them, these were stories of the endless possibilities the adventure of life held in store for them. To me, they were stories of my own miserable failure.

- Like, *multi*millionaire, he said.

- From slime? I asked.

I desperately wanted him to be wrong, but a quick Google search confirmed his reports. I have no excuse for being surprised by this, but Karina, a YouTube slime influencer, was pulling down $200,000 a month.

From slime.

Slime was booming. Slime had never been bigger. Slime was everywhere. The CEOs of the slime companies were fifteen years old, their consumers younger than that, and I found it, in my deepening Zillowcholia, a dispiriting simulacrum of corporate America. There were the major slime manufacturers, like Nickelodeon and Elmer's – Big Slime, if you will – which were sold in the big-box stores like Target and Walmart. There were the independent slime shops – Mom-and-Pop Slime – who sold slime directly through their websites, and whose businesses lived and died on the reviews of the all-important slime influencers, teenagers who reviewed and promoted slime in exchange for paid sponsorships and free products. There was even an annual Slime Mania convention, the biggest slime event of the entire slime fiscal year. Karina Garcia, the self-proclaimed Queen of Slime, was twenty-four years old. She had recently purchased a six-bedroom house.

She was adding a guesthouse.

By the pool.

I despised her.

- And make sure to smash that *Like* button! Karina sang at the end of her videos. - And click here to subscribe!

She represented everything I loathed about the modern world, compressed into one despicable, phony, singsongy capitalist.

And I wanted Lux to loathe her too.

- Yes, I said to him. - But do you think she's happy?

- Of course! said Lux. - Why wouldn't she be happy?

Lux has always been a deeply caring and compassionate soul. He sees the best in all people, all the time. It's very annoying. When he was younger and we watched *Scooby-Doo*, he felt bad for the zombies being dragged off to jail; when we watched *Phineas and Ferb*, he felt bad for the evil Doctor Doofenshmirtz, whose plans always went so terribly awry; when we watched *Star Wars*, he felt bad for Darth Vader. He thought Darth might be lonely. He imagined that it pained Darth to be reviled by the entire universe. He felt sad that everyone hated the Dark Lord, that he had no friends. It only made it worse when, at the end of the film, we all cheered Vader's downfall. Lux sat in bed afterward, his eyes filled with tears.

- It wasn't nice to do that, he said. - Everyone was mean to Darth Vader.

I held him and said I was sorry.

- You're right, I said. - That wasn't very nice.

I wondered what Schopenhauer would have made of this large-hearted child. It was difficult to condemn human nature as inherently self-interested when your six-year-old is saddened by Darth Vader's loneliness.

- Yes, says Arthur, but his concern is rooted in selfishness because he's worried about the possibility of his own rejection from the tribe.

Shut up, Arthur.

I'd always admired Lux's generosity of spirit, but lately, thanks to Nextdoor, his goodness was beginning to concern me. He was nine years old now, and I worried his kind heart in a cruel world would be broken, that his honesty in a world of lies would prove a liability, that his boundless love would be met with bloody hate. To see this being of pure light on the streets of this city of darkness only made me hate Los Angeles all the more.

I will devastate this city and make it an object of horror and scorn. All who pass by will be appalled and will scoff because of all its wounds.

Jeremiah 19:8.

Here's a good life tip for those who may not know it: If you start quoting Jeremiah, something has gone very wrong in your mind. You are heading toward a very dark place. You are not merely gazing into the abyss; you are the abyss. If you don't yet take antidepressants, take some. If you are already taking some, take more.

Jeremiah was my mother's favorite prophet. He was, in the words of one biblical commentator, a miserable cunt. That commentator was me. Jeremiah wept, all the time, about everything. He wept so much he was known as the Weeping Prophet, and the other biblical prophets weren't exactly a barrel of laughs. My mother would quote his bitter denunciations whenever I did something wrong, and his violent threats when she wanted to remind me of God's wrath. When I drove on Shabbos, she said:

Rachel is weeping for her children; she refuses to be comforted because they are no more.

When I left her home and traditions, she said:

There is hope for your descendants, declares the Lord. Your children will return to their own land.

Jeremiah is perhaps most famous for wearing an actual wooden yoke around his neck, inscribed with his warning to sinners that God would soon destroy their nation. Here's another good life tip for those who may not know it: Don't take advice from people wearing yokes.

I always hated Jeremiah, but now, after just a year in Los Angeles, I was thinking of getting a yoke myself. The city seemed cruel to me, cruel as Sodom, and so I decided, then and there, to combat Lux's positivity with a healthy diet of bitter cynicism. He would be miserable, but he would be safe.

- Well, buddy, I said to him as he squished his slime, think about it. Karina took something she loved, and what did she do? She commoditized it.

- What's that mean?

- It means to turn something into a means for making money. She's prostituting herself.

- What's that mean?

- It means to sell your body for money.

- Oh.

- Now she has a *job* where she once had a *passion*. Now she sees dollars and cents. She sees product and marketing.

- I don't think she just wants to make money, Dad, he said. - I think she's doing what she likes, and it *happens* to make money.

Idiot.

- Do you know what internalized capitalism is? I asked him.

He did not.

- It's when people begin to believe that their self-worth is linked to their productivity and income. She's not happy, buddy, she can't be, because capitalism tells her that her only value is her ability to produce income.

- What's income?

- Money.

- Dad, he said, *look* at her. She looks pretty happy.

He showed me a video of hers.

She looked pretty happy.

Fuck.

. . .

ZOO

In a remote zoo, in the middle of a vast desert, resides a family of pigs: Father Pig, Mother Pig, and their young son, Jonah Pig. Jonah Pig is a deeply caring and compassionate soul. He sees the best in all creatures, all the time. He stops to smell the flowers.

   - It's very annoying, says his father.

The pigs live in the Petting Zoo. The humans feed them and pet them and show them love. Then, one morning, a nuclear blast wipes out all mankind and destroys the earth. Somehow, the zoo survives. But the cage doors have been ripped open from the blast, the humans are all dead, and the once-restrained animals are now loose, alone — and very, very hungry. Mother Pig and Father Pig must now raise their large-hearted son in a dangerous, postapocalyptic world possessed of a terrible and deadly secret:

They're delicious.

The network executives looked at me blankly.

- It's *The Road*, I said. - But with bacon.

It is a heartfelt story of a family in a heartless world, I explained, but here's the rub: Mother Pig, despite the now-dangerous world, wants to protect her son's optimistic, positive nature. Father Pig, because of the now-dangerous world, wants his son to be more wary, more cynical.

They said they were interested.

They said they would discuss it.

They said they would get back to me.

...

THE INSPIRING TALE OF
THE RAPIST ARCHITECT

Once upon a time, there was a man named Howard Roark, who designed buildings and raped women. The people liked his buildings. The women liked being raped. Howard was very proud that he cared only about himself.

- I am a man, said Howard, who does not exist for others.

He was the hero of the story.

The End

The Inspiring Tale of the Rapist Architect, more commonly known as *The Fountainhead*, is a story written by a woman named Alisa Zinov'yevna Rosenbaum, more commonly known as Ayn Rand. Lately, Ayn, which rhymes with *pine*, and nearly *slime*, was everywhere. Republicans were quoting her, Conservatives were lauding her, the president was reading her. Ayn was an Assholist, and the pseudo-contrarian pseudo-philosophy she pseudo-developed is known as Assholism. Assholism maintains that selfishness is courageous, arrogance a virtue, and coldheartedness the mark of genius.

Said Ayn:

If any civilization is to survive, it is the morality of altruism that men have to reject.

And:

Until and unless you discover that money is the root of all good, you ask for your own destruction.

And:

Only if one feels immensely important can one feel truly light.

At her funeral, there was a six-foot-tall wreath.

In the shape of a dollar sign.

She would have loved Zillow.

- Here's a nice one, I called to Orli from the living room. - It's only a hundred thousand dollars a month.

- To buy? she called back from the kitchen.

- To rent, I said. - But it has seven bathrooms.

- That's a lot of assholes, said Orli.

Lux came in and sat down beside me, slime in hand.

- Wow! he said, glancing at my screen. - Is that our new house?

- I don't think so, buddy.

- It would be nice to live there, he said, don't you think?

A teachable moment.

- Well, I said, you can't live there. Nobody can.

- Why not?

- Because it's a hundred thousand dollars a month. And to earn a hundred thousand dollars a month, you have to give up your soul, you have to be dead inside, so you can't really *live* there, since you're dead. Nobody earns a hundred thousand dollars a month ethically.

Orli entered, not liking the conversation she'd been overhearing. The names Lux and Orli both mean *light*; my name means *peace*, but it also means *goodbye*, which I had been sensing Orli was getting ready to say to me, permanently.

- What's *ethically* mean? Lux asked.

- It means being a good person, I said.

He shrugged.

- Karina earns two hundred thousand dollars a month, he argued, and she's a good person.

- She's sponsored by Coca-Cola, buddy.

- So?

- So it's poison, I said. - She's literally making money by selling poison.

Back in my advertising days, I had worked on the Coca-Cola account. This was the slogan they were using:

Choose Happiness.

For rust remover.

They cling to deceit; they refuse to return.

Jeremiah 8:5.

- Dad, said Lux, I'm sure if she knew it was poison, she would stop.

Idiot.

- Have you ever heard of Ayn Rand? I asked.

- Okay, said Orli, flashing me an angry look. - I think that's enough . . .

. . .

- Come with me, Jonah, says Father Pig, leading him toward what remained of the Petting Zoo's front gate. - I want to show you something.

Jonah is frightened. The pigs all agreed, after the blast, to never venture outside the Petting Zoo, for it was far too dangerous now among the uncaged animals. But Father Pig takes him by the hand and tells him not to worry, that he's old enough to know certain things, that indeed now he must know them.

They head cautiously into the main zoo, staying off the pathways, making their way via the relative safety of the dense woods. Soon they arrive at a clearing where a large group of chimpanzees are swinging from the trees, screaming, fighting, and throwing feces at each other.

- What are those? Jonah asks.

- Chimps, says Father Pig.

- Are they crazy?

- Batshit crazy, says Father Pig. - Don't go near them.

They continue on their way, whereupon they come to a large area full of boulders and shattered bones. Atop the boulders sits a ferocious lion, who roars like thunder, his teeth like daggers.

- What is that? Jonah asks.

- That's a lion.

- What's a lion?

- Your worst nightmare, says Father Pig.

They continue on their way, whereupon they come upon a pool of water beside which sleeps an enormous polar bear, his razor-sharp claws red with blood.

- What's that? Jonah asks.

- That's a polar bear.

- What's a polar bear? Jonah asks.

- Your other worst nightmare.

Jonah trembles.

- I want to go back, he says. - I don't like it here.

- Okay, says Father Pig. - But first, there's something you need to know.

- What? asks Jonah.

Father Pig sits, and Jonah sits beside him. Mother Pig has warned Father Pig about telling Jonah their secret, but he feels he must.

- Jonah, says Father Pig with a heavy sigh, we're delicious.

- We're what?

- We're delicious, says Father Pig. - We're moist, we're meaty, we go with everything. We're bacon, buddy. We're sausage.

- What's bacon?

- Our cured bellies.

- What's sausage?

- Our intestines, stuffed with our blood and head meat.

- Head meat?

A rustling in the woods behind them causes them to spin around in fright. It is Mother Pig, and she has heard the whole discussion.

- Okay, she says, flashing Father Pig an angry glance. - I think that's enough . . .

. . .

- I'm worried about Lux, I said to Orli.

We were at a bar on Wilshire Boulevard, just up the road from our apartment. During the day, an old woman slept in the bar's doorway with a sign that read *Help*. At night, they served a cocktail they called a Gold Fashioned.

It was made with XO-grade Cognac, a dash of Angostura bitters, and 23-karat gold.

- He's too happy, I said.

- He's too happy?

- Too trusting, too . . .

- Young? she said.

- He's too kind, too good. People suck.

- This isn't about him, she said. - This is about you.

It wasn't going to be a pleasant night.

- You were raised by people who judged, she said, so you grew up judging too. Is that what you want for him? To judge everyone? How long will it be before he's judging himself?

On the television above the bar, a Lakers game was about to begin. The players were just arriving. The announcer was talking about LeBron's cars, about his three Ferraris and his Lamborghini and his Rolls-Royce. LeBron fixed an arrogant countenance upon his face and strode past the camera like a man with three Ferraris and a Lamborghini and a Rolls-Royce.

Ayn Rand, on her first crush:

What I liked about him most was his arrogance.

Jeremiah:

The arrogant one will stumble and fall . . . I will kindle a fire in her towns that will consume all who are around her.

The woman beside me ordered another round of Gold Fashioneds.

- I really like the gold, she said to the bartender.

- It works, right? said the bartender.

- *Indeed*, I said to Orli, *on every high hill and under every green tree you lay down as a whore.*

- Schopenhauer?

- Jeremiah.

- Marvelous, she said, signaling for the check. - Your mother would be proud.

...

CHOKE ON IT

Once upon a time, Moses went up to Heaven to visit God. While he was gone, the Israelites built a golden calf. When Moses came down from Heaven, he found his people on their knees, praying to gold. Moses attacked the golden calf, crushing it beneath his feet and turning it into powder. He put the gold powder into water and forced the Israelites to drink it – men, women, and children, everyone had to drink gold.

Everyone who rejected the gold survived the gold.

Everyone who prayed to the gold died from the gold.

The End

That is what's known in storytelling terminology as a happy ending.

- How's LA? Ike asked.

- It's Hell, I said. - I'm in Hell. No, it's worse than Hell. In Hell, evil people get punished. Here they get mansions and infinity pools.

I had been developing a theory.

- It's the pools, I said to Ike.

- The pools?

I called it the Shit-Stirrer Infinity Pool Theory.

- The shit what? he asked.

- The Shit-Stirrer Infinity Pool Theory, I said.

Here's how it goes:

Shit-stirrers, I explained, have a long and noble history. Shit-stirrers ask questions, point out problems. Shit-stirrers can be writers, artists, or comedi-

ans. They can be Jews or Lutherans or atheists or suffragettes or abolitionists. They can be Jesus Christ or Dick Gregory, Voltaire or Vonnegut. They
have one thing in common, though, whatever shit they happen to be stirring: Power despises them. Power runs a tight ship, and it doesn't tolerate
boat-rockers. In earlier times, to shut them up, shit-stirrers, like Jesus, were
crucified, or, like Voltaire, chased out of their countries, or, like Dostoyevsky,
thrown in hellish gulags. Today, to shut them up, shit-stirrers are given infinity pools. It's devilishly simple: A shit-stirrer looks at the world around him
and decides that something is wrong, something is off, something is unfair or
corrupt or immoral. He decides, say, that religion is just a system of popula-
tion control, or that capitalism is incommensurate with democracy, or that as
dangerous as heroin is, it doesn't compare in the history of the world to the
destruction wrought by testosterone. And it bothers him. He gets indignant.
He gets defiant. He wants to tell the world, to fix the world, to stir the shit. He
decides to write a book about it, or tell a joke about it, or sing a song about it,
or make a film about it. And he does. And it works. It hits. It blows up. Suddenly, he's making it. And he gets a book deal or a film deal or a music deal or
a Netflix comedy special. He buys a house with a flat roof and glass walls.
And he gets an infinity pool. And the pool is wonderful, and it is warm, and it
is infinite, and he gets some pool floats with cup holders in the armrests, and
he makes himself some Gold Fashioneds, and he floats around in his pool with
his Gold Fashioneds in the cup holders in the armrests of his pool floats, and
pretty soon he forgets what he was so indignant about in the first place. Something about poverty? Inequality? Can't remember. All that caring, all that
outrage, seems like a long time ago, a time before Gold Fashioneds and infinity pools. It is a kind of spiritual hush money; they're not being paid millions
to be quiet, it's more devious than that – they're being paid millions so they
have nothing left to say. Why rock the boat when you're the captain? And the
system works. No gulags, no crucifixions, none needed. Jesus, living in a mansion in Bel-Air with a Bentley and an infinity pool, doesn't call for revolution.
He doesn't chastise the rich, because he is the rich. He renders not unto Caesar

what is Caesar's; on the contrary, he cheats on his taxes like all good million-aires, he rushes to Nextdoor whenever he sees a black man on his street, and the only Caesar he knows is his Mexican landscaper, who he's never actually spoken to and whose name he thinks is José.

- That's my theory, I said to Ike.

There was a long pause.

- I'm working on it, I said.

- Didn't you have a pool? Ike asked. - In Woodstock?

- Yes, I said. - But it was a small one.

- What's happening with *Zoo*? Ike asked.

- Waiting, I said.

...

We were getting ready for bed when Lux burst into our bedroom in a panic.

- I'm out of snow! he cried.

Slime is made by mixing ordinary white glue with Borax, a household de-tergent. Lux had begun making his own slime, and the apartment was buried in jugs of glue, boxes of Borax, and packets of a white powder called Instant Snow, the secret ingredient in cloud slime, a soft, fluffy slime that was all the rage. Orli told him to calm down and assured him we would get some more.

- We have to get it *now*, he said.

- Why? I asked.

- I checked on Amazon, he said. - There's only one packet left!

- There's more than one packet left, I assured him.

- But I checked! he said.

I motioned him over, put my arm around his shoulder, and tried to shatter his naive view of the world.

- It's called scarcity marketing, buddy, I said. - It comes from the word *scarce*.

- What does *scarce* mean?

- It means in short supply, I said. - You know all those tall buildings in Los Angeles and New York, in every city, in every country, all around the world?

He nodded.

Orli crossed her arms.

- Well, I said, they're filled with grown-ups who do nothing all day long except sit around, in meetings, trying to figure out how to take your money. That's their whole job. That's all they do, morning to night. And one of the ways they take your money is to lie to you and tell you that there's only one item left.

- Even when there's more?

- Yes.

- Why would they do that? he asked.

- Because they're scumbags, I said.

- Bedtime, Orli said to Lux.

She took him to bed and tucked him in.

- Why would you tell him that? she demanded when she returned.

- I want him to know what they're up to, I said.

- If they're up to something, she said, he'll see it on his own.

She climbed into bed and turned off her lamp.

- If you hate yourself so much, she asked, why do you want to turn him into you?

...

The network passed on *Zoo*.

- We already have a talking horse, they said.

- But this isn't about a talking animal, I explained. - It's about how we see the world and how we raise our children, about the competing stories we tell of optimism and pessimism, of the choice between taking a chance on your fellow man or giving up, deciding that no one can be trusted, that it's every man for himself, which, on an ever-shrinking planet, is perhaps the most important question of our times.

- Yes, they said. - But we already have a talking horse.

I came home to find Lux at the dining table, his usual bright cheer replaced with heavy gloom. Spread out before him was his slime-making equipment – glue, water, Borax, lotions, dyes – and a mail package that had been hastily torn open as only an excited child can do. But he wasn't excited. A few weeks earlier, he'd held a small yard sale to earn money to buy himself slime. He sold his books and his old toys, he sold his plushies, he even sold his beloved Harry Potter magic wand. He made almost fifty dollars, and that evening, after watching a video of a YouTube slime influencer named Talisa Tossell, he spent it all on a slime she had recommended.

- And make sure to smash that *Like* button! Talisa said. - And click here to subscribe!

Every day since ordering, Lux had raced home from school, hoping to find that his slime had arrived. And at last, that afternoon, it had.

- So what's wrong? I asked.

- There's no extras, he said, fighting back his tears. - And the slime is *awful*.

As in all commerce, the real work of the slime business takes place under the table. Influencers are just the influenced – by money or gifts or favors. And so slime makers, in an effort to influence the influencers, send them free samples along with other freebies – bags of candy, homemade cookies, scented stickers, plush toys – whatever they can to ensure a positive review of their slime.

- Ooh! Talisa had squealed about this particular slime. - It's so great when they include candy! Hershey's Kisses! And what a great slime – this is my new favorite!

Alas, Lux was no influencer, and so his slime didn't come with anything – no candy, no cookies, no free samples, no stickers. Worst of all, the slime was crap; it didn't stretch, it felt dry and old, and the scent Talisa raved about in her YouTube video was less Fresh Watermelon than Week-Old Sushi.

Lux felt cheated.

He felt tricked.

He felt like a fool.

I felt this was an important opportunity. If I was ever going to replace his rose-colored glasses with a pair of my dark midnight blues, now was the time. I sat beside him at the dining table as he angrily squished all the new slimes together into one great glob of late-stage-capitalist mediocrity.

- I'm sorry, I said. - That really sucks. But it's not your fault.

I told him that it was a tough lesson to learn, but that, ultimately, capitalism encourages deceit.

- Deceit? he asked.

- Dishonesty, I said. - Have you ever heard the term *caveat emptor?*

He shook his head as he kneaded the slime, adding water and glue as he tried to salvage it.

- It means *buyer beware*, I said. - It means that it's the *buyer's* responsibility to not be stolen from. Can you imagine that? The *seller* is allowed to lie and cheat – in fact, it's *encouraged*. It's like saying it's a woman's responsibility to not be raped.

- What's rape?

I checked to make sure Orli wasn't nearby.

- I mean, what kind of a basis for a society is this? I continued, deciding to leave forcible violation for another time. - A system that rewards predatory behavior will be dominated by predators; there's no other possible outcome, and yet we're all so surprised when . . .

- Fixed it! he suddenly shouted.

- What?

- I fixed it!

He held the slime in his hands, squishing it between his fingers.

- I added some hand lotion and water, and now it's good! Talisa was right, this is *really* good slime!

He held the slime up to my face.

- And hey, he said, now it *does* smell like watermelon, doesn't it?

It did.

Fuck.

- But have you really fixed anything? I asked him.

- Yeah, he said. - I fixed the slime.

- I understand, I said, but the system that . . .

But just then Orli came bounding into the room, her eyes alight, a huge smile on her face, waving a handful of tickets overhead.

- Guess what I got? she sang.

- What? asked Lux.

- TICKETS TO THE SLIME CONVENTION! she shouted.

- YAY! shouted Lux.

Fuck.

...

Lux was beside himself with excitement as we headed to Anaheim for the convention. All his favorite slime brands were going to be there: Slime Obsidian, Kawaii Slime, Luminati Slime. There would even be a special guest appearance by Talisa Tossell, part of what they called the Slime Celebrity Meet & Greet.

- In Hollywood they call that lunch, I joked.

Nobody laughed.

As we headed down the 405, Paix read salaries to me from his cell phone.

- You know how much LeBron made last year? he asked. - Thirty-five million.

- Wow, I said.

I was sure he was doing it to bother me, to make me feel inferior, but I wasn't going to take a fourteen-year-old's bait.

- Why do I have to go to this capitalist nightmare? he'd complained.

He's becoming me, I thought. *Fuck.*

- Anthony Davis made twenty-five, Paix said.

- Wow, I replied.

- Million.

- Great.

- A year.

- I know.

- For playing a game.

- Crazy.

- Karina Garcia makes two hundred million a *month*, Lux said.

- Two hundred *thousand*, Paix corrected him.

- That's still a lot.

- It is, said Paix.

- Wow, I said.

I was determined not to ruin the show for Lux. I was determined to withhold my cynicism and disgust. I failed.

The doors of the Anaheim Convention Center opened at ten a.m., and I was borne in upon a wave of frenzied eight-year-old consumers and huckstering preteen entrepreneurs, a Randian wet dream of money, power, and greed. The enormous ballroom, lit by enormous crystal chandeliers, was filled with folding tables arranged in long aisles, each of the tables piled high with various brands of slime.

- This is AWESOME! Lux shouted, and he and Orli ran off into the crowd.

- Kill me, said Paix.

- TWO FOR ONE CLOUD SLIMES, TWO FOR ONE! one ten-year-old entrepreneur shouted as we walked by.

- BUY THREE SLIMES, GET A FREE SLIME OF YOUR CHOICE! shouted an eight-year-old girl wearing a T-shirt with her company's logo on it.

Behind the pint-size capitalists toiled their parent-investors, dreams of Karina Garcia's mansion in their heads, restocking the tables, hauling product from the back room, making change, and stuffing the cash into their pockets for safekeeping.

My people have exchanged their glorious God for worthless idols. Be appalled at this, you heavens, and shudder with great horror.

Jeremiah 2:11–12.

And shudder I did. Silently, in my mind, I condemned, and I loathed, and I prayed for God to bring destruction upon these people.

- Well, at least they're entrepreneurial, I said to Paix, trying not to darken his world too.

- So are hookers, he said.

Fuck.

An hour later we met Lux and Orli at the ballroom door. Lux ran up to me, his face flush with excitement, his swag bag filled with slime and candy and free samples and coupons for future orders.

- Let's go meet Talisa! he said.

He and Orli dropped their bags with us and hurried off down the hallway for a quick bathroom break. As they disappeared into the crowd, I hoped I hadn't ruined his day. I hoped I hadn't made her angry. And then, subtly, almost imperceptibly, the floor of the grand ballroom began to tremble. The walls began to shake, the crystal wall sconces tinkling gently as they shook. A lifelong New Yorker, I assumed the subway was passing beneath us, only remembering a moment later that I was no longer in New York City. I was in Anaheim. And there wasn't a subway around for miles.

It was, I realized with horror, an earthquake.

Because of God's indignation, the earth will quake, and no nations will endure His denunciation.

Jeremiah 10:10.

- Dad? said Paix, his eyes wide. - Dad . . . is that . . . ?

The chandeliers began swinging wildly back and forth. They looked heavy, too heavy to be swaying that much without crashing down.

Now? I thought. *Now he answers my prayers?*

I grabbed Paix by the arm, dragged him to the side of the room, out from under the swinging chandeliers; the quake intensified; I watched as the floor began to rise and fall in terrible waves, rolling from one end of the long ballroom to the other, upsetting tables and chairs; slime tubs toppled from their displays, splattered on the floor. I held Paix's hand tightly, ready to dash through the crowd to find Lux and Orli, trying to recall where the restroom was, to remember where I had noted the emergency stairway that morning, which exit was closest, which floor we were on – the third? the fourth? Fuck me, were we on the fourth? – how far we had to run to get out . . . when the tremors suddenly stopped.

As suddenly as they had begun, they ceased.

The waves rolling across the floor softened, weakened, came to a stop.

And then, as if nothing at all had happened, the conventioneers returned to conventioneering.

- TWO FOR TEN, one called, FIVE FOR TWENTY.

I imagined that when Earth finally collapsed beneath the weight of unsustainable capitalism, those would be the last words spoken by the last human being as he fell to his knees and exhaled the last lungful of breathable air on this now-despoiled planet:

- Two for ten, five for twenty.

The End.

The mother beside me, holding her baby, looked at me and shrugged.

- Aftershocks, she said.

There had been a quake the day before, she explained, some distance from Anaheim. Aftershocks can occur for days following the initial quake.

The chandeliers stopped swaying, found their center. Convention workers replaced the fallen slimes, sellers sold, buyers bought. Lux came hurrying back from the bathroom, Orli just behind him, completely unaware that anything at all had happened.

- Can we go see Talisa now? he asked.

Paix smiled.

- What a God, Paix said, smiling widely.

But Lux, I knew, was as unlike God as anyone could ever be. God was miserable. God found fault. God sent fires and floods and earthquakes. God, like me, sat in stone-faced, acid judgment.

We met Talisa, who was charming and self-effacing and as surprised as anyone about her odd success. She said she was sorry that the slime he ordered had dried out, but she explained that can happen in the mail, and then she gave him a hug, and he beamed and we headed back home. In the back seat of the car, Lux chatted excitedly about the convention, and about the photos he had taken with Talisa, and about the aftershocks he was upset to have missed, and he played with his slime and traded candy with Paix, who admitted he'd had fun after all. Orli drove and played cheerful music and offered to trade Lux her Reese's Peanut Butter Cups for Twix, but he said *No way!* and they laughed.

I stared glumly out the window at the passing traffic. Lux had spent the day in a fancy convention center with gold carpeting and grand chandeliers, in an elegant high-ceilinged ballroom filled with excited children and brightly colored tubs of fun that for every four he bought, he got one free. I, meanwhile, had spent the day like a miserable prophet, judging and condemning all around me.

All I was missing was the fucking yoke.

The last story Kafka ever wrote was about a creature in its burrow, desperate to keep the world away from him. The world was perilous, hostile. From the safety of his burrow, the creature looked out at the world and said this:

Feh.

A burrow sounded nice. A burrow sounded like a good idea. To protect me from the world, sure. But perhaps more importantly, I was beginning to suspect, to protect my light-filled family from the plague of darkness that was me.

34.

Natasha was raised with a very different story than Flynn's. We adopted Natasha when she was just eight weeks old, and her every day was filled with love and affection. If Flynn was raised with *Most People Suck*, Natasha was raised with *Most People Are Good*. And it shows. Natasha loves everyone.

- Look at all these other dogs! she said when we got to Los Angeles, eager to play with them all.

- Look at all these fucking dogs, Flynn growled, eager to kill them.

I was walking her one morning when Craig phoned from New York.

- Did you hear? he asked.

I assumed it was about Israel.

- About Ike, he said.

Craig was Ike's patient as well. Ike had helped him through a long and bitter divorce, which Craig, being a Feh, had blamed upon himself.

- What about him? I asked.

I worried it was about Ike's shaking hands. He had Something, Craig would tell me. Advanced Something. Stage 4 Something. I would phone Ike, beside myself, and he would tell me not to worry, that he would fight it, that the prognosis was good. Three months later he would be dead.

I wasn't totally wrong. Craig told me that the podcast about Ike had premiered and was currently the number one podcast on Apple. My heart began to pound. I knew what that kind of publicity meant.

- And? I asked.

- And they're starting hearings.

- Hearings about what?

I heard the worry in his voice.

- About revoking his license, he said.

I'd have preferred news about Israel.

I felt dizzy, my knees weak.

He was my lifeline. And then, one day, he was just . . . gone.

Natasha, on cue, took a shit on a patch of grass beside the street. She was scratching at the grass with her hind legs when I heard a man behind me shouting.

- Hey!

I turned to find him storming toward me, the veins in his neck bulging.

- Your dog's getting grass on my car!

He pointed to the luxury BMW sports sedan parked on the street behind us.

- Where? I asked.

- There!

It took me a moment to spot the single blade of grass that had settled on the fender.

- There? I asked.

- Yeah, there! That's rude!

- She's not being rude, I said. - She's being a dog.

I brushed the blade of grass off the car. This only made him more incensed.

- No! he shouted. - You have oils on your hand! I'll do it, I'll do it!

He stomped off to his garage and returned a moment later with a cordless leaf blower, with which he proceeded to blow the single blade of grass off the hood of his car. As I watched him, I had an idea for a business.

Don't steal it.

It's going to make millions.

Here it is:

I'm going to purchase an open-top bus, the kind they drive tourists around in in Hollywood, and I'm going to paint the words *Instant Self-Esteem Tour* on the side. People who feel bad about themselves will get on – the Mes, the Phils, the Craigs, the Fehs – and I'm going to drive them around the city: I'm going to drive them to where the Lamborghini owner was refusing a hungry woman a dollar; I'm going to drive them to Skid Row, where shattered Army veterans live in cardboard boxes; I'm going to drive them to Bel-Air, a short Rolex throw away, where people live in multimillion-dollar palaces; I'm going to drive them to the home of the man who got paid by TMZ for spying on Phil; and I'm going to drive them to watch the kettlebellers on Wilshire walking past the homeless; and then I am going to drive them here, to this street, to my street, to watch a furious man using a leaf blower to remove a blade of grass off the hood of a $125,000 car while in the alleyway behind him an old man in rags sleeps on a soiled mattress and wonders if he'll live to see tomorrow.

And you, I'm going to call to my passengers, you think you're despicable?

35.

FEH II

Once upon a time, a sensitive young girl lived with her wealthy family. They had a cook and a maid and a nurse and a governess. They were very happy. The girl loved her father very much.

Then, one day, the mobs came. Mobs of people who hated them for being Jews, mobs of people who hated them for being rich, mobs of people who took over her father's store and stole all he had.

The little girl's world was destroyed.

Her father was broken.

Her paradise was gone.

The End

That was the little girl's story. It was a terrible story full of terrible people, a story that forever blackened her sensitive artist's soul. Years later, the girl would write her own stories, stories based on the only story she knew, stories about good, rich men like her father who deserved to be rich, and about bad, poor people like the mob who deserved to be poor, stories about how greed was good and altruism was bad and that all that mattered in this world was the individual and everyone else could go fuck themselves. Everything she ever wrote, from *The Fountainhead* to *Atlas Shrugged*, is the sorrowful wail of a brokenhearted child, a sorrow turned to rage, a rage that points its tear-stained finger at the world and shouts, *Feh*.

36.

In a survey sponsored by the Library of Congress and the Book-of-the-Month Club, Americans named *Atlas Shrugged* the book that had most influenced their lives. It was second only to the Bible.

So, to recap:

In first place: *Feh*.

In second place: *Feh II*.

37.

William James believed that every philosophy is nothing more than a reflection of the philosopher's own temperament. This creates, he wrote, *a certain insincerity in our philosophic discussions: the potentest of all our premises is never mentioned . . . What the system pretends to be is a picture of the great universe of God. What it is — and oh so flagrantly! — is the revelation of how intensely odd the personal flavor of some fellow creature is.*

A century before the Schopenhauer family stopped by the Bagne of Toulon and forever soured Arthur's personal flavor of the world, another philosopher, Blaise Pascal, declared unequivocally that man was wretched. Blaise had his own miseries. His mother died when he was young. He had few friends. He suffered poor health. He was a hunchback. He led a lonely life. And so, unsurprisingly, he declared:

Lust is the source of all our actions.

And:

No religion but [Christianity] has taught that man is born in sin . . . therefore none has spoken the truth.

And:

The more I see of Mankind, the more I prefer my dog.

Pascal's writings were hugely influential. He is quoted to this day. On the plus side, he invented the bus, which we can jump in front of after reading him.

38.

How Paul Rudd Died an
Unimaginably Horrible Death

It was morning and Paul Rudd woke, as he always did, without a care in the world. And why wouldn't Paul Rudd wake so? The world, after all, was Paul Rudd's oyster, there for him to rip in half, dip into lemon garlic sauce, and devour alive. And so Paul Rudd was surprised to find that carefree morning that his bedroom was filled with deadly Bengal tigers.

- It's a good thing I'm Ant-Man! said Paul Rudd as the tigers crept closer. - I'll just transform into a giant and defeat them all!

But Paul Rudd wasn't Ant-Man. Ant-Man was merely a one-dimensional fictional character Paul Rudd portrayed in a cookie-cutter superhero film in the embarrassing last years of the failed American empire. And so, all at once, the Bengal tigers attacked. Normally, of course, Paul Rudd would have died quickly. But alas, these were very special Bengal tigers, which had decided earlier that rather than tearing Paul Rudd to shreds quickly, it would be more fun to slowly torture him over the course of months and years, tortures beyond the imagination, tortures that would make the Grand Inquisitor himself lose his lunch, which, ironically, was oysters with lemon garlic sauce.

The End

Ike had phoned earlier that morning. The podcast about him had been a hit, and there was talk that Apple was going to turn it into a feature film starring Paul Rudd. We both knew that Hollywood involvement meant Ike's license would be revoked, whether it deserved to be or not, and we both knew that I would never be allowed to speak with him again. The man who had tried to show me that I wasn't *feh* had been declared *feh* himself.

The mentor, in storytelling terminology, was dead.

- Did he phone you? I asked Ike.

- Who?

- Paul Rudd! Did Paul fucking Rudd fucking call you? Did Paul fucking Rudd ask for your side of the story? Did Paul fucking Rudd show any curiosity at all beyond how much money they would shove up his prolapsed asshole?

I ranted and raged. I couldn't help but think of Phil, who agonized over his every acting role, who relentlessly examined the morality of the projects he took on, who used his art as a way to expose his pain and reveal his fallibility. And then there was Paul Rudd, who seemed to me to be concerned only with using other people's pain, other people's fallibility, without hesitation, without inquiry, without any concern beyond how it would further his own riches and career. Judging by the final product, I was correct.

Ike assured me that everything was going to be okay. The film wasn't confirmed, he said, but he wanted me to know in case I heard it somewhere else.

- Besides, he joked, of all the people they could get to play me, Paul Rudd isn't so bad.

He was my lifeline, Phil had said to me about his own shrink. *And then, one day, he was just . . . gone.*

I remembered thinking back then:

Better you than me, buddy. Better you than me.

I closed my eyes and prayed to God. It had been a long time. I prayed to Him to kill Paul Rudd and to wipe all of mankind off the face of the earth. *Please, God*, I prayed, *unleash YOUR fury, what the fuck are YOU waiting for, YOU coward, YOU fraud, kill off this hideous species one by miserable, despicable one, until there is not so much as a single man, woman, or child left upon this blighted, shit-stained planet at all.*

For the first three days, the Egyptians couldn't see, but they could move about. For the next three days, the darkness was so heavy that they could not move. Those who stood could not sit; those who sat could not stand.

Darkness fell.

Day Four.

Maybe Five.

Make it Six.

I needed a fucking burrow.

39.

Soon after Phil came out of rehab, we met at a burger place in SoHo. He was talking about art and expression and pain and Arthur Miller. I was in a foul mood.

- Fuck Arthur Miller, I said.
- Fuck Arthur Miller?
- Fuck Arthur fucking Miller.
- Arthur Miller's a genius.
- No, he's not, I said. - He's an asshole. What's genius about shouting that life is unfair and doomed? I know shit stinks; I don't need Arthur fucking Miller to remind me. Dragging me through shit isn't genius; it's lazy, it's easy. You want sad, I can give you sad. Give me a stage at Lincoln Center for two hours, and I'll make you jump off the motherfucking roof. Big fucking deal.

I felt better.

- I think about it, he said after a moment.
- About what?
- Suicide.

I felt worse.

- Yeah, I said. - Me too.

A long moment passed.

- But it's too late, I said.

- For what?

- For us. To kill ourselves.

- Why?

- Because we have kids, I said. - That's the trouble with suicide. You have to do it early, before you have kids. If you kill yourself after you have kids, you're just a fucking asshole. Sorry, brother, but our window for killing ourselves has closed.

- That's true, he said with a smile. - That's why I could never do it.

40.

The Unfortunate Man Who Had a Head

Once upon a time, a man decided to set out into the world to try to make it a better place because he was insane. The first thing he did before setting out into the world was to change his name to Don Quixote. The second thing he did before setting out into the world was to put on a helmet.

Maybe not so insane, then.

...

My burrow was getting crowded. It wasn't much of a burrow, to be fair, just a run-down coffee shop a few blocks from our apartment, but it was the best I could find. It was dark and grim, the coffee bitter, but at least the filth kept the customers away. Lately, though, it had been unseasonably cold and wet for Los Angeles, and my burrow had filled with customers.

- Fifty-one dead, an old man called from behind his newspaper.

I tried to ignore him. He was at the table beside me, an old white man wearing a tan velvet tracksuit and a heavy Rolex watch; his thinning hair was dyed shoe-polish black and slicked back over his head. If he'd never been in a Scorsese mafia movie himself, someone playing him had. Beside him sat an even older man in a wheelchair.

- Forty injured, Old Man added.

- When? asked Older Man. - Here?

- In New Zealand, said Old. - Couple of weeks ago. Christchurch.

- In a church? Older asked.

- In a mosque! Old shouted at the hard-of-hearing Older. - In Christchurch! New Zealand!

- A mosque in a church? Older asked.

- Ach! said Old with an exasperated wave of his hand.

The oldest of the group, meanwhile, sat at the head of the table, dressed in a pristine white suit, a white fedora, a long white beard, and a furious scowl. He looked like the Lubavitcher Rabbi, if the Lubavitcher Rabbi had raided Mark Twain's closet.

- AR-15, Oldest said, shaking his head as he read from his newspaper. - It will happen here tomorrow, don't you worry.

- The shooter was playing music, said Old.

- The shooter was from Munich? Older asked.

- He was playing *music*! Old yelled in his ear. - *Music!* While he was killing people, he was playing music!

Kafka's burrower, at peace in his burrow, soon begins to hear sounds. Annoying, incessant sounds, a *whistling* as the burrower describes it, a *gurgling*.

A whole swarm that has suddenly fallen on my domain, a huge swarm of little creatures.

All at once, the old men's phones began pinging. In frenzied unison, they fished them from their pockets.

- Man with a knife in Culver City, Old read aloud from his phone.

- Police responding, said Oldest, doing the same.

A quick glance over their shoulders revealed that they were all using the same app, an app called Citizen. Citizen, originally named Vigilante, is a mobile app that monitors police and fire rescue communications and informs you of every incident within a specified radius. Every fire, every mugging, every stabbing, every confrontation. A *feh*-stival.

Police activity, 2 miles away.

Vehicle stolen, .5 miles away.

Person assaulted near skate park.

Citizen had launched only recently in Los Angeles, but it was already at the top of the app charts.

- You can't live with your head in the sand, said the app's fans.

- Knowledge is power.

- Forewarned is forearmed.

I imagined the commercial. Paul Rudd addresses the camera.

- Nextdoor can make you think the world is a toilet . . . he says.

Pull back to reveal he's safely barricaded behind the heavily fortified gates of his mansion.

- But Citizen can prove it.

A black man walks by. Rudd's phone dings. He checks it, smiles, gives the camera a thumbs-up.

Logo up.

Citizen. It's Worse Than You Think.

Old shook his head and tutted.

- Hell in a handbasket, he declared. - Hell in a handbasket.

Later that night, Lux climbed into our bed. He was frightened. His teacher had told them about the mosque shooting.

- Fifty-one dead, he said.

- I know, I said.

- Forty injured.

- I know, I said.

Curious, he had gone online to find out more. The news story about the mosque shooting had led him to a news story about a mass shooting in Illinois, which had led him to a news story about a rise in school shootings, which had led him to an infinity of nightmarish YouTube compilation videos of school shootings, mug shots, gunmen, shell-shocked students fleeing their schools, and terrified parents searching for their children.

And click here to subscribe.

I assured him there was nothing to be frightened of. I explained to him that his school was very safe. And I pointed out to him that fifty million children went to public school every day, just like his, and that according to experts, the chance of being involved in a school shooting was less than one in half a billion.

- That's five hundred million, I said. - Okay?

- Okay, he said.

I hugged him.

- Can I sleep in here tonight? he asked.

...

I first met Wolf Blitzer in 2001, in the black, smoke-filled months following the attack on the World Trade Center.

I've been trying to get rid of the bastard ever since.

Orli and I lived on Hudson Street at the time, twenty blocks from Ground Zero. Death was everywhere. Terror had settled on the city like the ashes of the dead. A neighbor told me that he'd come home the evening of the attack to find his apartment window shattered, a seat from one of the doomed planes in his living room. A coworker lost her husband – they had only recently been married – who worked on a high floor of the North Tower.

- War, said Wolf.

I turned up the volume.

- Hate, he added.

I settled in to watch.

- Misery, he continued. - Sorrow. Ruination.

- Of what? I asked.

- Of everything, said Wolf. - Now here's John with the weather.

I couldn't look away. I watched him in the morning with my coffee, I watched him at lunch on my laptop, I watched him at night, on the couch, until I could watch no more and crawled full of hatred and despair to bed.

- Let's go live to Ground Zero, Wolf would say, and I went with him: to Ground Zero, to the White House, to Tora Bora, to Baghdad.

- What a fucking ghoul, said Orli.

- He's a news anchor, hon.

- Look how *excited* he is, she said. - Three thousand people are dead, and it's literally the best thing to ever happen to this fucker's career. Fuck him.

Me, I watched. Even after the rubble was cleared, I watched. Even after the dead were buried, I watched. I couldn't take my eyes off the yellow, all-caps news crawl at the bottom of the screen, which before 9/11 had been used only for emergencies. Now it was there day and night; it never ceased, a shrieking Scheherazade with a thousand and one stories that all ended the same way:

- Devastation, said Wolf.

- When? I asked.

- Now. Collapse.

- Where?

- Everywhere.

- Why are you watching that shit? Orli asked.

I was shocked at her apathy and indifference.

- Because terrorists attacked New York City, I said.

- That was four months ago, she said. - Come to bed.

- We'll be right back, said Wolf, with Donald Rumsfeld.

After Rumsfeld, Cheney.

After Cheney, Rice.

After Rice, suicide.

- Stop watching, Ike said.

- Stop watching? I asked.

I was shocked at his apathy and indifference. Did he have any idea what was going on out there? Did he know how ill-equipped our twenty-first-century military was for a nineteenth-century guerrilla desert war? Did he know that our government had spent billions on the XM2001 Crusader Self-Propelled Howitzer, only to find it was neither mobile nor precise enough for the Afghan geography, an infernal hellscape where even the mighty Soviets were defeated?

- No, he said. - Why do you?

- Because I watch the news, I said with a news junkie's self-satisfaction.

- Why?

- To know the story.

- You know the story, he said. - It's the same story they tell all the time: horror, death, tragedy. What are you waiting to hear?

I couldn't believe I looked to this man for guidance.

- It's just so easy to live with your head in the sand, I said.

I got home, turned on Wolf, poured some gin, and spent the evening watching sickly-green night-cam footage of bombing runs, of buildings exploding, of lives ending. Two martinis and five Special Reports later, I crawled miserably to bed. This is what I thought of me and of you and of all of mankind when I did:

Feh.

...

Esther is an elderly Asian woman possessed of a serenity I will never in this life know, who runs her small acupuncture practice out of her modest home in the Sawtelle neighborhood of Los Angeles. She watched from her front door, hand on her heart, as I limped up the walkway, wincing, stopping now and then to let the pain in my hip subside, a pain I had been suffering for months now, a pain that began deep in my joint and now radiated down my leg, making every step an agony. I had been to internists and specialists, taken X-rays, CAT scans, MRIs, had nerve tests and epidurals, all to no avail. No impact had preceded the pain, and no doctors had been able to relieve it. My Western doctors, eager to be rid of me, suggested I try something Eastern.

Esther was eighty-six and looked forty-five; I was forty-five and felt like I was eighty-six. She helped me up the front steps and led me through the living room, its walls hung with Chinese silk prints, it shelves lined with delicate carvings of the Buddha, to a small, softly lit treatment room at the back of the house. She helped me onto the treatment table and, in her halting English, asked me how I was feeling.

- Did you hear about the shooting? I asked.

She shook her head.

- New Zealand, I said.

- Mm-hmm, she said.

- Fifty-one dead.

She motioned for me to lie down.

- He was playing music, I said.

She dimmed the lights.

- The killer, I said.

- Mm-hmm.

- As he killed them.

- Okay, she said. - No more talk.

She placed a lumbar support beneath my knees and a warm cloth over my eyes. Then she stuck needles in my face.

An hour later, she helped me to the front door.

- Now more peace, she said.

...

- How's the hip? Orli asked when I got home.

She was on the small patio at the rear of our apartment, enjoying the last warm rays of the day's setting sun while sketching in her notebook.

- Lousy, I said.

My phone pinged.

Report of man armed with machete, Citizen notified me. *Two miles away.*

- There's a man with a machete two miles away, I said, reading from my phone. - Maybe he can cut my fucking leg off.

I could see her Early Warning Defense System light up at the introduction of this new app. Her eyes narrowed, her shoulders tensed. I believe I mentioned her Middle Eastern descent. Orli's grip on happiness is as tenuous as mine, but while I often sabotage mine, she defends hers. Violently.

- How do you know that? she asked.

It was bad enough the outside world did all it could to besiege our home with negativity; for me to bring in a new source of misery was tantamount to an inside job.

I told her about Citizen. I told her my infirmity had me feeling weak and vulnerable, and so I had decided to download it. To be safe. To know.

- To know what?

- The stuff, I said. - That's going on.

- What stuff?

- You know, I said. - The bad stuff. Crimes.

My phone dinged. She glared at me.

- And you find that helpful? she asked.

- I can't live with my head in the sand, hon.

- What does it tell you, exactly?

- Lots of things, I said. - What happened, how many are hurt, if the perp has escaped.

- Perp?

- Perpetrator.

My phone pinged.

- Does it tell you the good things? she asked.

- There are good things?

- Does it tell you when someone feeds a homeless woman or when someone falls in love or when someone helps an old man across the street?

My phone pinged.

- So instead of burying your head in the sand and saying life is good, she said, you're burying it in a sewer and saying life is shit.

I asked her if she'd ever read *Don Quixote*. We live, I explained, in a world that requires helmets. I'm not happy about it, Don Quixote wasn't happy about it, Sancho Panza wasn't happy about it. We should, after all, be able to walk around without worrying about getting our heads bashed in. Our non-bashed-in heads should not have to be filled with thoughts of who will be bashing our heads in, or of what we can do to prevent the eventual head-bashing-in. In a better world, yes, we'd have no need for helmets, or Citizen. But this is a helmet world, I said. A Citizen world.

- But aren't most of Don Quixote's fights his own fault? she asked. - Doesn't he go looking for trouble?

I didn't see how that was relevant. She stood and gathered her pens and pencils, her afternoon ruined. By me.

- Fine, she said. - But don't fucking tell me about it. Whatever you hear, I don't want to know.

She turned and went inside.

My phone pinged.

Man with machete still at large, said Citizen. *One mile away.*

He was getting closer.

Things were looking up.

...

A woman at the counter was berating the weary barista.

- This is supposed to be a *caramel* macchiato, she tutted. - I can't even.

This is what her sweatshirt said:

Spiritual Gangsta.

- CO_2, said Old.

- What about it? asked Older.

- It's rising, Old replied.

I stopped not writing and went online. Nextdoor had led to Citizen, Citizen had led to news. Boldly I set out, Quixote-like, into the bleak digital landscape of news, blogs, vlogs, tweets. There on CNN and MSNBC and Fox and *The Huffington Post* was on display all the naked hideousness of mankind — war and violence and hate and fear and revenge and rising CO_2. Suddenly, as if to confirm the awfulness of humanity, a fight erupted at the coffee counter. A homeless man had stolen a sandwich from the cooler. The manager was trying to get him to leave. The man was furious, eyes bulging, the veins on his neck threatening to burst.

- I'm Hot Sauce! he yelled. - You think I can't afford a sandwich? I sold a million records last year! I'm a millionaire, bitch, I'm Hot Sauce!

Hot Sauce pulled out a pair of rusty scissors and threatened to stab him.

Sirens began to wail in the distance.

Pain shot down my leg.

Spiritual Gangsta was the first one out the door.

My phone pinged.

Armed man in coffee shop, said Citizen. *Zero miles away.*

...

The noise can be heard everywhere, Kafka's burrower grieves, *and always at the same strength, and moreover uniformly, both by day and night.*

- Hypersonic nukes, I said to Orli. - Russia has hypersonic nukes.

- What are hypersonic nukes?

- What's the difference? I asked. - They're hypersonic.

- So?

- So? So, we're going to blow ourselves up. We're going to destroy the planet. We're going to commit species suicide.

- Why are you reading that shit? she asked.

- You can't just kill the messenger, hon.

- But it's not just *a* messenger, she argued. - It used to be *a* messenger. One messenger, standing in front of a king. But that was a long time ago. There are thousands of messengers now, millions, the damned messengers never let you alone — news, Twitter, Insta, it never ends. They're swarming all over the house, crawling in through the windows, sliding in under the doors, they're on your phone, on your laptop, there's no escape from the messengers, we're under bloody attack by bloody messengers, so yeah, I MIGHT WANT TO KILL A BLOODY MESSENGER OR TWO!

- We're fucked, I said. - It's Genesis all over again. It's the same old story. We ruin paradise; that's what we do. We're destroyers, ruiners. *We're a virus with shoes.*

- Who said that?

- Bill Hicks. *Cursed is the ground because of you.*

- Bill Hicks? she asked.

- God, I said.

- I preferred it when you were quoting Jeremiah, she said.

...

Esther was concerned. Her treatments weren't helping. My hip was getting worse, despite her needles and vitamins and potions and teas. She asked me to show her my tongue. She asked me if I was sleeping well. She asked me if I was eating healthy foods — vegetables, fruits, protein. I told her that a container ship sank near France and spilled five million pounds of hazardous material into the bay.

- Mm-hmm, she said.

- Chemical weapons.

- What about them?

- Assad's using them, I said.

- Who?

- Assad, I said. - In Syria.

She motioned for me to lie back.

- Okay, she said. - No more talk.

She placed a lumbar support beneath my knees and a warm cloth over my eyes.

- Mustard gas, I said as she did. - On his own people.

Esther had had enough. She pulled the cloth from my eyes and shook an angry finger in my face.

- You eat bad with your eyes! she said.

- I what?

- You eat bad with your eyes!

- With my eyes?

- Yes.

- I eat bad with my *eyes*?

She was annoyed. Many of her clients, she explained, are so careful with what they eat: They don't eat meat, they don't eat bread, they don't eat sugar.

- But what do they eat with their *eyes*? she asked. - Filling their eyes all day with garbage, with poison. With their phones, with news. They won't eat meat, they won't eat milk, but they eat garbage with their eyes!

She clamped her hands over her ears and squeezed her eyes shut.

- From now on, she said, all poison out!

Later that night, Lux climbed into our bed. He was frightened. His science teacher had been teaching them about global warming. That afternoon, after school, he had gone online to find out more, where he watched terrifying You-Tube videos about rising sea levels. The terrifying rising sea level videos led to terrifying algorithmic recommendations for terrifying earthquake videos. The terrifying earthquake videos led to terrifying algorithmic recommendations of terrifying tsunami videos.

- They're happening more, said Lux. - Tsunamis. Because of climate change. Because of us. Because we ruined the ocean.

Cursed is the ground because of you, said Wolf. *Now here's Tom with sports.*

I felt a sudden fury boiling inside me — at YouTube, at Wolf, at Arianna and

Twitter and Facebook. Because it wasn't just that my child was eating bad with his eyes, it was that he was being *fed* this poison for the sake of profit, of clicks, of money. It used to be scowling bearded men who told that story. It used to be miserable men of God, miserable philosophers, miserable writers. These days, though, everyone told it, a million times a day. I held him close and explained to him that while climate change was a genuine issue, tsunamis were very rare. I told him the odds of being killed in a tsunami were 1 in 500,000. I assured him that scientists say they are so rare, in fact, that it's difficult to estimate just how low the chances are of experiencing one.

- Okay? I asked.

- Okay, he said.

But it was too late.

The story had been told.

- Can I sleep in here tonight? he asked.

...

- Chemical weapons, Old announced from behind his newspaper. - In the ocean.

- In your colon? Older asked.

- In the *ocean*, Old shouted. - There are chemical weapons in the *ocean*.

D'Fuck You Looking At was sitting at a table in the back, his right eye black and swollen. He'd been in a fight. A blonde woman in white trackpants and a matching white hoodie got her coffee, sat down beside D'Fuck You Looking At, noticed him, then got up and moved to a table across the way. This is what it said in large black letters on the side of her pants:

Empathy.

- How did chemical weapons get in the ocean? Older demanded.

- They buried them, Old said. - To get rid of them. Now they're leaking, killing everything.

- It'll be in the air soon, said Oldest. - Soon we'll be breathing it.

- All we do is destroy, said Older.

This time, though, I was prepared. I had decided to take Esther's advice, to go on an information diet, to fight tech with tech. The evening before I had installed Simple Blocker on my laptop, an extension that I set to block all news and social media. I downloaded Freedom, which restricted my internet access. And on my phone, I installed Coffitivity, an app that was both brilliantly simple and terribly sad: Coffitivity provides the sounds of a coffee shop – mugs clinking, milk steaming, people talking – the critical feature being that the conversations of the people in the Coffitivity coffee shop are muted to such a degree that they are impossible to discern.

They should have called it Burrow.

And so, reader, this was where I found myself in the suffocating years of the information-blighted twenty-first century, relentlessly pursued by Nextdoor and Citizen and Wolf and Arianna and Drudge and Sean: sitting in a real coffee shop, trying to write fake stories, while listening to the sounds of a fake coffee shop, in a desperate attempt to keep from going mad from the terrible stories being told at the table beside me.

And it worked.

In my fake coffee shop, I heard nothing.

I began to write.

I began to smile.

A moment later I looked up to find Hot Sauce, inches from my face, livid, shouting at me, eyes bulging. I took off my headphones.

- You think I'm gonna steal from you, motherfucker? he roared. - I'm Hot Sauce!

I had no idea what he was talking about or why he was talking to me.

Empathy headed for the door. Her fear only encouraged Hot Sauce, who turned to the café and warned everyone that he would be back in five minutes with his gun.

- I'll kill all you motherfuckers, he shouted. - *Pow, po-pow!*

He kicked the door open and left, miming shooting me as he went.

Old and Oldest made their way to the door, pushing Older's wheelchair before them. I thought they were overreacting, but when D'Fuck You Looking At got up to leave, I figured I should too.

Ultimately, Kafka's burrower fails. The noises continue to torment him. No matter what he does, he can find no peace.

I shake my head, he writes. *I have not yet found any solution.*

The story is unfinished, as if Kafka himself could find no escape from the noise.

I set out the next morning to find a new burrow, a burrow to end all burrows, but the pain in my hip had intensified overnight, and I couldn't limp more than twenty feet without having to stop and wait for it to subside. On one such stop, I spotted a homeless man being led out of a nondescript building I hadn't noticed before, a simple cinder-block structure with a glass door at the front. It isn't unusual to see the homeless being led out of one doorway or another, angry shop owners or homeowners beside them shouting for the police, but this interaction was different. The man leading him out was an older man with a trim silver beard; there was no yelling or pushing or cursing. They stood together on the sidewalk a moment, laughing and chatting like old friends, until the bearded man handed the homeless man a hot cup of coffee and a small pastry bag, patted him on the back, and wished him good luck before heading back inside.

Curious, I crossed the street and entered the building, only to find a coffee shop there, this one light-filled, warm, and welcoming, the thrift-store couches and long wooden farm tables and mismatched secondhand chairs lending it a casual, informal air. Here and there about the bright and sunny space, people sat with their laptops, working quietly, greeting each other pleasantly. Nobody was reading news stories aloud, nobody was threatening to shoot the customers.

What is this place? I wondered.

The bearded man, behind the counter now, welcomed me warmly. I ordered a coffee.

- How much? I asked.

- There are no prices, he said.

- No prices? I asked.

- No prices, he said. - You pay what you want.

- I pay what I want?

- You pay what you want.

- I don't think you get how this whole capitalism thing works, I said.

He smiled, introduced himself as Steve, and asked me how much I would like to pay.

- What do people usually pay? I asked.

- Anywhere between three and five, he said. - But it's up to you.

I gave him ten because I'm Jewish and I don't want people to say we're cheap. I sat down at one of the farm tables and took out my laptop. As I did, a destitute homeless man walked in, muttering to himself, dragging his no-wheels wheelie suitcase behind him with one hand, holding his pants up with the other. His lower leg was wrapped in dirty bandages; a doctor had seen to it, but that had been some time ago.

- Hello, Steve said to him, as warmly as he'd just welcomed me. - How's it going today?

The man stopped, wary. He didn't want any trouble.

- Good, he mumbled as he began to make his way back out.

- Are you hungry? Steve asked.

The man eyed Steve suspiciously. He nodded. He was hungry. Steve came out from behind the counter, led the man to a nearby couch, and returned a moment later with a coffee and pastry. The man mumbled his thanks, wrapped the pastry in its wax paper for later, and stuffed it in his torn coat pocket as if someone might steal it if he didn't. Steve sat down beside him, asked him his name, asked him where he was living, asked him where he was from and how long he had been in town. The man began to relax. He sipped his coffee. Steve gave him the name of a nearby help organization, the address of the local shelter, and guided him to an urgent care facility up the road where he could have his leg looked at. The man thanked him and stood to go. Steve walked him outside, where they chatted a few moments more before the man limped off in the direction of the urgent care center.

What is this place? I wondered.

- I think I found a burrow, I said to Orli that evening.

- A what?

- A place to write.

- A coffee shop?

- I have no idea.

I returned the next day and the day after that. One morning the door swung open and D'Fuck You Looking At walked in.

- D'FUCK YOU LOOKING AT? he shouted at the room.

I expected everyone to head for the door, for Steve to phone the police. But the people in the café took only minor notice of him. Steve came out from behind the counter and approached him.

- I'm sorry, he said firmly, but you're going to have to leave.

- I just want a fuckin' coffee! D'Fuck said. - I have money!

- Not now, said Steve. - Come back later, and if you can control yourself, you can have it then. We're open until three.

D'Fuck's entire demeanor changed. His fists relaxed; his shoulder dropped. He appeared contrite, regretful.

- I'm sorry, he said, really. I'll be cool.

Steve shook his head and showed him to the door.

- Come back when you're feeling better, he said without a hint of judgment. - We'll see you then.

- Okay, said D'Fuck, and he turned and left.

What is this place? I wondered.

Once D'Fuck had gone, Steve turned to face the café, raised his hands, and asked for everyone's attention. In a loud voice, he thanked everyone for their patronage and announced that together they had raised enough money for five hundred meals for the community's elderly and homeless.

- We couldn't have done it without you, he said.

Everyone cheered.

I could no longer contain my curiosity. As Steve passed by, I stopped him. I told him I had been watching him the past few days with the customers, observing him with the homeless, and that I had been moved, heartened even. He was happy to hear it.

- So, I asked, what is this place?

- It's a church, said Steve.

I waited for him to laugh.

He didn't.

- I'm the pastor, he said.

- Fuck, I said.

And then Steve laughed — a loud, head-back, full-throated laugh. It wasn't quite Orli's laugh, or even Phil's. But it was pretty damned good.

41.

As I write this book, Andrew Frame, the founder of the app Citizen, is worth a quarter of a billion dollars. Nextdoor is valued at two billion dollars. Sean Hannity, Wolf Blitzer, Arianna Huffington, and Bill O'Reilly are all multi-millionaires.

It is the best of times for people telling us it is the worst of times.

42

THE MAN WHO GAVE A FUCK

Once upon a time, there was a man who cared. He cared about the poor and the destitute. He cared about the weak and the sick. He didn't like the way they were being treated by the powerful and the wealthy, how they were maligned by the government, cheated by politicians, and manipulated by clergy.

- Stop treating people poorly, the man said to the powerful. - Stop lying. Stop cheating. Stop with the money.

He was a shit-stirrer.

- Fuck you, said the powerful.

This was in the time before infinity pools, so they nailed his skinny ass to a cross.

The End

- The Lord is my shepherd, Steve said to me.

Steve had a very different story from mine. In Steve's story, God was good.

\- You do know what shepherds do to their sheep, right? I replied. - They slaughter them. They literally lead them to slaughter.

Over the next few weeks, we sat in his church/café and spoke for many hours. Suspicious at first of his motives, I made it clear that I wasn't looking to find God, I was just looking for a burrow. If anything, I was looking to re-write God. I wasn't an atheist, I explained – the idea that there was no God was a bit optimistic for me. I was a misotheist; there is a God, and He's an asshole.

\- I can understand that, he said.

Steve volunteered as chaplain at a nearby hospital, offering solace to the dying, and had seen enough pain and suffering to understand my position.

When Voltaire was dying, I told him, a priest came to offer him the last rites.

\- Will you now renounce the devil? the priest asked the dying philosopher.

\- This is no time to be making enemies, said Voltaire.

Steve laughed.

Orli came by, met Steve, met his family. She was happy to see me writing. We began to refer to the coffee shop as Scarbucks, since so many there were scarred and damaged in such heartbreaking ways. Steve helped them, fed them, spoke with them, rehabilitated them. Some of his employees had lived on the street themselves; some were recovering addicts; some had cuts up and down their arms from their days of self-harm. The regular customers came in, joked with Steve, and settled into their seats. Strangers strolled in, expressed wonder at the pricing system, and chatted with employees about the different coffee bean origins. And when the homeless came in, Steve went to them. Some had nothing; some insisted on paying with whatever spare change they had. Often, if they had nothing, other customers paid for them. Being there made me feel something I'd never felt before. Pot made me leave myself, gin made me forget myself, and GHB made me like myself. But this place made me like mankind. It made me proud to be human.

It was weird.

Don Quixote was fifty years old when stories finally drove him mad. I was approaching fifty and began to wonder as I sat there if I had been driven mad by stories too – stories from the Bible, stories from history, stories from philosophers, stories on social media, stories on news sites, so many stories, all the same, all named *Feh*. Perhaps the late comedian Bill Hicks, a hero of mine in my youth, had been mistaken. Perhaps we humans aren't the virus. Perhaps the virus is the story that tells us we are.

- Do you know what the word *feh* means? I asked Steve one afternoon.

- *Feh?*

- *Feh.*

It was a Yiddish word, I explained, used to convey disgust and disapproval. It was also the name of the story I had been told ever since I was a child. It was what God said about us, about humankind; and ever since, humankind has agreed. I wondered, knowing what damage that story had done to me, what damage that story might be doing to others. Steve nodded. In all his years doing community outreach, he said, he'd never met a single man or woman who didn't come from an abusive family. Sometimes the abuse was sexual, sometimes violent, always emotional. Everyone's story was different, but everyone had been told by someone they needed, by someone they loved or respected, that they were *feh*.

Steve was from Oklahoma. His father had been a literature professor. Out of college, Steve began working in finance. He did well – bought a house, a BMW, flashy clothes – until a brush with death caused him to begin questioning it all. He moved to California, where he began working with impoverished Hispanic children in El Monte. He studied Christianity and decided to become ordained. The Jesus he admires is the Shit-Stirrer Jesus, the Jesus calling out the religious leaders, the Jesus knocking over tables at the Temple.

- Stop treating people poorly, Steve once said at a large Christian convention at which he'd been invited to speak. - Stop hating. Stop cheating. Stop with the money and the power.

Steve isn't invited to Christian conventions anymore.

Scarbucks became my regular coffee shop. Every week, twice a week, Steve held feedings for the local homeless and elderly. They had a weekly art therapy group in the garden, just for the indigent; and every November they organized a Thanksgiving dinner where they handed out hundreds of turkey dinners to the needy. Inspired by Steve's own generosity of spirit, I began reaching out to the homeless sitting beside me, buying them lunch or coffee when they seemed without. One of the regular customers was an elderly African American man, blind, always sharply dressed in a suit and tie regardless of how hot it was outside, who held a cane with one hand and mopped his brow with a silk handkerchief with the other. Every day, having finished his coffee, he would stand, unmoving, waiting for Steve or one of his staff to help guide him outside. One morning Steve was busy with a line of customers when the man stood, and so I went to him and offered him my arm. I led him out to the sidewalk, where his daughter was coming to meet him to drive him home. As we waited, he told me that he was ninety-two years old. Ten years earlier, crossing Wilshire Boulevard, he had been struck by a car. He fell, hit his head on the curb, and went into a coma. When he woke from it, days later, he was blind. At first, he refused to believe it, to accept it. Eventually, though, he did.

- The good thing about being blind, he said, is that you have to rely on the kindness of strangers.

- That's a good thing? I asked. - In Los Angeles?

- Oh yes, he said. - Until I was blind, I didn't know just how many people *were* kind.

My cynical comment felt ugly, easy. Blind.

- If you hadn't helped me, he said, someone else would have soon enough.

- So wait, I don't get credit for this? I asked.

He laughed, a joyful laugh, his shoulders hopping as he *kee-kee-kee*d into his free hand.

The café was a small oasis of kindness in what seemed a cruel city in a cruel nation in a cruel time, a time of growing hatred and brutal judgment. I found it peaceful and inspiring, and I was glad to have discovered it. And so, knowing God as I do, it didn't surprise me when I arrived one morning a few weeks later to find a notice on the front door:

Closed, it read, *due to pandemic.*

We'll be back with more hilarious Auslander *after these messages.*

COVID-19 had arrived.

And behold, the world and all that was in it turned to darkness.

43

- You're going to get us sent to Hell, says Elijah.

- Nobody's getting sent to Hell, says Gabriel. - Just listen to me.

They are at the bar again, huddled together, whispering.

- I *did* listen to you, says Elijah. - You said God is wrong.

- I said the story is wrong.

- What story?

- The Bible story.

- How is it wrong?

- Let me ask you a question, says Gabriel. - Whose story is it?

- Whose story?

- Yeah, says Gabriel. - Who's the protagonist?

- Of the Bible?

- Of the Bible. Who's the hero, the one we like, the one we admire, the one we want to be like? Because it isn't mankind.

- No, says Elijah, mankind sucks. So who's the hero?

- Well, Gabriel says, look at the story. In most stories, the protagonist is the first character we meet. In the Bible, that's God. Genesis 1:1. *In the beginning, God.* Our hero. And we like God. He's powerful, successful, loves nature, appreciates beauty. He is sensitive, creative, something of an artist. He doesn't just save a cat, as Hollywood executives demand heroes do, He creates one.

- So, God's the protagonist, so what?

- So then what happens?

- I don't know, says Elijah. - He creates Man?

- Exactly, says Gabriel. - Man. The antagonist. Genesis 1:27. Man comes in, steals God's apples, and God kicks him out. Man kills, Man rapes, Man prays to golden calves. God good, Man bad.

- Okay.

- No, says Gabriel. - Not okay.

- Why not? asks Elijah. - Man *is* bad.

- Sure, says Gabriel, that's the story. We all know the story. But who *told* us the story?

- Who?

- Yeah, who?

- Moses.

- Nope.

- Moses wrote the book, Gabe, I was there.

- Moses wrote it, yes, but who *told* it to him?

- God.

- Exactly. God. It's *God's* story.

- I know it's God's story, Gabe; it's the fucking Bible. So?

- So, it's akin to the story of the Three Little Pigs being told by the wolf. Once upon a time, there was this flawless wolf, perfect in every way, who lived in a beautiful forest. *In the beginning, Wolf.* Then, one day, some asshole pigs come in and start building houses. They're jackhammering, clear-cutting, ruining everything. No notice, no permits, nothing. *Fuck this*, says the wolf. *I will not contend with pigs forever.*

- So, he blows their houses down, says Elijah.

- So, he blows their houses down. *The End.*

- And?

- And we cheer.

- Right, says Elijah. - Fuck those pigs.

- Right. But that's the *wolf's* story.

Elijah considers this a moment.

- That's true, he says.

- But the pigs, says Gabriel, they tell a different story. For the pigs, the wolf is the antagonist. The wolf is cruel, angry, violent. And I don't want to take sides, but I think we can agree that, objectively speaking, the pigs are the weak and helpless ones here. The wolf's the asshole.

- So, what are you saying? asks Elijah.

Gabriel leans forward, lowers his voice.

- I'm saying, he says, that God's the wolf.

- God is the wolf?

- God, says Gabriel, is the asshole. God is the bad guy.

He stands, tosses some cash on the bar, and turns around, only to find God standing behind him. Furious. Seething. He's heard it all.

- H-hey, God! Gabriel stammers. - Buy you a round?

God grabs him by his neck.

- Go to Hell, says God.

44.

THREE BURROWS

Burrow One

And Moses stretched forth his hand toward Heaven; and there was a thick darkness in all the land of Egypt.

- What kind of darkness was it? Rabbi Scold asked.

- The darkness of Hell, said Rabbi Scold. - And the Egyptians grew frightened, and angry, and each turned on his neighbor and killed him.

- Yay, we cheered.

. . .

COVID-19 cases reached twenty thousand. People began buying surgical masks in bulk to sell at hyperinflated prices. On Amazon, a hundred pack of masks, which originally went for eight dollars, was going for over two hundred dollars.

This is what it said on the window of our local pharmacy where the masks were sold out:

We're in this together.

...

Here's how you know the prophets of the Holy Bible were full of shit:

They never mentioned the toilet paper fights.

In all the thousands of words they composed about the inhumanity of end-times, about the horrors of the apocalypse, in all their foreseeing this and foretelling that, with all their lakes of fire and rivers of blood and lambs hanging out with lions, they never once mentioned that at the end of the world, human beings, created in God's image, would stand around in Target department stores fighting over toilet paper.

I call bullshit.

If they had been *actual* prophets, if they had *actually* been able to see ahead to March 2020, then they would have seen us fighting over twelve-packs of two-ply lavender-scented double-quilted toilet paper, and if they *had* foreseen us fighting over two-ply lavender-scented double-quilted toilet paper, over Charmin Ultra Strong and Angel Soft with Fresh Scented Tubes, there's no *way* they wouldn't have put that in their sermons, there's no *way* they wouldn't have mentioned that in their books, because that right there, in aisle 8, is the *summa summarum* of humanity: two strangers fighting over toilet paper in the ransacked paper goods aisle of a Target department store.

- That's mine! the woman shouted at me, pointing at the twelve-pack of Cottonelle Ultra Comfort toilet paper in my hands.

This is what her T-shirt said:

Fun Gal.

Fungal.

- How is it yours? I demanded.

- I saw it first!

- I'm literally holding it, I said. - In my hands.

COVID cases had reached forty thousand. The schools had closed. The cafés had closed. The parks had closed.

- Fucking Chinese, said the Republicans.

- Fucking racists, said the Democrats.

- Fucking white people, said black people.

- Fucking black people, said white people.

- Fucking city folk, said rural people.

- Fucking rednecks, said city people.

Mankind would not contend with mankind any longer.

- I saw it first! she shouted.

- So?

- So, it's mine!

- I saw a Porsche outside, I said. - That doesn't make it mine.

She became utterly incensed. She began shouting, calling me a misogynist, a shithead, and a privileged white person.

Note: She was white.

I didn't know how long it had been since she wiped herself, but it must have been a while.

- You know what? I said, hurling the package at her feet. - Take it. You're way more full of shit than I am.

She picked up the toilet paper, called me a faggot, and walked away. A Target employee, witnessing the confrontation, came over, shaking his head.

- People are going nuts, he said.

- Tell me about it, I said.

- You looking for toilet paper? he asked.

He led me down the aisle to the back of the store, to a door marked *Employees Only*.

- Wait here, he said.

As I did, a woman in a red Trump hat began arguing with a young man in a black Supreme T-shirt who had told her to put on a mask. She was shouting that COVID was a hoax, that her rights were being violated.

- Read the Constitution! she shouted in his face.

The Pomeranian in her arms looked at me and whimpered.

Kill me, it begged.

The stockroom door opened, and the employee allowed me a glimpse of the pristine six-pack of Charmin Ultra Strong in his arms.

- Great, I said, reaching for it before someone else could grab it. - Thanks so much.

He pulled the package away.

- Fifty, he said.

- Fifty?

- Dollars.

- Fifty dollars? I asked. - For toilet paper?

- You want it? he said. - Fifty dollars.

What if I find ten good people? Abraham asked.

You won't, said God.

- Fuck off, I said.

- Suit yourself, he said.

The man in the Supreme T-shirt stepped up beside me.

- I'll give you sixty, he said to the employee.

- Seventy, said the woman in the Trump hat.

- Republican scum, said Supreme T-shirt.

- Snowflake, said Trump Hat.

A land of deepest gloom, said Job. *All gloom and disarray, whose light is like darkness.*

This was the sign in the store window as I left:

We're All in This Together.

...

The streets were deserted. Not even the kettlebellers were out. The only people I saw were the homeless, already sick, already dying, who pushed their three-wheeled shopping carts and rusty wheelchairs down the middle of the now-empty roadways, shouting at no one. In the doorways of the closed shops whose owners once chased them away, they set up camp – tents, boxes, shopping carts, sleeping bags.

- They're like the rats in the park, someone on Nextdoor said of the homeless. - There's no one on the streets left to feed them.

- LOL, said someone else.

...

Job's wife tried to hold her family together. She took a job as a water carrier. When her boss found out who her husband was, he fired her. Then, to keep them from starving, she cut off her hair and bought bread with it.

- I'm sorry, I said to Orli.

- For what?

COVID had destroyed any chance of my earning money. Hollywood, theater, publishing, advertising – all had gone dark. I considered driving for Uber, but the pandemic had frightened passengers away, and many current drivers were looking for other jobs themselves. Orli had been temping in offices around town before they started closing down; fortunately, in the days just before everything shut down completely, she landed a remote job for a company based in New York City. Her salary was just enough for us to cover our bills, but she was working twelve-hour days, chained to her desk in the makeshift office we set up in the kitchen between the trash bin and the dog crate. Her art supplies were in a drawer, waiting for me to stop failing.

I had never felt more *feh* in my life. About myself, about mankind. Orli assured me it was just a change of roles; when we were younger, she said, I had earned money while she took care of the house and family, and now she earned the money while I took care of the house and family. But her words had no effect.

- I should have, I said.

- Should have what? she asked.

I should have stayed in advertising. I should have gone after the money. I should have climbed the corporate ladder. I should have gone to the Iowa Writers' Workshop. I should have stayed in Edgar's workshop. I should have written books about boy wizards and killer clowns. I should have saved Phil. I should have known he was on heroin. I should have saved Ike. I should have killed Paul Rudd. I should have stayed in New York. I should have gone to college. I should have gone into finance. I should have stayed on God's good side. I should have kissed His ass. I should have prayed. I should have repented. I should have fasted on Yom Kippur. I should have bought Apple stock in the nineties. I should have bought America Online stock before it split. I should have saved more money. I should have stuck to a budget. I should have embraced social media and maximized my brand. I should have tweeted. I should have amassed thousands of followers. I should have posted positive reviews of my own books on Amazon. I should have played the game. I should have networked. I should have been on LinkedIn. I should have lied. I should have cheated. I should have made slime. I should have been a slime influencer. I should have gone to film school. I should have ordered less from Amazon. I should have saved more for a rainy day. I should have been nicer to people on my way up. I should have laughed at my boss's lame jokes. I should have been a lawyer. I should have been a doctor. I should have known this was going to happen. I should have seen this coming. I should have been more practical. I should have been more responsible. I should have taken the road more traveled. I should have been less arrogant. I should have been less stubborn. I should have worked on Wall Street. I should have gone into real estate. I should have been a ruthless capitalist. I should have been a heartless corporate raider. I should have struck when the iron was hot. I should have made hay while the sun shined. I should have been a go-getter. I should have kept my nose to the grindstone. I should have read more Seth Godin. I should have read more Timothy Ferriss. I should have leaned in. I should have made friends with people in high places. I should have focused on my résumé. I should have learned a trade.

I should have flipped that goddamned truck over that goddamned cliff.

I should have fried my pancreas.

I should have killed myself when I had the chance.

- I should have drank more poison, I said.

...

Flyers began to appear around town, bearing a fake seal of the World Health Organization, telling residents to avoid Asian American businesses because of the corona outbreak. Wolf Blitzer told me that an Asian middle-schooler had been assaulted by students claiming he had COVID.

- Why are you watching the news? Ike had asked me during my post-9/11 news binge.

- I'm looking.

- For what?

- Hope.

- But they don't sell hope, Ike said. - They sell fear. You're in the wrong store.

Now, in my darkness, I was looking again. I scoured the web for news sites, science sites, anything I could find that might indicate this nightmare was going to end.

- The bodies are piling up, said Wolf Blitzer.

And:

- The virus is mutating.

And:

- COVID cases have passed ninety thousand.

Orli went on the emotional defensive; her homeland under attack by news of the terrible and the awful, she fought back with news of the uplifting and the hopeful. She was full of shit and we both knew it, but the boys didn't. She told them about New Yorkers cheering from their balconies every night in honor of health-care workers. She told them about the people around the world sewing face masks to help with the shortage. She told them about the five-star hotels providing free rooms for hospital workers. But behind her every ray of sunshine, I pointed out a storm cloud.

- They don't need cheering, I said of the NYC health-care workers. - They need better pay.

Of the people providing masks:

- The fucking government should be taking care of that.

- Probably just a write-off, I said of the hotels. - They're empty anyway.

- What are you doing? Orli demanded once the boys had left the table.

- What are *you* doing?

- I'm trying to cheer them up.

- It's fucking desperate.

- Of course it's fucking desperate, she said. - There's a pandemic going on! That's what you do in the darkness, you look for light!

But Fehs only see the *feh*. We know how to find flaws, to deride, to criticize, to knock down – ourselves and others. But when real *feh* comes, when darkness so dark you can touch it settles upon the land and the only way to survive it is to find some light – that we have never been taught to do.

Said Rabbi Scold:

- The Egyptians, stricken with the plague of darkness, went and stood beside the Israelites to share in their light. But even beside those standing in light, the Egyptians could not see.

Said Wolf:

- There is no treatment.

And:

- Any vaccine is at least a year away.

And:

- You can contract COVID through your eyes.

- Through my eyes? I asked.

- Through your eyes, said Wolf.

- Come to bed, said Orli.

- We'll be right back, said Wolf, with Doctor Fauci.

...

I needed a burrow, a hole, a grave. I needed somewhere to go, to hide, to not see Orli on her tenth straight hour of Zoom meetings, to not see the boys in their eighth straight hour of Zoom classes, bored and lonely and pale.

And for them not to see me.

I set up a makeshift office in the subterranean garage below our apartment. A flickering fluorescent overhead, a plastic chair on the uneven concrete floor, a small folding table between the hot water heater and the car. I brought down my laptop, a coffee maker, some pens, a bottle of gin, and a pack of cigarettes.

Burrow One.

I drank gin.

I smoked cigarettes.

I wrote nothing.

Twenty feet away from where I sat, in the trash-strewn alley behind the apartment, homeless people fought over food and clothes they pulled from the dumpsters. A woman in a nearby apartment shouted at them from her window. They shouted back.

I drank more gin.

I smoked more cigarettes.

I wrote more nothing.

...

- Anything funny? I asked the bookseller.

He was reading a book called *The Uninhabitable Earth: Life After Warming*.

- No, he said without looking up.

I picked up the shelf copy. These were the reviews:

Remorseless.

Near unbearable.

Read it and weep.

Horrifying.

It was a bestseller.

I roamed the aisles. Had books always been so miserable? I wondered. Is this why nobody reads anymore? Every book on the New Releases table was the same: *You Suck. You Suck Because You're Male, You Suck Because You're Liberal, You Suck Because You're Conservative, You Suck Because You're a Racist, You Suck Because You Don't Think You're a Racist, You Suck Because You Think Other People Are Racists, You Suck Because You Don't Care About the Planet, You Suck Because You Care Too Much About the Planet, You Suck Because of Your Past, You Suck Because of Our Future.* I settled for a book called *Sapiens: A Brief History of Humanity,* by a man named Yuval Noah Harari.

Bill Gates, on the cover, said it was fun.

That's how utterly desperate the situation was.

I was looking to Bill Gates for ideas about fun.

- Anything else? the bookseller asked.

- Got any nooses? I asked.

- Sold out, he said without looking up.

...

Chapter One, Harari begins, *An Animal of No Significance.*

That'd be us then.

Humans.

If you're waiting for it to pick up, don't. It's downhill from there. We are cruel and dangerous, Harari writes. We are an ecological disaster. We are a terrestrial menace. Harari was as disgusted with mankind as Yahweh was.

314 | SHALOM AUSLANDER

- *Feh*, said Yuval Noah Harari.

It was a bestseller.

…

Wolf Blitzer showed me a video of people in a Walmart fighting over diapers. Some people began to suggest that COVID was a deliberate attack on the West. They said it was biological warfare instigated by the Chinese. This is what the president of the United States said:

- Kung flu.
- Yay, cheered his supporters.

Maybe, I thought, Harari had a point.

…

Orli could smell the cigarettes and gin on my breath.

- Are you smoking? she asked.
- No.
- Are you drinking?
- No.

She glared at me.

- Second cases of pancreatitis, she said, don't always respond to treatment.

I was counting on it.

…

Rumors began to circulate on Nextdoor that the city would be closing the schools for the rest of the semester, not to reopen until the following school year. The boys were devastated. They had just established friendships in their new California schools, and now they were isolated, again, and worried that their fragile new friendships would wither by the time school reopened. I assured them that everything would be okay and that we would get through this together. In the mornings I put on cheerful music, scrambled them eggs, fried them bacon, and poured them juice.

- Love you, Dad, they said.

Idiots.

Then I took my laptop and a cup of coffee down to my burrow, locked the door, smoked the cigarettes, and drank the gin.

- This lockdown, said an overcaffeinated YouTuber with a fake tan and even lower self-esteem than my own, is a great time to focus on your glutes and abs.

I decided to work out.

It would be good for me.

It would change my mood.

I did three burpees, had a cigarette, went upstairs, and pretended to be surviving.

- You have to take care of yourself, I said to Orli, before sneaking off to the bathroom to take a hit of pot.

- You have to keep your spirits up, I said to Paix, hoping he didn't smell the booze on my breath.

- You can't give up on your schoolwork, I said to Lux, having given up on everything.

At some point in the burrow, I started a new story:

VICTORIA'S SECRET IS SAFE WITH ME

Eleanor, a troubled young woman seeking a cure for various self-destructive habits, travels to a remote hilltop retreat run by the enigmatic Doctor Limburger, an eccentric man with a devoted following. Many of the guests have been there for years. Eleanor is skeptical, expecting to be told, as she has been told by so many gurus before, to love herself.

But Limburger tells her something different. Her problem, he claims, is not that she is self-loathing but that she is not self-loathing enough. She hates herself because she thinks she should love herself. But why? Why should anyone? We're awful, he tells her, and he takes Eleanor's hand in his and tells her a secret. Victoria's secret.

- Victoria's Secret? she asks.

- Victoria's secret is this, he said. - We're disgusting. Every one of us. That's Victoria's secret. We're vile. We're hideous. We're repulsive. Sweat, skin, pores, shit, piss, earwax, fingernails, eye crud, nose crud, pus, snot, semen, blood. And that's just the human body; the human mind is even worse. That's why we have thongs and panties, silk and lace, pushup bras, strapless bras, demi bras, sports bras. Victoria's Secret doesn't sell lingerie; they sell lies, lies we can bring home in a bright pink bag, lies we can cloak ourselves in to pretend we aren't repulsive.

- But these lies lead to pain, Doctor Limburger continues, and the truth will set you free. And the truth is, Eleanor, we suck.

Harari would love it, I thought.

Orli did not.

- He sounds like God, she said of Limburger.

It wasn't a compliment.

Fake websites appeared online, purporting to sell medical supplies that were sold out in stores. Email scams featured fake CDC doctors who, in exchange for Bitcoin, would tell you the secrets to surviving COVID. Spammers collected funds for COVID victims, which they then kept for themselves.

Maybe, I thought, God had a point.

Burrow Two

Park Closed Due to COVID.

Uh-oh, I thought.

The stabbing pain in my bowels was intensifying, and I was on a walk, far from home. Orli demanded that I go for walks, that I get out of the dark garage, that I get into the light. That I try.

- Are you giving up? she had asked.

- On what?

- On yourself, she asked, weary, disgusted, disappointed. - On us, on life? I can accept being down, I can accept being depressed. But I can't accept giving up.

The walk was meant to prove to her that I hadn't. But a lockdown is no time for an IBSer to be far from home.

I have suffered, since late adolescence, with crippling IBS (irritable bowel syndrome), no doubt a punishment for eating *treyf* (Yiddish for *nonkosher*). Nature calls for everyone now and then, but for me it calls a dozen times a day. IBS is Schopenhauer's Will made manifest; it is neither concept nor metaphor; it is actual, physical, and resides within my obstreperous bowels, *The World as Will and Defecation*. For me and other sufferers of this grievous affliction, the upside to nuclear holocaust is how easy it will be afterward to find a vacant public restroom. With the rest of mankind wiped out, there will be no waiting outside locked and occupied bathrooms, as we sufferers do a dozen times a day, writhing, grimacing, wondering if this is the day we finally shit ourselves in public. I have long envied early man, *Homo crappus*, hurrying doubled over across the plains of Africa, every thicket an opportunity for alleviation. Hurrying, of course, is the key word here; there is no negotiating with this colonic terrorist. My bowels wait for no one. But when the restaurants and stores shut down for COVID, their bathrooms shut down with them. Every outing, no matter how brief, was now a terrifying journey into the excretory unknown, like swimming out into the open ocean uncertain you'll make it back to shore. I thought the park would be a safe haven, but large public gatherings had been prohibited, and the parks – and thus the park bathrooms – were locked tight.

This is it, I thought as the pressure built in my bowels. *This is the day I shit myself in public.*

I seethed. I groaned. Everybody was talking about how difficult the pandemic had been on doctors and nurses, but nobody mentioned the plight of IBSers. Doctors? Nurses? Please. Hospitals were *filled* with bathrooms. Spend a day with my colon, Doc, we'll see who the hero is.

A passing police officer, patrolling the park, noticed my distress.

- They might have a bathroom, she said, pointing me to the exclusive, gated, five-star, six-hundred-dollar-a-night Alighieri Hotel & Spa across the street.

I had always despised the Alighieri, but I had no choice; judging by the fury in my belly, I had three minutes, tops. I hurried across the deserted, garbage-strewn avenue and fast-walked through the tall wrought-iron gates of the Alighieri . . . and behold, it was as if I had been transported to a magical land of luxury, wealth, and peace. Twenty yards away, outside the hotel, the apocalypse was in full swing; anger, hatred, death. But here, gentle music played on the outdoor speakers. Here, white lawn chairs and white patio tables were arranged on the lush green lawn. Here, a grand cobblestone drive encircled an enormous, ancient eighty-foot-tall fig tree, a breathtaking natural marvel in this world in which nature seemed to have become our enemy. Here, the front doors opened on their own, and the cool air-conditioned air embraced me, and the staff smiled and said, *Good morning, sir*, and *How are you, sir*, and *The bathroom? Yes, sir, of course, sir, down the hall and to the right, sir.*

And what a bathroom it was. Marble floors. Oak stall partitions. No-touch toilets and no-touch sinks. I was in heaven. But the miracles were not over, for as I left the bathroom, I spotted the small hotel coffee shop down the hall-way, and behold, it was open. The entire world was closed, the end-times had arrived, the Four Horsemen were strolling down the 405, but here in the Alighieri Hotel & Spa, the coffee shop was open, offering rich espresso and delicate pastries and artisanal sandwiches with pesto and aioli. I approached it as one might a mirage, waiting for it to disappear as I drew close.

- Are you . . . open? I asked the barista.

- We are, he said with impossible cheer.

- How? I asked.

- I have no idea, he said. - I'm just glad we are.

His name was Alex, and he was originally from Arizona. Before COVID, he had three jobs, but because of the pandemic, this was the only one left. Money was tight. He handed me my coffee.

- Can I offer you a muffin? he asked.

- How much?

- Nine dollars.

- Nine dollars? For a muffin?

- It's an Alighieri Apple Almond Crumble, he said, handing me a small sample. - It's very moist and flavorful.

And behold, it was.

Burrow Two.

- I found a place to write, I told Orli that evening.

- Where? she asked.

- Heaven, I said.

I was way off.

...

I took a seat in the Alighieri beside the large picture window overlooking the tree-lined front entrance. An exotic Audi R8 sports car rolled through the front gates, revved its engine loudly a few times, and pulled up to the valet at the front door. The driver emerged. He was wearing white pants. He handed his keys to the valet and went inside.

A moment later, an orange Lamborghini rolled through the gates, revved its engine loudly a few times, and pulled up to the valet at the front door. The driver emerged. He was wearing white pants. He handed his keys to the valet and went inside. As he did, though, he noticed with some chagrin the Audi R8, and he doubled back, directing the valet to park his orange Lamborghini beside it. The valet did as he was instructed, but Orange Lamborghini shook his head, frustrated, and indicated with his hands that he wanted it parked at an angle, as if in a showroom.

Outside the Alighieri, stores were closed, many to never reopen. Windows were boarded up. The few people who ventured outside did so cloaked in masks and face shields, scurrying away if they saw another human passing too close.

Orange Lamborghini entered the lobby. He stood at the front window to watch people admire his car.

I'm no politician, and I think by this point you know how I feel about news and world events, but if you'll permit me to weigh in on matters politic for a moment, I do think that the world would be a better place if we were all permitted, by law, to punch Lamborghini owners in the face. Not to beat them to death, of course – we're not monsters. Just one punch, in the face.

Hard.

- Why did you punch that man in the face? your child will ask.

- Well, Son, you see that car parked over there?

- Yes.

- That's his car. It costs two hundred fifty thousand dollars.

- Wow.

- And do you see the desperate woman lying in the gutter in a puddle of her own urine eating rotten food she pulled out of a trash can?

- Yes.

- That's why.

A camo-wrapped Mercedes-AMG rolled through the gates, revved its engine loudly a few times, and pulled up to the valet at the front door. The driver emerged. She was wearing white pants.

There were two groups of early man, writes Yuval Noah Harari. Neanderthals were the kind group, the caring ones, the generous ones. We were the other group. The Sapiens, the brutes, the beasts.

A man at the table beside me was conversing loudly on his speakerphone.

- And did your back injury occur at work or at home? he asked.

- Well, said the man on the other end of the call, both, kinda, y'know?

- So, the lawyer continued, would you say that the injury *occurred* at work but *affects* you at home?

- Definitely.

- Would it be correct to say that it affects every aspect of your life?

- It would, yes.

- And this has had emotional repercussions, hasn't it? the lawyer asked.

Orange Lambo came into the café and ordered a latte.

- We just got back from New Mexico, he said to Alex.

- Wow, said Alex. - How was the flight, with the COVID and all?

- You know, Orange Lambo said, we were going to fly commercial this time, but a private jet was only a few grand more, so we thought what the hell?

- Sure, Alex said.

- I mean, why not? said Orange Lambo.

Camo-Wrapped Mercedes-AMG entered the coffee shop. In addition to her white pants, she was also wearing a white blouse and white shoes and a white straw hat. She was carrying a white Pomeranian. She was dressed for Heaven while the world was going to Hell.

Sapiens, I thought.

Feh.

So much for my new burrow.

...

Late at night, while Orli and the boys slept, I would creep down to the garage and phone Ike's office. I knew he wasn't there. I couldn't talk to him even if he was. I closed my eyes and listened to his answering machine message, relieved, for a moment, just to hear his voice. Some nights I phoned twice.

...

The schools closed indefinitely.

- Why the *fuck* did you bring us here? Paix shouted at me. - I hate this city, I hate it here, I hate you!

I went to hug him, but he pushed me away.

- I'm sorry, I said to him.

I shouldn't have forced him to move here. I shouldn't have taken him away from his friends. I shouldn't have brought him into this dying world. I shouldn't have forced this existence upon him. I shouldn't have condemned him to life. I shouldn't have been so foolish. I shouldn't have been so selfish. I shouldn't have had a second child. I shouldn't have made him share our love and attention. I shouldn't have raised him in a small town. I shouldn't have made him think life was good. I shouldn't have taught him to hope. I shouldn't have traveled so much when he was a baby. I shouldn't have given him a cell phone. I shouldn't have let him play video games. I shouldn't have let him watch R-rated movies when he was thirteen. I shouldn't have angered God. I shouldn't have written what I did. I shouldn't have risked His wrath. I shouldn't have given Him a reason. I shouldn't have fucked with Him.

I shouldn't have been me.

...

Of all the people at the Alighieri Hotel & Spa, I loathed none more than Ambulance Chaser.

- Tell me about tingling, Ambulance Chaser said to his speakerphone. - Do you have any tingling?

Always speakerphone. Was this fuck actually *proud* of his job? Did this bottom-feeder *want* us to hear his devious machinations? Did he think we'd be impressed?

- Tingling like in my hands? his client asked.

- In any of your extremities.

- No, not really.

- Numbness?

- No.

- For Christ's sake, John, you fell off a goddamned ladder. You must have *some* tingling or numbness.

I tried to ignore him, to focus on Victoria's Secret. Doctor Limburger was counseling a certain patient considering gender reassignment surgery.

- I am not a puritan, he says to his patient. - I am not a prude. But remember this: After surgery, you will — sadly, regrettably, unfortunately, and unforgivably — still be a human, a Sapien, an animal of no significance, an ecological disaster, a terrestrial menace. Believe me, if there existed a procedure to transition from human to panther or tree or stone, I'd sign your paperwork immediately and operate tonight. And do you know why? Because I'd be having the same procedure done myself in the morning.

A homeless woman entered the hotel. Security quickly surrounded her.

- Can we help you? they asked.

- I'm hungry, she said.

- The kitchen's closed, they said. - COVID.

Camo-Wrapped Mercedes-AMG hurried in with her white Pomeranian, all in a panic.

- I need something I can feed her, she said to Alex.

He told her that there was a CVS three blocks away, which carried all kinds of dog food.

- I can't feed her that, she said. - What do you have here?

There was a big board over the counter that listed all the food the café offered. Alex patiently read the menu aloud to her: fresh-baked muffins, home-style cookies, a classic breakfast burrito with cage-free eggs and *pico de gallo*, a munchies breakfast burrito with organic chicken sausage and avocado, a vegan burrito, an egg and cheese croissant, chocolate croissants, pizza with barbecued chicken and mushrooms, acai bowls, protein shakes, chicken Caesar wraps, and portobello mushroom wraps.

- That's it? she asked. - Can they make her a burger?

- There's no one in the kitchen.

- How come?

- COVID.

- So, I can't get a burger? she yelped. - What does COVID have to do with making my dog a burger?

- We have sashimi, Alex offered. - With caramel ginger and lime sauce. Three pieces for twenty dollars.

Security dragged the homeless woman down the cobblestone driveway to the front gate. They waited there, hands on their hips, until she shuffled off.

Camo-Wrapped Mercedes-AMG bought two plates of sashimi and set them on the floor for her dog, who devoured them hungrily. Camo-Wrapped Mercedes-AMG cheered and clapped her hands.

- She doesn't usually like fish! she said.

She ordered the dog another plate of sashimi.

- How about sleeping? Ambulance Chaser asked his client. - Do you have trouble sleeping?

. . .

Trudging home, I passed the local Christian Science Reading Room. In the window hung a large framed reproduction of the iconic painting *Sermon on the Mount* by Carl Bloch. It's an awful painting. It's bloodless, clichéd, dull. Bloch made twenty-three paintings of Jesus's life, the real miracle being that they are all equally shitty. In this one, Jesus sits at the top of a hill, in a red flowing gown, his finger raised to Heaven. His followers gather around him.

- Boo, says Jesus. - Hiss.

A man covered in rags was asleep in the Reading Room doorway, his arms clasped around the axle of his wheelchair to keep it from being stolen. Down the road, a hungry woman was being thrown out of a hotel while a Pomeranian was eating sashimi with ginger and lime sauce.

Amen, I thought.

...

Why didn't Job kill himself after all the misfortune that had befallen him?

The ancients say it is because he never lost his faith.

I say it's because he never read Yuval Noah Harari.

There is no way out of the imagined order, Harari writes. *When we break down our prison walls and run towards freedom, we are in fact running into the more spacious exercise yard of a bigger prison.*

I wasn't impressed. I'd already read the original, written by God. If Bill Gates found Harari fun, there's some German porn buried in Monsey, New York, he might want to check out. I imagined the commercial for this miserable book. We open on Yuval Noah Harari at his writing desk. *Sapiens* is propped up in front of him. He has the barrel of a 9mm handgun in his mouth. He notices the camera.

- Oh, hello, he says. - Would you like to kill yourself but can't quite pull the trigger? Well, have I got a book for you! My name is Yuval Noah Harari . . .

I went back to the bookstore.

- Anything funny? I asked the bookseller.

- No, he said.

They had some new display tables out. One was for books about systemic racism. One was for books about climate catastrophe. One was for books about late-stage capitalism. Over on the Staff Recommendations table, Jorge had recommended a book about anti-Natalism. *Is life bad?* Jorge wrote on his recommendation card. *Yes! Is extinction good? Maybe!* Janet recommended a book about how love is merely a biological function we need to overcome if we hope to survive, and William recommended a book about how we are all racists even if we aren't (especially if we aren't).

- Can I help you find something? the bookseller asked.

He was reading *Sapiens*.

- Heroin, I said.

- Sold out, he said.

According to the ancient Midrash, the angels God sent to bring the plague of darkness over Egypt got out of control. They made the darkness darker than dark, they made a darkness so dark it could be felt.

Even God had to learn the hard way: Darkness spreads. Darkness feeds off itself. Once you start darkness, it's hard to stop it.

. . .

Ambulance Chaser was beside himself, distraught, his head in his hands.

- Your Honor, please, he was imploring into his phone, his hands clasped together in debased supplication. - Please, Your Honor . . .

I hadn't noticed his advanced age before. He appeared to be seventy, maybe seventy-five, too old to be doing this desperate work, too old to be begging, too old to be prostrating himself. Only now did I notice the holes in the soles of his worn shoes, his threadbare suit jacket frayed at the cuffs. Too busy judging him before, I realized that I had never seen him buy a coffee; he always brought his own, from home. I had judged him for that too.

Cheapskate, I had thought. *Tightwad lawyer won't even part with a few bucks for a coffee.*

He tapped his worn shoe anxiously on the marble floor as he pleaded with the judge on the other end of the line. The courts had closed because of COVID, and from what I could gather, he wasn't navigating the move to virtual very well; he had missed a court date, or a filing, or a deadline of some kind.

- That is not my problem, Counselor, the judge said stiffly.

- Please, he begged her. - If you could just let me file the necessary documents now . . .

The judge ended the call.

Ambulance Chaser slammed his laptop shut, ran a trembling hand through his thin gray hair. He glanced at me, shame beneath his anger, and I quickly looked away.

A plague was spreading across the land.

It had been for many years.

A plague of sneering and contempt, a plague of judges and judgment, of finger-pointing and disdain.

And I was sickest of all.

Fuck me, I thought.

On the way home, I passed Jesus.

Judge not lest ye be judged, he said in Matthew 7:1.

Twenty-five sentences later, in Matthew 7:26, he judges anyone who disagrees with him.

Fools, he spits.

So fuck Jesus too.

Burrow Three

I filed for unemployment.

It wasn't much.

We took out a loan.

It wasn't much.

Job, after losing everything he had, went and sat on a dung heap. Taking his lead, I went to the alleyway behind our apartment. Black flies swarmed around the overfilled dumpsters. Shattered liquor bottles were strewn across the pavement. The homeless scrounged through the recycling bins for clothing and cans. I found a discarded three-legged dining chair and propped it up between two rancid dumpsters.

- I'm going for walk, I would tell Orli, then creep around back to the alley-way, sit in the chair, drink gin, and chain-smoke cigarettes.

Burrow Three.

...

Eleanor, having fallen in love with a young man at the Shame Center, is harshly reprimanded by Doctor Limburger. Limburger is furious. Love, he reminds Eleanor, is strictly prohibited.

- Do you know what Photoshop is, Eleanor? he demands. - A modern computer can accomplish three billion tasks a second. With it mankind should have cured every disease, solved every crisis, brought world peace, explained the origins of the universe and the existence of God! But what has Man, that hideous beast, used it for? For Photoshop! For erasing wrinkles! For getting rid of cellulite, pimples, stray hairs! And do you know what Man used before Photoshop? Before filters and layers and eraser tools? To hide his hideousness? To pretend he was noble? Love! Love, Eleanor, is an invention of a species that can't bear its own foulness. Love is the Photoshop of the soul.

I didn't laugh.

I didn't show it to Orli.

...

By chapter 2, Job's wife has had enough of him. No money, no children, no courage. She goes to his dung heap.

- Fuck this, she says to him. - And fuck you. I'm done.

And that's it. She leaves. We never hear from her again.

Probably a wise move.

- I'm going for a walk, I said to Orli.

I crept around the apartment to my dung heap, to my garbage-strewn bur-row, a cup of gin in one hand and a pack of cigarettes in the other. I threw back my gin, hoping to at last convince my pancreas to begin eating itself again. I took out my phone and began to dial Ike. I stopped. He was gone.

Feh, said the world about Ike.

Feh, said the world about Phil.

Feh, said everyone about me.

Feh, said me about everyone.

- Do you still hold on to your faith? Job's wife demands of her pathetic husband. - Bless God and die.

Job 2:9.

Despite that being the literal translation of what she said – the Hebrew word used in the text is *baruch* (bless) – the ancients claim she was being sarcastic, that by *bless* she really meant *curse*. If you curse God, you will die. Wages of sin and all that. But what if she meant what she said? And what if she was right? What if she saw someone she loved believing the cruel judgments passed upon him, and she saw the damage those judgments had wrought? Bless God, Job's wife thus warns him – praise those who do nothing but hate you, judge you, condemn you – and it will kill you in the end.

She would have hated Rabbi Hammer. She would have hated my parents. She would have hated Nextdoor and Schopenhauer and Twitter and Harari. I imagine Job's wife strong and beautiful; I imagine her defiant and resolute; I imagine her of Middle Eastern descent but raised in the East End of London; I imagine her with brown skin and green eyes and a laugh that could fill the world. I imagine her being much, much happier after having left Job in his dung heap.

I lit another cigarette, downed my gin, and closed my eyes as the familiar fire burned its way down my throat. Next stop, emergency room. I thought of Phil's hand on my shoulder.

Hang in there, fellow Feh, hang in there. It will all be over soon.

When I opened my eyes, Orli was standing in front of me. Her eyes were red with tears, but her face was a mask of anger. She looked at me, and at the booze in my hand, and at the cigarette between my fingers.

- Fuck this, she said. - And fuck you. I'm done.

And she turned and walked away.

Probably a wise move.

Asked Rabbi Scold:

- The Torah says that during the plague, the Egyptians could not see their fellow man. Why does the Torah need to say this? It was a plague of darkness after all.

- Because, said Rabbi Scold, with all the other plagues, the Egyptians could seek out their friends and family to commiserate. But not with the plague of darkness.

With darkness, each Egyptian suffered alone.

I heard Orli enter the apartment and slam the door behind her.

Darkness.

Day Seven.

45.

Orli and I checked into the Oasis, the same hotel we'd stayed in after moving to LA. It was one of the few still open during the pandemic. This time, though, we didn't bring gifts for each other. We didn't bring lingerie, or sex toys, or chocolates, or candles. We brought anger and resentment.

We pulled into the empty lot, parked, and sat in the car, not speaking. An abandoned hotel golf cart was parked haphazardly on the front lawn, unused for months, covered in cobwebs and leaves.

The pool was closed.

The restaurant was closed.

The bar was closed.

We had come here to save our marriage.

- Okay, I said, opening the car door after a long, bitter silence. - Let's get this over with.

...

In the early years of our marriage, before we knew we were crazy, before we knew we needed help, we fought. We fought and we fought, and every fight reached its nadir with my declaring that we were getting divorced. That was the only story I knew, the only ending I deserved, the last *feh* chapter in a thoroughly *feh* life.

- Please, Orli would beg, please stop saying that. We can argue, we can disagree, but please stop saying it ends with divorce. Or it will. Or it will.

Stories are powerful things.

...

We didn't jump on the beds.

Everything in the hotel room was covered in plastic. The cups, the toilet seat, the desk chair, the ice bucket. *Due to the ongoing epidemic*, read the note card on the nightstand, *we will not be changing towels or bedding. We're all in this together.*

Orli showered.

I didn't know why. Habit, I supposed. The sound of the shower only deepened my sense of despair, reminding me of a joy I could now not even imagine. Our room was on the ground floor at the rear of the hotel, complete with sweeping views of the utility room and AC condenser bank. As Orli showered, I pulled open the rusty sliding door that opened onto a small concrete patio set into overgrown, weed-infested grass. Nearby, on the narrow pathway that led around the side of the building, sat another golf cart, as if everyone had simply fled or disappeared. I sat at the small patio table, lit a cigarette, and drank from my bottle of gin.

Fuck you, I said to my pancreas.

I would not contend with me forever.

In the days following Phil's death, the New York City newspapers ran the most humiliating, sickly photographs of Phil that they could find, photoshopped to make him look even worse. They all bore the same headline: *Feh.* That's the *feh* ending, after all. Not just death, ignominy. Collapse. Shame. The inevitable body-hitting-the-sidewalk of the fall that began so long ago in Eden and ends sometime later in a pile of dirt. In our defense – Phil's, mine, all the Fehs, in all the world – there is an old writing axiom: Third-act prob-

lems are just first-act problems. You can't tell us we're *feh* in act 1 and take issue with the tragedy it causes in act 3.

So fuck you too.

When I looked up, Orli was sitting beside me.

- What is it? she asked. - What's going on?

Fifty years, I thought.

Six hundred months.

Eighteen thousand days.

Eighteen thousand days of this interminable trial. Eighteen thousand days
at the defendant's table, facing bitter accusations from relentless prosecutions,
and the same eighteen thousand days at the prosecutor's table too – condemning,
blaming, finger-pointing, hating, judging all around me. Eighteen thousand
days of a trial called to order in my earliest youth, before I could read, before
I could write, before I could possibly understand that the judge was a mad-
man, the jury bloodthirsty, the verdict sealed before the case began.

The storm blows over, goes an old Yiddish expression, *but the driftwood*
remains.

- I'm just so tired, I said to Orli.

- Of what?

- Of the hate.

- What hate?

- Of myself. Of everyone.

Your body, Doctor Superior explained that first night in the ER, can only
process a certain amount of poison. Too much poison, and it breaks.

I broke. There was just too much poison in my mind, too much hate. I
couldn't bear that voice one more day, that endless hateful hissing, that destructive storyteller whispering in my ear that I am awful, that we are all awful,
that man is a virus, fallen, reprehensible. I couldn't take it one moment more.

In an interview after David Foster Wallace committed suicide, his sister
said she wasn't angry at him. She never thought, *If only he'd tried harder. To*
stay alive. To be.

- I knew how hard he tried, she said.

To stay alive.

To be.

Orli took my hand in hers.

- I wish you could see yourself as I do, Orli said.

- I don't want to be here anymore, I said. - I want to leave. I want to go back, to wherever I came from, to the darkness, to the void. I'm in Hell. This has to be Hell.

Tears ran from her eyes.

I darken all.

- Maybe it is, she said. - Maybe it is Hell. Maybe they were right. Maybe you're awful and I'm awful and we're all awful. But what if we aren't? What if it *isn't* Hell? What if you go up on that roof, right now, and you jump, and you die – and you find out they've been lying to you? That they were full of shit, every one of them. That they've cheated you, robbed you of life and love and joy. What if you drink enough poison, and your pancreas finally fails, and you finally die, and you wake up in some afterlife only to find, much too late, that this right here hasn't been Hell, but that it's been Heaven all along?

She took my hand, urging me to listen to her, to let her light in.

- What if you're not awful? she said. - What if you're okay? Not great, but not evil. What if we all are? What if they lied? What if they told you a sick story, over and over and over, and the only mistake you made was believing them?

A wave of nausea came over me, so strong I thought I might faint. The smoke from my cigarette made me want to gag. The gin turned to bile in my throat.

- I love you, she said.

- We'll deal with your issues later, I said.

My desperate *heh* in this world of *feh*.

- Look at me, she said. - Look at the boys. Look at the world around you. Can you? Can you see it?

- No. I'm broken.

- You're not broken; you're blind. Someone blinded you. To yourself, to life.

But I will see for you. I will be your eyes. But you have to trust me; you have to take my hand and trust what I tell you I'm seeing.

- I can't.

- Why?

- Because you love me.

- So?

- So, my Seeing Eye dog is an idiot.

- Less of an idiot than you, she said.

With that I could not argue.

I am not, you may have guessed, a big believer in miracles. I do not believe as most Americans do in the existence of angels. I do not hang winged cherubim from my rearview mirror. I don't have angel statues in my yard with a quote from Jesus inscribed on the base about peace or love that nobody who has these statues ever seems to practice. In fact, here's a tip: If you're ever lost in the woods, and you stumble through a dense thicket to discover a small cabin, lights on inside, the smell of delicious food wafting from the kitchen window, and you stagger toward it as if in a dream, and with the last of your strength you climb the patio steps to the front door, saved, and you are about to knock, and you look down, and there beside you stands a little angel statue with a quote about love from Jesus Christ – run. Because you, weary traveler, are about to get shot in the face.

And yet.

Behold.

Suddenly.

A miracle.

No splitting seas, no burning bushes, no walking on water. Just . . . laughter.

I heard laughter.

I hadn't heard laughter in a long time. Not mine, not Orli's, not anyone's. I looked at Orli to see if she had heard it too. She had, and she glanced around now, as puzzled as I. In this plagued world, laughter sounded frightening, dangerous, prohibited. It grew closer. I realized it was the laughter of children, shrill and ecstatic and defiant, entirely out of place in this locked-down, hate-filled world.

All at once, from around the side of the building, came charging a small group of young girls, seven or eight years old, squealing and laughing, all billowy skirts and sunlit hair and bright eyes and knobby knees and ponytails and joy, a whirlwind of pink and yellow and life. They stopped in their tracks to see us. I expected them to run, to flee. That was what you did when you saw people those days: you covered your mouth, you crossed the street, you ran. But they didn't.

- You're smoking! one ponytailed girl shouted at me, and they all burst out laughing.

- Am not, I said.

- Yes you are! they cheered.

- Am not, I said.

- What's that, then, huh?

- A cigarette, I said.

- Ha!

- It's not mine, I said. - It's hers.

- Liar! squealed Ponytail, and then, for no reason and needing none, she executed a perfect cartwheel, her toothpick legs and frilly socks and pink shoes a windmill of impossible happiness.

- Good, huh? she asked.

- I can do better, I said.

- Liar! she shouted again.

- I'm a much better liar than you! shrieked a pointy-elbowed girl in a pink Disneyland T-shirt.

- Who are you? Orli cheerfully asked Disneyland, the joy on the children's faces now mirrored on her own.

- Who are *you*? Disneyland asked back.

- I'm Orli!

- YOU'RE SO PRETTY! Disneyland shouted.

- Thank you! said Orli. - So are you!

- What about me? I asked.

- You're pretty too! shrieked Disneyland, and they all exploded with laughter and cartwheels.

One of them, the tiniest of the crew, wearing bright yellow ribbons in her bright yellow hair, pushed her way through to the front of the pack, struck a defiant Wonder Woman pose, hands on her hips, chin up, and said - Guess what I have?

- What? asked Orli.

- SUGAR! she shouted, raising her skinny arms overhead in victory, and indeed, in her tight fists were a dozen pink packets of sugar.

- We stole them from the dining tables! she squealed. - The whole restaurant is empty!

The girls cheered.

- Hand one over! said Orli, beside herself with laughter now.

That laugh, that laugh.

Yellow Ribbon tore the top off one of the packets, threw her head back like a frat boy at a kegger, and dumped the entire packet into her mouth.

The girls went apeshit. They screamed, they cheered, they downed their own sugar packets. Ponytail did more cartwheels. Yellow Ribbon did handsprings. Disneyland jumped on the golf cart, which someone fleeing the apocalypse had left the key in, and hit the gas. The cart lurched forward, and Disneyland, shocked it had moved, hit the brakes, and they all began shrieking and skipping and cheering and cartwheeling back around the corner of the building to whatever paradise they had come from.

I realized once they were gone that I was crying. They were so un*feh*, so okay with themselves, so okay with others. *Is it possible?* I wondered. *Have I ever been so?* I couldn't recall a time when I wasn't giving myself shit, or getting shit, or giving other people shit. But once upon a time, I knew, long ago, I had been like them. I'd been okay, I remembered, with myself, with mankind, with this world. It was a long time ago, so long ago that I couldn't remember how long ago it was. But I remember this: It was the days of laughter and joking. It was the days of flipping baseball cards. It was the days of playing *kugelach* on the tile classroom floor. It was the days of light.

Then people began telling me a story.

And behold, the world and all that is in it turned to darkness.

Later that evening, as we lay together in bed, Orli told me about a rare disorder called Anton syndrome she'd read about in one of her many brain books. Yes, brain disorders are our pillow talk. Sufferers of Anton are blind but insist they can see. They will describe with total assurance the room around them, the furniture they are sitting on, and the clothes you are wearing. Then they will thank you for the coffee, stand up, and walk straight into the wall. They aren't faking. They aren't in denial. They are absolutely convinced they can see. Not much is known about the pathophysiology of the syndrome, but two things are certain – the cause and the cure. The cause is trauma. Harm. Something, someone, at some point, causes damage to their head. A stroke, say. Or a baseball bat. Or a story. And just like that, the world that is, is forever lost to the world he imagines it to be.

As for the cure, there isn't one.

There is only a diagnosis.

But that's a start.

I am now halfway through this shrouded life. Certain for so long that I could see, I now know, at last and at least, that I cannot. That what I have been told is a hell might just be a heaven. That perhaps we are not odious vermin, that we are not always cruel and dangerous, that our every inclination isn't always evil. And that the people who told me we were, they were blind, too, and only thought they could see.

It's not much. It's not a cure. It's only a diagnosis.

But it's a start.

Stories are powerful things.

46.

In 1520, in the Basque region of Spain, a man named Ignatius of Loyola was recovering from leg surgery when, to pass the time, he asked his sister-in-law to bring him some of his favorite stories – the chivalric, knight-filled romance stories so popular in Spain at the time. Unable to find any, she instead brought him a book about the life of Christ and the Christian saints, of judgments and sinners and *feh*.

Ignatius read the stories.

He read them and he read them and he read them.

He went mad. He began to have visions. Two years later, he composed *The Spiritual Exercises*, a set of meditations to be recited by believers. This is the one of them:

Let me see myself as an ulcerous sore running with every horrible and disgusting poison.

Not long after, in Spain, not far away from where Ignatius found *feh*, a man named Miguel de Cervantes wrote a chivalric, knight-filled romance story, just like the ones young Ignatius loved. But Cervantes didn't love those stories. He hated them. So he wrote a story about a man driven mad by them.

Phil's funeral was held in the St. Ignatius Loyola church on Park Avenue. He hated churches.

- They make me feel like shit, he told me. - The books, the paintings. I walk in, and I feel like shit.

This is what he wrote in one of his last emails to me:

I want to have worth.

This beloved man, this adoring and adored father, this gifted artist, so full of worth, yet so convinced he was worthless. It occurs to me now, ten years after his passing, that perhaps that was what we truly had in common. We had been blinded, and we were still blind. Two men, in the middle of their lives, sitting in a bar in Tribeca, blind still, blind forever, and yet so so certain we could see.

47.

*N*ow *the truth of the matter,* Kafka's burrower admits, *is that in reality the bur-row does provide a considerable degree of security, but by no means enough, for is one ever free from anxieties inside it?*

It wasn't the burrow that was the problem, he comes to realize.

It was the burrower.

No matter how deep he dug, no matter how secure his walls, no matter how strong his defenses, every time he entered, he brought the noise with him.

Because the noise, he finally realizes, is inside him.

48.

- I would like to end with this thought, Adichie concluded her talk, that when we reject the single story, when we realize that there is never a single story about any place, we regain a kind of paradise.

49.

In 1912, Kafka wrote one of his first stories, *The Judgment*. It was, like the story of Job, about a man who did nothing wrong but was wrong. The man's name was Georg Bendemann. Georg's disapproving father accuses him, judges him, and sentences him to death.

- *Feh*, says Georg's father.

Georg accepts the judgment. He doesn't question it. He seems, even, to agree with it. He flees from their apartment, throws himself into a river, and drowns.

Two years later, at the age of thirty-six, Kafka wrote a letter to his own disapproving father.

What was always incomprehensible to me, he wrote, *was your total lack of feeling for the suffering and shame you could inflict on me with your words and judgments.*

Kafka is beginning to question the judgment. Not just his father's judgment of him but judgment as a whole.

Four years after that, Kafka writes a new story, *The Trial*. Spoiler alert: There is no trial. There is only more judgment, endless judgment, judgments even without judges. And just like in his earlier *The Judgment*, K, the main character in *The Trial*, is sentenced to death.

- *Feh*, says the official.

But Kafka the writer is older now. He has grown. And this time, in this story, Kafka rejects the judgment. K refuses to commit suicide. It's no Hollywood ending, I know: K dies, bloodily, like a dog. But in the story of Kafka himself, of the human being named Kafka, Kafka is no longer accepting judgment, and he is not merely questioning it. He is rejecting it. He will not kill himself. He will not succumb to *feh*. He will not contend with those who will not contend with him.

50.

Blindness, by Portuguese novelist José Saramago, is a story about an epidemic. One day, everyone in an unnamed land begins losing their sight. The story is told through the local eye doctor, one of the first to be blinded. The blindness causes everyone to go mad, to hate, to fight, and the society begins to crumble.

Blindness was spreading, Saramago writes, *not like a sudden tide flooding everything and carrying all before it, but like an insidious infiltration of a thousand and one turbulent rivulets which, having slowly drenched the earth, suddenly submerge it completely.*

The *thousand and one turbulent rivulets* reference to Scheherazade, the ancient teller of stories, is no accident.

Stories can be a plague too.

···

A few weeks after our stay at the hotel, COVID began to subside and Scarbucks cautiously reopened. It seemed even sunnier and more pleasant than I had remembered, despite the mandatory masks and awkward social distancing. All who entered were greeted warmly; those who had suffered from

COVID or lost loved ones to it were consoled. People, grateful for the chance to be around other people again, paid even more for their no-pay coffee than they had before. I sat at a table in the back with Steve, and, after inquiring about his family and he about mine, told him I was working on a theory. I called it the Theory of Feh-lativity.

- Feh-lativity? he asked.

The seeds of it had taken root fifty years ago, I told him, in a yeshiva in Monsey, New York, in a dysfunctional family where all was fury and shame. But it came together the day Orli and I watched half a dozen carefree young girls mainline sugar packets and hijack a hotel golf cart. Here's how it goes:

Philosophers, writers, and scientists have long sought to distinguish mankind from the lower animals, to identify that one thing that makes us unique among the creatures of the earth. William Hazlitt suggested that man is the only creature that laughs. Two hundred years later, we now know that dolphins laugh too. That pigs chuckle. That even cockroaches giggle with excitement when they discover their way into your pantry. Mark Twain declared that man is the only creature that blushes or needs to, but then he hasn't seen Flynn when I catch him peeing in the living room. Camus took a drag of his Gauloises, squinted through the smoke, and declared that man is the only creature that refuses to be what he is – that is, the only animal that strives – but all living things strive through the process of evolution, and so it may be said that even the lowly caterpillar, cocooning himself upon my garden fence, yearns to become something better.

Are we the only creature that mourns?

Nope.

The only creature that mates for life?

Nope.

The only creature that rapes?

Nope.

Here's my theory, arrived at in the year of our disdaining Lord 2021, besieged by the Bible and Nextdoor and Twitter and Yuval Noah Harari and

Wolf Blitzer: There are actually two things that separate mankind and animals, two things that, in regrettable concert, might go some way toward explaining the misery, pain, suffering, anger, and strife we humans experience on this earth. This is the first one:

Mankind is the only creature that hates itself.

Not mere shame, not mere guilt – I'm talking full-on loathing, for himself and the rest of his species. I have not conversed as Solomon was said to have with the various creatures of this world, but I've watched rabbits in my backyard, and I'm pretty sure they don't think themselves a scourge upon the planet. Deer don't berate themselves for overpopulating the woods. Flynn seems ashamed when I catch him peeing on the rug, but more likely he's just afraid of my giant human feet chasing after him; either way, he doesn't go off to his crate, pour himself a gin, and declare himself and his whole species vile and repellent. He doesn't wish he was a cat. Goats don't go to confession, cross themselves, and beg forgiveness for eating garbage. Elephants don't think they're fat. Only one creature looks upon himself and thinks, *Feh.*

Us.

Me and you.

Mankind.

The depravity of mankind is so easily discoverable, Samuel Johnson wrote, *that nothing but the desert or the cell can exclude it from notice.*

This is a guy we build *statues* of, folks.

Here's the second difference between man and animal:

Mankind is the only creature that tells itself stories.

We are the only animal that crafts tales, with beginnings, middles, and ends, with heroes and villains. We are the only animal that learns from the stories we tell, whose views of ourselves are formed by these stories, and whose subsequent actions are determined by the stories we are told.

Human beings, writes literary scholar Jonathan Gottschall, *are storytelling animals. Story is how we communicate, it's how we make sense of the world, it's how we evolved.*

And yet the story we tell most, the story of stories, the ur-story of our species, is this:

Feh.

We are not just the storytellers, though. We are the storytold. I don't know if we told stories before we decided we suck, or if we decided we suck before we told stories. But the Bible is one of our oldest stories, and from beginning to end, it's the story of *You Suck.*

The Bible, according to *Time* magazine, *is the most influential book ever written. Not only is the Bible the best-selling book of all time, it is the best-selling book of the year every year.*

Says Guinness World Records: *It is impossible to know exactly how many copies have been printed in the roughly 1,500 years since its contents were standardized, but research conducted by the British and Foreign Bible Society in 2021 suggests that the total number probably lies between 5 and 7 billion copies.*

- That's a lot of *feh*, said Steve.

- That's my theory, I said.

Job begins with a bet, a sick experiment. I've begun to believe we have been part of a sick experiment too. What if, the experimenters wondered, we were to take creatures that understand the world and themselves through story, whose very operating system is story, and tell them, from a very young age, a terrible story about themselves? What would happen? What would they become? Would they hate themselves? Would they hate each other? Would they divide themselves into nations? Would they build weapons capable of destroying their own world? Would they seek comfort from the pain of that self-hatred in drugs and booze? Would they overdose on heroin trying to numb the hate, mourning for the worth they had but couldn't see?

What is art? asked Leo Tolstoy.

His answer:

Emotional infection.

Have I been infected? Have we all? Have we been blinded – by rabbis, novelists, philosophers, thinkers, writers, all telling us the same darkening tale?

Perhaps, somewhere on these books, on the spine or just below the title, they should be required to print, in clear and readable text:

Danger.

Toxic.

Not for Human Consumption.

Because that shit will kill you.

I am no cheerleader for humanity. I am a descendant of the Holocausted and Inquisitioned, the enslaved and the pogromed. I am no stranger to man's inhumanity to man. Perhaps that's why this concerns me so; surely this constant refrain of self-contempt and derision becomes self-fulfilling at some point. We stand in the wreckage of a world laid low by a terrible story, a story whose horrific ending my children or children's children will have to endure, a story we never tire of telling:

Feh.

51

Not much is known about the Danish artist Carl Bloch. Primarily a painter of mythology and Danish rural life, he never painted religious subjects until he was paid to. And yet his paintings, *The Sermon on the Mount* in particular, have become some of the most iconic images in modern Christendom, adorning everything from churches to living room walls, couch pillows to tote bags. To the devout, *The Sermon on the Mount* shows their glorious Lord preaching, surrounded by rapt believers, their hands clasped, taking in his every word.

They should look more closely.

It wasn't unusual for painters in the Classical Realist tradition to place subtle jibes in their works, clues to the artist's true feelings about their subject, like Rembrandt (a major influence on Bloch) subtly mocking the wealthy who paid him for their portraits.

And so where others look at *The Sermon on the Mount* and focus on the man, center right, with his finger in the air, lecturing, hectoring, judging, I focus on the young man to his left, sitting at the fiery preacher's feet yet turned away from him, his eyes on the cheerful child across the way, an innocent young girl utterly uninterested in the furious finger-pointer sitting before her, delighted instead with the brightly colored butterfly that has come to rest on the bowed head of the self-flagellating old woman beside her. I see a man turning his back to Jesus. I see a man in the middle years of his life, at last rejecting the finger-pointing judge, wondering if he will ever again be able to see himself and the world around him as clearly as that enchanted young girl.

Art, of course, is open to interpretation. Christians refer to this painting as *The Sermon on the Mount*, and that's what they see in it. But I wonder if Carl Bloch – devoted father of eight children, who filled so many of his paintings with children who didn't seem to belong in them, who never painted about religion until he was paid to – called it something else.

I wonder if he called it *Fuck Judges*.

...

COVID cases began to rise, and the schools, coffee shops, and stores were once again shut down. The city-run food drives were canceled. Thanksgiving came, and Orli, the boys, and I decided to volunteer at Scarbucks, preparing and distributing Thanksgiving meals for the homeless and elderly.

Dozens of people showed up, masked and gloved, to offer their assistance.

Someone had donated a carload of new Disney backpacks for the homeless children; volunteers cooked turkeys the day before and began dropping them off at the church early that morning. It was a busy few hours; there were mashed potatoes to make, stuffing to prepare, and endless cans of cranberry sauce to open and spoon out onto hundreds of plates. Orli and Lux were assigned to the group inside the church, cutting up long trays of cornbread and carefully wrapping each piece in tinfoil. Paix and I, outside in the parking lot with the others, helped place finished meals in plastic bags, ready to distribute to the needy who were already beginning to line up on the sidewalk out front. Steve cranked some seventies R & B through an old speaker a volunteer had brought with her, and people began to sing and dance as they sliced the turkey and filled to-go cups with gravy.

Suck My Dick Faggot showed up early. I learned that his name is George. He is an Army vet with severe PTSD, who has struggled with alcoholism ever since he returned.

- Happy Thanksgiving, I said to him.

- Happy Thanksgiving, he replied.

D'Fuck You Looking At was there (Mark, a talented soccer player in his youth with an abusive father who beat him so badly he ran away), and Peaches showed up too. Nobody knew his name, but he seemed happy, and when he looked inside his bag, he said, - Cranberry sauce, my favorite!

I know what you're thinking.

I know because I was raised *feh*, and I've heard all the *feh* before, and I know that *feh* sees only *feh*.

And so yes, I know that Thanksgiving is a bullshit holiday. I know about the horrific Native American genocide it conveniently glosses over. I also know about the Armenian genocide, and the Rwandan genocide, and the Holocaust; and I know about the Holodomor, and I know about the My Lai massacre, and I know about the Inquisition; I know we're destroying the earth, and I know about that desperate polar bear stuck on that ice floe in the middle of the rising sea, and I know about the Great Pacific Garbage Patch; I know about systemic racism, and I know about white nationalism, and I know about neo-Nazism, and I know about sexism; I know about late-stage capitalism, and I know about libtards, and I know about MAGAts; and I know that the turkeys we were serving were innocent victims of a vicious, marauding tribe of Sapiens driven by an indomitable will, and that the world would probably be better off had we never been born. But right now, right here, people are giving their time to help others (I know, it's just because they selfishly want their species to survive), and they are feeding people who have no food (I know, they are just virtue signaling for their Instagram feeds), and George is on his third piece of cornbread (I know, America should take better care of its veterans), but for this one brief moment, for one brief fucking minute, can I just be allowed to imagine that I don't suck completely? That maybe I'm not rotten, maybe I'm not a *gonif*, maybe I'm not *feh*? That maybe we humans are a half-decent species after all, or even just a quarter-decent? And maybe, please, just for this one afternoon, can we all agree that God and all the other judges, here and online, in the past and in the future, the preachers and the academics, the writers and the philosophers, can just go fuck themselves, because Paix is handing food bags to the poor, and I'm handing Disney backpacks to homeless children, and Orli and Lux are cutting up their hundredth tray of cornbread, so will you all just shut the *feh* up for one fucking minute because they need me inside to help mix the mashed fucking potatoes?

Thank you.

Six hours later, all had been fed. There were still some plates of food left over, so we helped Steve and his sons load them into their car (which causes global warming), which they were going to drive over to Compton (a neighborhood blighted by systemic racism) and distribute to the hungry people there (perpetuating the myth of white messiahs and that people of color can't help themselves). After that we said goodbye and headed home, our feet aching, our clothes covered with cranberry sauce and turkey gravy, where Flynn would be lying on his back, legs stretched out, waiting for a belly rub in this not completely *feh* world.

- I'm *shepping naches*, I said to Orli as we walked behind the boys.

Yiddish for *I feel proud*.

She laughed.

- About the boys? she asked.

- About everyone.

- Best Thanksgiving ever, Lux said to Paix.

- *No cap*, Paix said to Lux.

Teenager for *true*.

The trouble with midlife, of course, is that the damned thing is half over. The life I wanted to end when I was younger, I now want to last forever.

At the end of Saramago's story, the doctor's wife comes to his rescue. She takes him away, to a remote place, and there, Saramago writes, she tells him a story. The story is a new story. When she is done telling it, he can see. His blindness is cured by a new story.

I've been working on a new story too. It's called *The Very Bad Man in the Very Good Place*. This is how it goes:

THE VERY BAD MAN IN
THE VERY GOOD PLACE

Once upon a time, a man and a woman lived in a very beautiful place. The moon was beautiful, and the stars were beautiful. The land was beautiful, and the sea was beautiful. The trees were beautiful, and the grass was beautiful. There was something called the aurora borealis, and a place called the Grand Canyon, and a field of dew-dusted lavender bell-flowers waking their petals in the early-morning sun.

The only bad thing in the place was someone called God, a nasty old man who hated the man and woman, who found fault with them, who judged them, who told them stories in which they were the villain.

- Thou art a stiff-necked people, said God.

- From dirt you come and from dirt you shall return, said God.

- I shall not contend with thee forever, said God.

Etcetera.

- What a dick, said the woman.

- Fuck this, said the man.

And so one day the woman and man arose in the morning, and they left. They found a new place to live, this one perhaps not as beautiful as the last, but at least nobody there judged them and nobody there hated them, and so they didn't judge or hate anyone either. Life wasn't always easy. Sometimes, the man would get angry at the woman.

- *Feh*, he would say.

- Whoa, she would respond. - You sound like God.

- Sorry, the man would say.

Once, their son threatened to kill his brother.

- Hey, said the man. - You're behaving like God.

- You're right, said the son. - What's wrong with me?

And the man and the woman never told their children they were *feh*, and their children never told their children they were *feh*, and soon they populated the whole un*feh* world, and every weekend, on Saturdays and Sundays, all the people all over the world would gather together in beautiful temples, much like they do now, and there would be images upon the walls of suffering and torture, much like there are now, but in this place, a human being would stand at the lectern at the front of the room and point to the images and say, *Look! Look with your eyes at the terrible suffering brought about by judgment!* and then he would read to them from a story called *The Very Bad God.*

- And then God drowned everyone, then God burned Aaron's sons, and then God made a giant winepress and put millions of people in it and killed them.

- Boo, the congregation would call.

- Amen, he would respond.

And everyone in the congregation would lower their heads, and look within their hearts, and ask themselves if they had behaved like God that week, and as the service concluded, they would turn one to the other and apologize if they had judged them, or if they had belittled them, or if they had harmed them in any way, and they would promise to try their very best, in the future, to be more like man than God.

The End

Thanksgiving is often cold in New York, but in Los Angeles the sun was warm as we walked home, and the sky was blue, and even the police sirens in the distance couldn't darken my mood. I looked at Orli and smiled; I was feeling love for her, because love is the chemical reaction that the human brain relies on to encourage the successful pairing and reproduction of mates, thereby ensuring our species' survival.

Still, it was kinda nice.

I told her that I loved her.

She told me that she loved me too.

She put her arm around my waist.

I wondered if she thought I was fat.

Heh.